1

The Code

Volume Four of the God Book Series

This book is not a work of fiction and has been intentionally unedited.

The book cover art was designed by God and painted by Celest.

A special acknowledgement for special people.

We wish to thank Tim and Mike, our computer genius friends, and our good friend Thor for the job they have done with all the technical aspects of taking this book from its manuscript form, proofreading for typos and formatting it into book layout for the printer.

The Code

Volume Four of the God Book Series

This book contains information God transmitted to Celestial (Celest) Blue Star of the Pleiades and David of Arcturus. In this book God continues to provide pertinent information to benefit all people regardless of their preconceived beliefs. These are the words of truth and wisdom as presented to humanity by the God of this Universe. This information is relevant to the further pursuit of truth and the debunking of the illusions that so many people on the planet still cling to.

Included in this book is a chapter that God transmitted to Chako Priest. There is also a special presentation by the Master "Kato."

My Codices

Forward

One of the most beautiful gifts that God shares with all of humanity is His willingness to cope with the foibles that humans create for themselves. Especially in the times we are now all living in. The problems people have are acknowledging how much each individual who has shamelessly indulged in feckless and abominable behavior have caused this beautiful world we live in to arrive at a spatial tipping point in consciousness. It has become the norm unfortunately for people to point the finger at others instead of assuming personal responsibility for their own actions and lack of actions in these crucial matters. Yet, when all is said and done, it is the people of this world themselves who lack the steadfastness of true belief and the less than acceptable determination of mind and Spirit who have been the true culprits in this melancholy and unwholesome state of the affairs of this world. While this has all been occurring, God in His greater wisdom has permitted people to play out **their last hand of cards.** Yet the God of this Universe sees the potential for many people to continue the changes they have barely begun in their lives, even though many individuals do so out of fear of **not** doing so. So many People do not want to be left behind...but they do not want to move ahead...well, what is wrong with this picture?

All illnesses have remedies. God's remedies lie in His words. He is not responsible for how many people read them; that is not His job. It is yours. He did not cause the Spiritual turpitude that assails all living beings here, only the human race has accomplished that with seemingly no remorse on many peoples' parts. We find it odd that so many people here do not truly want to know when something is really wrong, <u>unless</u> it impacts on them personally. This is very selfish! What about when times were "good," how many people actually cared about others they had never met especially if they were people from other countries? The answer is, *very few.* We see God as a counterbalance to the mishmash of erroneous beliefs and deliberate manipulations that so many have instigated here. God is His own Scales of Justice. The time is long past now to hold the Illuminati accountable for all the things still taking place here. They too will have their comeuppance. That event has already begun.

We appreciate God. We are completely dedicated to receiving His words because we can do this and because He asked us to do this work as a means of touching those hearts, minds and Souls of all those here that He can.

It has not been easy for us to accept the private knowledge we have of the "happening" events that will soon take place which will effectively cause so many people here to leave the planet. However, as we have stated before, our method of dealing with this information is to repeat to ourselves, *"if God can handle this, so can we."* This is helping us enormously to better cope with the things we can not change. Many people of late have sent supplications to God about their own requests for personal help and also are asking for aid for the welfare of the planet herself. We would consider this to be a more touching moment if it were not for the fact that some of these people have spent their lives as self-serving individuals and what they are still doing now is not too commendable either. It is the people however who have always most generously asked for help for Terra and the human race as a whole, who have earned not only our own respect but our gratitude as well. Readers, we ask that each of you consider how much God loves all people, regardless of what less than favorable wheels they have intentionally set into motion. No true God could possibly bear witness to all that has transpired here since the early days of mankind *without understanding that children need to learn from the errors of their ways.* Although in all honesty, God has said He wished it would have taken less time. This is why it is that within His books, God has chosen to speak on so many subjects, each geared to assist all Earthizens in understanding that God is not malicious, wrathful or judgmental. Each book is also a "reminder bell" of who you are and WHY you are. If only we could find human words to express to each of you His unlimited compassion and the long work required for God to address all of you at this time. He does so with as He told us, "great expectations and incomparable knowledge that you WILL prevail, even if it is in spite of yourselves."

Please arrive at the understanding that these God books are far more important than you can possibly imagine, at this time.

We look around at this beautiful planet that was Created for all of us who arrived here from so many Star Nations. All races were meant to mature and ultimately evolve into finer expressions of themselves. We know that the wanton waste, pollution and unconscionable abuse of this world and its natural resources will *eventually* be rectified. However, that does not make us feel any better about the present happenings. So many people do so little to help themselves much less assuming a positive stance to be of assistance to everything else that matters. We understand just as God does, that many people have yet to recognize the inseparable, undeniable connection that exists in the coalition of all forms of life. Negativity, lack of foresight and an *"I don't want to know"* as well as, *"there is nothing I can do about it"* attitude, have seriously limited the available options of so many of our beloved human counterparts. We do not bear them any ill-will; however we do reserve the right to be disappointed in them. It was inevitable that so many would not hear or heed the wakeup call and thus they still falter as they walk aimlessly about while flirting with the dying winds of change. There are crucial times in any civilization's history when a species arrives at a precipice, one that demands change and an unwavering desire for the pursuit of the inevitable and enviable evolution of Spirit. We as a race, the entire human race, are at this juncture now; still so few actually see this timeline of gridline intersections as anything that is different from those in times past. God in His infinite wisdom has chosen this grid-time to refresh the dormant memories of all of His Earthbound Children. We understand that not everyone will have access to His messages here in the present. We also understand that these words of His will live on for the future generations; those who will come after us and gather insights from His words. The past will not repeat itself any longer; this in itself is a blessing for those who understand these implications.

The human races' petty differences, its antiquated belief systems have long held most of them back from blossoming into the true God I Am expressions they were, they are, all destined to be. We ourselves at times find it very difficult to be here on Earth. On our home worlds everything for the most part has a purpose; so much of it is centered in "knowing," it is about laughter and joy, harmony, unconditional love and a surreal sense of peace and serenity coalesces through the air. There are no illusions about who we are or our purpose for being. No one is any better than another, it is recognized that not everyone is on the same evolutionary level so there are never any judgment calls. Everything is offered openly and without conditions, we would know no other way of being.

In the not so distant future the way of life here on Earth is going to drastically alter. Life will out of necessity become simpler. The Golden NOW Child will be the divining rod that guides us, that carries us forward into our tomorrows. Time will no longer have meaning for anyone here, for everything will happen in the moment. The seasons will change; fresh infusions of new life will be abundant for all to revel in. Now all we need to do is to "get there from here." This is in but small part the purpose of these books.

Celest and David

Introduction (by God)

Well My Children, I can not say that this book has been a long time in coming. That is certainly not the case. I can tell you however that this book is one that should remain in your collective minds as a long series of defining moments. At least, that is what I have planned for each of you. I intentionally took My time so many, many, of your lifetimes ago, when I began the thought processing **for what at** <u>that</u> **time span was for the future.** I began by deciding what words I would choose to use and in what order I wanted My books to be written. Because I already knew who My scribes would be even way back then, it simply remained for Me to Create a long series of events so the scribes and I could speak without interruption, BUT at what I had deemed to be the perfect gridline intersection of humanity's affairs. Under the auspices of all Universal laws, all sentient beings in all Universes were told well in advance that this crucial timeline would take place and WHY it must. You see, Children, understanding the "why" is of even greater import than understanding the "when." "Why" defines a momentous occasion but leaves out no details of those events that are at the hub of the occasions, even though so many of the things that would take place were quite frankly, disgusting. "When" was easily seen to be the moment the human races here arrived at the *epicenter of themselves.* **You are all there NOW.**

I so truly wish this all could have happened differently Children; I desired that you not become enthralled by the abominable actions and thought forms of others. Also, I did not want YOU to create them for yourselves, either. *You can see how well that went!* What any Luminescent of any Universe desires for His or Her Universe, is the advancement of all Children and the uncompromising love of all the Children of the individual Universe.

Unfortunately, all Luminescents have during one span of growth or another; all observed indicial behavior on the part of some inhabitants that required modification. No, when the Golden NOW Child finishes her dance of change I will not appear to any of you and say, "OK, you have now been modified."

You have each in one manner or another received specific "transmutational" information. This USUALLY is given to you in increments by small monads that are segments that comprise the whole of pertinent information. They are either embedded in your Soul Voices or sent to you at a specific timeline that complements a thought or action that you are involved in. It is an activation of an actualization process. Perhaps what I just explained to you will not make much sense to you now; I did not expect that it would. But eventually you will understand and remember. This is why in great part I chose *The Code* to be the 4th. book of My series. Due to the lack of time so many Children have left here, I have gone ahead as I said I would in My last book and changed the format for this book and the remainder of the books in this series. By Celestial and David combining My words instead of their previous individual segments, I believe I can say more in less time. Oddly enough even though time is an illusionary occurrence, I must still adhere to the fact that for many of you, the linear world still exists. Now, I shall see if I can change that!

Those of you who require quantifiable proof of My existence and those who still erroneously believe My Son Jesus is going to come down and save you from yourselves, are all going to be sadly disappointed. To see Me, IS to become Me. Think on that for a while if you are up to it. My words are My own, they need no proof to substantiate themselves either. Those of you who are ONE with Me "*know*." It is up to the rest of you to seek and find Me. The rekindling of Our combined Spirits is all that I seek from you. No Father could ask anything more. You see, this world's corruption created by people and their self-destructive ways have long interfered with Our union. This is at an end. Together you and I have the perfect marriage. It is not for convenience nor is it to procreate a species. Our unison is to be felt from the heart and lived through the Soul. One thing I can guarantee you is that I will never judge you and that I will never leave you in "aloneness." This has been a big problem for many of you there on My Earth. You feel so crowded, as if everyone is on top of each other yet at the same time you feel as if you are so alone. As My Celestial daughter would say, *Is it better to feel alone, or to feel alone together?* I will let you be the judge of that.

My words of this day come from a heavy heart and yet from an elevated place. I see that many of you will not survive the transition from one state of Earthly being to the other state of Earthly being; this is the state that is soon to rise to meet those of you who are ready. This saddens Me, yet I know that in time most, if not all, will return here once again to take part in all that the human experience has to offer. When times get tough in the days ahead, and tough they will be, raise you head high, walk tall with pride and reach out a helping hand to others so that they may in turn do the same for you. Your dusty and dirty faces will retain the expressions that are earned...not the ones that are purchased. The waters may run dry but mind you, that replenishment is on the way. I ask that you hold on just a little longer, even longer if you must. The climax to all your idiosyncrasies and all your triumphs and tribulations will dim in the Dawning of My New Day. We, you and I have come a long way together from the beginnings of you as Soul. We have traversed the great unknown in search of heightened awareness and newfound dreams. All of this has brought us here, here in the gatherings of the Light where many still fear to tread. The Earthly Dream is now a reality.

What was once just a thought, an idea consummated by inspiration is now blossoming into reality. My Children are awakening one by one while the world has been in anticipatory wait. Can you not feel the excitement in the air? Can you not breathe it into your lungs and feel the emotions swell up inside of you? You and I have journeyed to this planet for so very, very, long. We, together you and I, have rebirthed here to bring the dream into the realm of the known. Are you as pleased as I am? I sure hope so. It has been by the sweat of your labors that the human race is now lifting beyond the precipice and ready to take the next step. Together We will navigate the uncharted waters of a future that lies in wait. No, I do not know precisely what lies ahead for there are always possibilities and probabilities to contend with. People change their minds; they change their wishes for themselves and others while some people want to try something new. Far be it from Me to stifle the Creative ventures as it arises from deep within them. I flourish as you flourish, you should all know that by now. Together you and I will right the wrongs that My less evolved Children put to the test of time. If you have learned one iota of what I have from all their meanderings, then you are a better person because of this. Try not to look on the dark side of things because of what appears to have gone wrong. There is always a silver lining for those of you who choose to wake up on the right side of the bed. As the finale of time evaporates into the shell of nothingness, believe and learn to understand that it is for the best.

My governing agent is no longer required when it comes to the affairs of the human race. This Universe is swaying to a new beat, one that you will find a treat. She knows a secret, one that She will soon share with all of you there on planet Earth. No, you will not miss it, it will be unmistakable. The Forces of Light will unveil themselves to each of you; the time of feeling utterly alone will vanish like the fog from a midsummer's night dream. Today is the beginning of the beginning of a new governing system that will take place on Earth. The reins have been turned over to one who loves you most sincerely. The Mother has awakened and she is about to lay rest all your fears. Like a nimble feline, she will flick away any disease and decay. This is the moment each of you has been waiting for. Again I say, rise and greet the new day.

In service, God

Codex 1

The Lives you change along the way

God... Children, I am thinking back at this moment to all the interactions I have long had with each of you. I am also thinking of all the wondrous meetings I have had with the Creator, with the Creation Processing and with all others of Divinity. Long ago, when you were each but a mere speck of a new but sparkling Light in the Universe, you were still cognizant of where you were and in "knowledge" of who I was. My, how things have changed! Today, most of you do not even know yourself let alone know Me. I have given life to multitudinous life forms throughout this Universe, as well as assisted in Creating life in other Universes. It is what WE do. I had during those times of the elongation and advancement of the Creative Processing, sought to gently awaken each new being, each newly Created aspect of the Creator and of MySelf. I sought to bring to the forefront of their Soul Selves the quintessential knowledge relevant to the eternal life of unlimited possibilities and probabilities. One of My Sons, Jesus THE Christ, was of great assistance even then. Jesus in His own serene and yet uncompromising manner, would brook no thoughts of any life being lived without each life having a purpose. Not a mission per se, but a purpose-a goal of surpassing each and every previous life existence that so many Children of Mine from My other worlds had. When I speak of My Jesus' uncompromising manner, I do so with sheer delight. I had watched Him evolve just as I had hoped each of you who are My Children here would. Of course We were in a different place, a realm where all things were made manifest by sheer mind-thought and dedicated resolution to and for just cause.

Jesus was one of My emissaries throughout His many, many, life experiences on other worlds, in other realms.

15

Although I love no one Child of Mine more so than another, there are those I love in different "fashions." One of Jesus' greatest attributes and it is was one that also exemplified **each** of His lifetimes here on the Earth Star planet as well, is His ability to glide in a sense, through absolutely disruptive conditions, yet reach out and gently touch those who are "kindred Spirits" while not breaking His stride for a nanosecond. Yes, of course Jesus, He who is Sananda, is a highly evolved being. Yet He did not simply "pop-up" on the God Scale as such. Evolvement is a process, those who tout their own perception of how evolved they are, are in fact the least of the lot. Jesus encountered many such beings throughout His many incarnations. Yet it was here on the Earth Star planet where He too was confronted by the greatest of challenges. Children, because of Jesus' many incarnations here, do not lose sight of the fact that it is not only I who knows you best!

I had desired that each of you live the Jesus THE Christ Consciousness not only "at home" the place where all of you actually do this, but everywhere I sent you or where you sent yourselves. However it was seen quite clearly that this was not going to take place here. It was however when each Soul that arrived here was one that was an elevated being, one that was enriched by the Christ Consciousness, one that refused to leave that Consciousness at home, that lives here became better for the **chosen few**. And yet I called you all....but few responded. Therefore, I had no choice but to bring throughout every century that has ever been, those stalwart Souls who would not be compromised.

I am going to attempt to explain a situation to you. Some of you will understand while others shall not. My Celest-Self has attempted on more than one occasion to explain to people how it is that I know what I know about all of your mind-thoughts. Envision a huge movie screen; one that is set into small fragments of images, each fragment contains different words, sometimes different pictures. Now try to do the impossible, I say this because again I must tell you that the human mind as a computer can only focus on so many things at once. Therefore, it really is not possible for the mind let alone your human eyes, to broaden the range into an unlimited scope. But please, try anyway. By viewing the screen which correctly displays all various thoughts and images of people, places and events taking place, you can compress all of this in a sense, thereby seeing all things, hearing all things, all at the same moment. This is the most simple explanation I can give you. I see, hear, taste and smell all the same things that you do but at what you would consider to be an unbelievable rate of speed. Also, I "hear" things at a vastly different frequency and vibration than you are capable of here while you are in mortal form.

OK now, if you can accept this fact and then combine it with another fact that is relevant to this issue, you will have more clarity about how it is that I do what I do. Remember please, I know each and every Soul agreement by heart; that includes all amendments that have been added. I can tell even if you decide to change your course in life, I will always know how dependable you as Soul will be to just cause. Or, conversely how detrimental you may become. Of course there is also the fact that I do these things *because I can.* Yes, Children, every step you take, every thought you each have is known by Me WHILE it is occurring. I am constantly reaching out to millions of you, I have always done so. I whisper in your ear, touch your brow and encourage you to never give up, by actively reminding you on both a conscious and SuperConscious level that I love you greatly.

You see, when it was clearly understood by all of We who are of Divinity, that so many millions of pure Soul types of all evolutionary status would need to be here from the beginning of linear time and through the Golden NOW,

17

We knew it was incumbent on them to be able to share their linked-minds and linked Soul Voices to all here who could withstand the assaults of the beast. Furthermore, these Souls who specifically volunteered for this mission knew full well that even Souls who were either already slightly tinged with darkness and those who would succumb to the darkness totally, still need to be touched by the Souls whose mission were to teach people how and why they should save themselves, while it was still possible. Obviously, I am sure that at least most of you reading My words are now beginning to better understand yet another reason for the necessity of reincarnation to be an ongoing processing of Souls. *If NONE of you understand the WHY, then perhaps I am addressing the wrong Children!*

Common sense in this matter can be your trusted friend. Without the provocative rebirthing process, how many opportunities for a Soul to change its course would remain? The answer is: **very few.** I am going to refer to the Souls who volunteered and the ones We selected for this processing as, "the Soul factor." I said, "Factor, not factory!" The Soul factor of yesteryear just as the factor of today, must always be prepared to link minds and peer all the way into the matrix of another person, to the depth of the other's being if necessary. Also, the factor must also present specific crucibles to those they are dealing with for the purpose of Creating opportunities for change that could otherwise have been denied to the other Souls. This all takes place on a conscious and SuperConscious level, but it is not a random selection process. All Soul agreements are mutually contracted; therefore they MUST be honored to the "max." Many millions of the most evolved Souls in the factor are adepts. Therefore, it is not a problematic situation for them to simply send their brain waves, the ones they have programmed for specific frequencies and altered vibrations, and then broadcast them to the world at large.

18

All but a few of the Soul factor of millennia past have returned yet again, this time for their participation in the Golden NOW. I applaud this factor for not only being the ones who determinedly keep working with the human races of this world, but also because they are not bellicose or embittered because of the formidable odds that they have always faced. They do not whimper or cry out in anguish begging Me to change this world. They do not see only the dark here; they see and greatly appreciate the enormous amounts of Light that so many of you are emitting regardless of your personal circumstances. Children, only the people here who are using their intuition, who are using their sentience, are the ones who KNOW when a link has occurred. This has always been the case. Sometimes they can easily trace back to the very moment it happened and by whom. Other times they are simply overjoyed to know that it has happened. Yes, it can happen through the written word as well. *HINT, HINT.*

The people who are in ignorance about what has happened simply wonder why they are feeling a bit better. You see, every nanosecond the Soul factor can touch another human's mind, heart or Soul, sends out a fast-moving beam of Light into the ethers. This Light then has the long sought opportunity to unite with the other Lights being transmitted and each Light then can gather more strength, more endurance for whatever lies ahead. It does not really matter in one sense if the persons being affected are aware of what really transpired. Although of course I would prefer that they did know. What matters is that Light is gathering more fields of Light and that dear Children is a priceless event. Those who are AWARE that a wondrous happening, a gift, has been given to them do in a short span of non-time go on to touch, affect, and connect with others. It is in this intangible manner that tangible events and new generations of more evolved people can be born. Do you understand? If you do not than I encourage all of you to please reread My words until you get it right!

19

As for the Souls who are tainted to one degree or another, yes, even they then possess the barest grain of Light that will have the chance to germinate at a future date. Perhaps **WAY** off in the future. If you wonder how long that link you have received will last, I shall tell you. It only requires a few moments of NOW for that precious gift to be assimilated by Soul. Then there is a spontaneous integration between all aspects of the physical body, the mind and of course this all radiates back to Soul. Essentially this means that Soul will ALWAYS have the benefit of those "telling moments." If not in the present incarnation then in future ones, notice please I used the plural form here; those iridescent precious gifts will assist you in achieving TRUE immortality. If for a moment you think that you must simply have blind faith to believe all that I am telling you, then I admonish you to be careful! I do not deal in blind faith; I deplore the fact that so many Children do this however. "Faith" itself is an energetic mass in its own right that lies in either dormant or activated form within the matrix of a Soul.

It is an energy streamer that has its own sentience; therefore it KNOWS truth and KNOWS deceit. Children here simply do not understand this however. Nor do they want to acknowledge that those who insist on having blind faith only accept at face value what they have been conditioned to accept. They are ultimately people who choose NOT to know the truth for and of themselves. I truly would not want to see you fall into this deplorable state of mind. However, when all is said but not done, it is still up to you.

You notice that I said, "Said but not done." Try not to lose this precious thought; it could very well be denotative of your many tomorrows. Although there are far too many of My Children who still sit on fences, now they do not know which side of the fence to sit on. May I suggest standing instead? Your individualized new perspective from this elevated position may offer you a more clearly defined view of what lies ahead of you. Then you would be in a much better position to "know" instead of guessing. Many of the fence sitters express themselves publically as being "in the know." Yet it is when they are silent, *when they believe no one is listening, that no one can hear them at all,* that they try to make sense out of what they privately know so little about. I can guide them out of the hole they are digging for themselves, however I can not make them admit to some fallacy that they themselves Created. This example of moral turpitude usual equates to some highly inflamed sense of ego. When this occurs it is not easily tamed. The truth is many do not want to change this stigma they unconsciously flaunt. I can not fault them for this, having the moral and Spiritual fortitude to confront oneself is not always an easy task. Try as I might to effectively reach into the hearts and minds of those who are **indulging in self-gratification,** it is not an easy task. I will not give up, I will simply bide My time waiting for the kernel or any kernel for that matter, of knowledge to sprout roots in their minds. The side effect to this manner of thought processing is that these same Souls who know themselves so *unwell,* will in all likelihood taint the minds of those who are not as wise or Spiritually mature as they ought to be. The dreary cycle then escalates as each Child of Mine who is touched by the flames of miscued information falters. It is due to their lack of diligence, they do not bother checking the information they received. Time after time I watch the downward spiral of otherwise goodhearted, well-intentioned Souls whose lives have been changed by someone else. These "someones" are the ones who should have been listening and trying to learn themselves instead of speaking. Their fates and destinies go round and round, like water funneling downward in a drain.

Do you think it is possible for you as an individual to change someone's life who may be thousands of miles away without ever meeting them? What about touching someone who is light-years away? Remember now, that pure refined energies know no bounds and that thought travels much faster than sound. *This is a fact!*

I want each of you to examine the encounters you made with others today. Think back at how many Souls you touched with just your own presence. It could be the shopkeeper, the postman *or woman*, the neighbor across the street. Did you add to their sense of importance, their confidence, or their serenity by offering them a kind word? Or did you burst their bubble before their day even had a chance to begin? If you walked about and paid them no heed, shrouded in your own cloak of anonymity, and paid them not even the slightest attention, then shame on you. You may have unknowingly been the guiding Light that was sent from above to nudge them in just the right way. As Gods and Goddesses in your own right, each of you needs to rise above the ho-hum doldrums of the day and rekindle the Spirit of magic. Rekindle believing in miracles; ignite a reason for being, in **self** and in others. Can you do this for Me? Will you do it for mankind?

This world is no longer on the teetering point of destruction; she will thankfully remain as an integral part of this Universe. Each of you has a vitally important choice to make NOW, one that will define your continued existences in this lifetime. Will you allow yourself to become expendable or will you live up to your Soul's name? As a Soul in activated form it is your responsibility to put yourself first, but not above others. Life has many learning arcs, each intertwined with the next. You must strive for balance in all that you do. Balance is the KEY to your evolution as a species as well as for you as your true self. The delicacy of a life well lived means that you have lived your life outside of a shell. This means you must be open and understanding to the pain and discomfort in others, while remaining detached all the same. I cannot stress to you the importance of YOU understanding the emotional and physical tribulations that others are going though. Yes, it is true that most of their dramas were created by none other than themselves. Weak willed, weak-minded others are just that, weak. They gravitate to disorganized chaos like a moth to a flame. These people you must be aware of and try as best you may to stay out of their way. Understanding what THEIR prevailing conditions are will at the very least help you NOT to make their mistakes.

Reincarnation has been a blessing to all of you, yes, I said all of you. I ask you to "Judge not lest you are prepared to judge yourself first." Reincarnation teaches personalities to speak as Souls. In other words, if I was to say that you were a free Spirit, would you think that you are completely free and unfettered from the bonds of "normal" man? Or would you think that your Spirit is one and the same with Me as MySelf? What if I then told you that your free Spirit, your non-committal self was causing you much pain? Would you then feel betrayed, offended? Would your protective shell then enclose you and shield you from the truth? Or would you understand that ninety percent of what you need to learn here on the Earth Star walk is to discover yourself? No, I did not say get in touch with your inner child, there is enough of that overstated least understood foolishness already. I watch sadly as many of you flounder through the day having no purpose, no joy in your lives. It equally saddens Me when I see those who gain such pleasure from causing others great pain. No longer will this be allowed, I have told you this before. No longer will I allow anyone to taint or suppress the incoming Souls who will journey here to this beloved planet. No longer can you or anyone else make excuses for being as you are. You are what you are until you see fit to be otherwise. I am here at this point erecting a mirror which will reflect **the true you** back to your mind's eye. If you do not like what you see then change it while you still have time. Inner reflection and hopefully the desire to enact great change in how you view yourself as a human being will be forever ingrained in your brain.

Let us briefly examine the inner workings of those of the Illuminati ilk. Although less evolved they still are very much in the know of great amounts of Universal knowledge that is currently out of your reach. They use the good in you to commit their wrongful deeds. You then take it upon yourself whether you do so consciously or not, to promote more of the same. This touches the beast which lies dormant in all of you. It is there because somewhere on your journeys through LIVES, you have either met with it, or been touched by another whose beast aspect was alive and had been well fed. It is up to you which to feed. *God or beast*. The Illuminati clans have long used the righteousness in you to promote their conflicts, these are the conflicts which cause others great pain. They are masterful in their planning and they consider all of you as expendable, as cattle or sheep at the very least. Why have they continued to do this? It is because they know that others will be sent to replace those of you who fall in their wake. This is an example of how **not** to reach out and touch others.

Long have you been innocent bystanders while watching your own demise. Longer still have you allowed yourselves to sit idly by while others are being mistreated or abused in other horrific fashion. Have you Children no heart for the forsaken people? Do you only feel pain when it affects you personally? What will it take for each of you to see yourself in others and say, "Enough is enough?" Is it tomorrow, or perhaps the day after? What about just before you die? Will this admonishment clear your consciousness so you can easily, peacefully transition off this plane? This planet herself and all of My Children who seek great change for the inhabitants of this world, are vanquishing the Illuminati and all of their legions from this world, once and for all. Who then will you then have to blame for your allegations of misfortune and mischievous ways, when the legions are no longer here to take credit for your lack of determination to change your lives for the better?

Have you ever beheld a child while that child was still free from limitations induced by years of conditioned training? The children are the Eye to My Soul. Through them I can do great works. Children open the eyes of the un-sensing adult. In many ways the children are the open windows to the veiled Soul of the adult. The children force adults through their childish charm and inquisitiveness of All That Is, to look within. They help them to remember a time when they too cared about something other than mortgages, alliances and acquisitions. They truly are a marvel to behold. If you have forgotten what it means to see through the eyes of a child then journey back to a moment of peace when all was right in your personal world. Remember the jubilation, the awe, the wonderment and the excitement you felt as you waited anxiously to peer around the next corner. Hold on to this moment and venture out into the world. Make note of the eyes that twinkle, the smiles that widen as others watch you in this heightened state of bliss. Be contagious for all the right reasons. Do it for yourself, do it for others, do it for Me, do it because you can.

I want you to understand something that so many have yet to realize. Each encounter you have, whether it is of a personal nature or just being in the right place at the right time, is important to the playing out of your intended roles there on Earth. No, you may not know it at the time. I ask you, is it really so important for you to know? Or is it enough to know that when you feel inspired, when you have followed the truth as you have seen it unfold before you, that this is enough? Many people touch the lives of others without ever knowing they have done so. This is an aspect of the grand design. The people, young and old of this world will never know how dearly they are loved. More still will never know the lengths and breadth of how I have tried to make each of your lives just a little more comfortable. Too many of you still equate comfort with lifestyle, I challenge you to understand that *comfort is a state of mind*, a way of being. If you can master this simple concept then the options that avail you will multiply exponentially.

The life you change most along the way *by reaching out to others* may well be your own.

In service to life... *God*

Codex 2

Uncivil Behavior

God... OK Children; in case I neglected to tell you before...do not expect Me to epitomize sweetness or to behave in any manner that can be construed as overly laidback in this book or the remaining books of this series. Although there is so much I want to tell you and so much more beyond that, that you need to know essentially I must work within the perimeter of the gridline that We are all now currently engaged in. This means that I must ask you to read between the lines if you are able to. If you can not then yes, that is a problem! However I will leave it to you to find the solution to that. I will not do it for you.

Every life experience begins with a *whoosh,* but not with the insurmountable problems you may suppose. Instead it begins with a continuation of what is termed, "unfinished business." That business however is aligned with each and all **new** beginnings that have been so carefully laid out for you, by you. Of course I have helped a bit with that. I have carefully inserted certain codes in each and every lifetime you have ever had. Each one however is specifically designed to meet all your fundamental Spiritual needs. That is to say that even if you decide to alter your course during any life experience the codes are always in place. Some may remain dormant throughout many of your lifetimes while others are always in a spectacular kinetic force field where nothing and no-things can displace the information I have given you. *However,* codes <u>can be</u> overrun; they <u>can be</u> brought to a standstill position IF the individual Child chooses the path MOST traveled. Those of you Children who are blatantly aggressive in your refusals to alter course, this means you remain on the path of the righteous and always maintain

27

your integrity, <u>can not</u> lose the precious gifts the ciphers house.

Some of the codes are in a type of alphabetical design, not in human writings as such, but in a type of geometrical pattern that can not be altered by you, even by your best intentions. At times, depending on who the Soul is I am affecting with the "God System," I simply have used numbers and symbols as a means that I have foreseen to best communicate with you each and all. At times this communication in My God System is predicated on secret information that is not meant to be shared by you with others. Some information is quite lengthy, while other information is very brief. All depends on not only the information to be accepted by you, but also on the circumstances you may be embroiled in here on the planet. There are instances when a Child or large cluster of My Children here may be so muddled in thought and deed, that it may require some time for them to disentangle themselves from that mess. They must do so in order to proceed with the INNATE understanding required. Your own levels of integrity clearly denote what areas of expertise you may have in decoding the System, as well as what is and what is not considered to be acceptable by you to know at any given time. No, I am most certainly NOT speaking of other people here who have ensnarled themselves in the "I don't want to know" syndrome. I am careful to never overwhelm any of you at any given moment.

If however, a Child here is caught up in the religious webs of deceit and injustice, then that Child of Mine will not want to know anything that could possibly conflict with the rhetoric he or she has long been exposed to. Their intellects would virtually shut down because of the massive shock they would receive in knowing that the very foundations of the lifetime had been a horrible lie. Again, this is all predicated on each individual Soul's ability

while in human form, to format correct choices in life by understanding what is a true reality and what is an illusion <u>disguised</u> as a reality. At times the illusionary world however takes on a whole new meaning in the minds of many Children here. They have become so subjugated, so truly indoctrinated with illusions that <u>they can not LIVE without them</u>. They are truly addicted to illusions! You did not know that now did you? That too is a life choice. It does not however in any manner negate the FACT that symbols, macrocosmic terms and infinite knowledge that is available in the altruistic design I have so carefully crafted for so many millennia still remain in place. I have striven to tell you repeatedly that **you are not alone.** Tell Me Children, how many of you bothered or even thought to look behind the meanings of those words? I do know the answer-very few.

"Civility" is also a term that I taught to all of you, many times in fact. Your meaning of the today word differs vastly from My own. I define civility as "an honor bound variant of highly displaced energy that lives and thrives only in a fertile environment." If you consider your mind to be fertile and your Spirit to be fertile then yes, THAT is an aspect of the meaning I have for the term. However, not one of you reading these words grasped that. I know you did not. I already looked. I said it was "highly displaced energy" because here on this planet of Mine, it is. At "home" it is simply an acknowledged unit of homogeneous macrocosmic energies that have intelligence and reign supreme as an integral and equal portion of unvarnished truth. It is designated to live as a partner to the individual Soul. It also functions as its own catalyst for assisting in the reaping of honors and rewards. *As you sow, so do you reap.*

OK, I had to search My mind to decide on the best manner to properly approach the subject of how civility has fallen into a state of such disrepair here and why it has.

You see if I am to tell you HOW then I am duty bound to explain the WHY. It can be no other way. Children, I implore you each to better understand not only how fortuitous it is that you are reading these writings, but I want you to clarify in your minds "why you and why not many others."

Understand this NOW: I have afforded every person on this planet the opportunity to read the God book Series of My writings to learn or relearn as the case may be, in order to not merely prepare yourselves for the things it is no longer possible to change, but to expand upon your individual and collective choices to remain on the Earth Star planet. Or you can choose to perish along with millions of others who shall continue to do so, because of all the choices they have made in this lifetime. Obviously, the first die has been cast and there are but a few die left. Yes, I heard a few of you thinking that perhaps, just perhaps, you are all encoded with the book information and have been led to Celestial and David's websites and thus to My books. Kudos to you! You are correct. But then again I did make this information available to all of you so very, very, long ago. As you each departed Nirvana and other realms to either begin a sojourn here or to pick up where you left off so you could arrive at final conclusions with your prior "unfinished business" here with the planet as well as with many of the Planetizens here, I then shared all My promises with you each.

Many of you Children had some qualms and a bit of hesitation at leaving home **again** and returning to the place where you had experienced so much pain in prior life experiences. Although I must say that there were still others who simply were ecstatic about rejoining Terra in order to be of even greater service than they previously had been, I treated you all equally and with great respect. It was through each and every incarnation that I reminded you just nanoseconds before you departed to arrive here in time to be aligned with your own specific gridline intersections, that **My written words would be revealed to you and would help to see you through.** Of course I did not make mention of the fact of exactly WHEN it would take place nor through whom I would speak. I **did** say that it would be through two highly evolved and strategically placed Souls whose very walk-in presence would cause many to gasp. I **did** say that the strategy that the Creator and I along with the able assistance of all other Luminescents and the covenant We all shared with The Masters and others, would all be reminiscent to each of you, as **one by one** specific spatial events unfurled here. Furthermore I **did** say that it would be during the times of the most tumultuous "incidents" ever to haunt humanity, that My words would be broadcast for all to read. No, Children, I did not tell you the whole of the matter back then. *Some secrets of Heaven should not be revealed.* At least not until the timeline is proper. **It is proper NOW.**

If you Children remember it was back in a previous book that I told you there would be born a New Book of Revelations. That new book is to be one that millions of you here are already writing; you just do not know it YET. This book shall not contain biblical pseudo writing. It will contain all your own thought forms that are not only regulating your own stability, they are assisting with the balance that Terra has requested of you. This will be part of the new but not anomalous "civil behavior" and will impact on millions of new Souls who will begin arriving here **after the lengthy reformation period has ended.** I ask you to bear that information in mind as you each continue to separate your new thoughts from your former ones. That is all I will say about that matter at this time.

Civil behavior and uncivil behavior are millions of Light-years apart in one sense, yet each is a part of the broadcasting of the true essence of your personalities in another sense. Although feminine energies had been despoiled and forced into submission and degradation by the carefully contrived plots of the dark agents of the dark overlords so very, very, long ago, still so many of you are terribly lacking in any understanding of **why** it happened. You see, the Illuminati always knew of the initial cycle and then of course all succeeding later spatial time cycles that were the heralds of the emergences of My Son Jesus THE Christ here on this planet. They were quite savvy to the fact that Jesus and His most beloved LIFE PARTNER Mary Magdalene, would be here together AGAIN. The missions Jesus and Mary accepted were and still are to **clear the path** that has been littered with the decayed and treacherous acts the Illuminati overlords laid out for humanity. Children, in this sentence above what I am now writing I INTENTIONALLY gave you a 3 word code. This code *when translated correctly by you* has a 4 word meaning. I shall sit back now and see how many of you "get it."

OK, back in the Stone Age days, women were easily conditioned to be submissive to the patriarchal energy simply because the Illuminati were "in knowing" of a fact that the people here were not. The dark ones were aware that many centuries later there would be a REEMERGENCE of Mary. They also knew that she would return again and again for as many times as she was needed. Have you Children already forgotten that I did tell you all rather succinctly I might add, that Jesus IS well known on all planets, all Universes? So it is that because of His continued journeys throughout all the galaxies, yes, including or should I say, especially the ones you know nothing about yet, He was often accompanied by His "TWIN FLAME." So it came to be known without a single break in spatial time that Mary would always be the ASPECT of Jesus who would strengthen all feminine principles. No, Jesus Himself has never attempted to fortify the masculine energies. Why would He?

He and she are the perfected coupling of male and female as ONE androgynous unit. Incivility towards all females here on the planet has ALWAYS been about Mary. To the dark overlords all females were but emblematic Souls descriptive of Mary. They had truly believed that they could stop the feminine principle from assuming her rightful place as CO-CREATOR with the masculine principle. The darkest of the dark ones were intent on destroying women's Spirits. In order to do this they concentrated on causing the deterioration of women's minds, MORALS, aspirations and intents. Have they succeeded? *What do you think?* I know what I think, because I know what I know. I will speak further of this matter in a bit.

OK, uncivil behavior is, "a wasteland of ill-conceived thoughts of the mind and Soulless matter, spread thin within the heart and Spirit of a human being, caused by the acceptance of disruptive, discordant and invasive energies." For all the time periods here, throughout all the ages that have ever been, the dark streamers have sought to further their unjust cause through the manipulation of mind and matter. By invoking invidious, spurious thoughts and intents spread like a slimy veneer in a bottomless trough throughout each human race, they did succeed. Ultimately this has caused gross loss of respectability and self-respect which then walks hand in hand with the loss of personal responsibility. Integrity is lost. The time of innocence is then over. Although this began on a one-on-one basis, over time the contagion has grown so massive that it now encompasses every human race. *Just as it was intended to.* There have long been few exceptions to this invasion. Moral decadence is the result, it then reigns supreme. THIS is what has been the prevailing corruption on this planet. You have no idea YET what else it has corrupted. This then is what happens as the civil encoding I gave you all then is transformed into uncivil codes, uncivil behavior. A part of the reincarnation selections of gender IS about Mary, while other parts are about learning to live as a female Goddess while understanding how to integrate with the masculine God. Men have not really had it so easy here you know. They have been as easily conditioned as have the women. *So, do not cast stones, verily I warn you, they will be cast right back at you.*

So many of you have been looking for a quick fix to the end of the old ways of life while concentrating on how you THINK it will be in the future. Children, I tell you all I will **never** condone a quick fix for any reason! Just so there is no misunderstanding in your collective minds about this. Quick fixes are what have caused the behemoth to feed on your fantasies, you know. How and why did you think your political agendas and medical smarminess came to be? And then there are the all encompassing lifestyles of certain people here who are among the rich and lameness. All these situations and people lacked tremendous credibility, yet it was My Earthbound Children here who always paid homage to those things that go bump in the night. And they did so, for as **long as the true natures of the beast Masters were not revealed.** For something to be revealed of those natures, it first must be suspect, it must be "persons of interest" who needed to be scrutinized. Of course that would require work on humanity's part, now wouldn't it? Although there have been many sycophantic people here who have most certainly contributed in one manner or another to the uncivil behavior here, they too must pay the price now.

All uncivil behavior must be eradicated here. This is the way it is! I assure you Children, IT WILL BE and it will happen with or without your assistance. This is one primary reason why the reformation and new birthing of all the Souls who will participate with Me in Creating an entirely new world here MUST of necessity take a long time. Yes, of course I am being unusually stern; the time for parades and media fanfares is long over. Truth must be emphasized and I assure you all, I am doing My part in this matter.

Now to speak further on the Mary Magdalene issue: I shall continue to do this in this part of the codex for she has so much bearing on every person of each gender here. My Mary-Self Child and My Son Jesus have long succeeded in circumventing certain situations that the dark legion attempted to make happen. Although the dark has always prided itself on its cleverness and its ability to shape-shift, thus confusing people who may not know WHAT they are dealing with, We have always had and carefully maintained a balancing of the Scales of Universal Justice. Due to the internal and external make-up that is the total composite of both Mary and Jesus, the Light without limit which is WHO and WHAT They each are, is the perfected antithesis that the dark sorely fear. Mary is in her own right royalty; she is of a very, very, long line of a lineage of what you may think of as, "true bloods." Each in her family possesses the most incredible Light, serenity and a totality of true passion dedicated to all Luminescents, all Universes, without restraint or any form of compromise.

They each have long been pioneers of the truest of truths and the harbingers of all greater realities. They have worked with utter dedication and self-discipline assisting in establishing all new worlds and giving of their genetic matter to all civilizations. Mary was born into herself and thus while she was but a speck waiting for the gestalt SEASON OF A SOUL to occur, she was even then promised to Jesus. No, we did not arrange their marriages, their eternal Sacred Communion with one another, We merely brought them together and the rest is spatial history. As it should be. Children, I do truly realize how difficult it is for all but a few of you here on this planet to deal with staggering numbers of ages that are all but incomprehensible to you. So, I will not attempt to give you human numbers regarding Mary's age, firstly because

35

there is none and secondly because you would not understand anyway. Simply stated, "Mary is eternal."

Long before the Earth Star planet was Created, Mary and Jesus traveled far and wide visiting different realms of thought and different citadels of knowledge. During the early beginning times of new worlds that had been Created, when they were under attack by some of the dark streamers, many evolved off-world beings always requested through a petition to the High Court, the assistance of these two Souls. Jesus and Mary each eagerly complied with the requests then set about doing what they do best. **They teach.** Oftentimes they teach by sheer example, indemnifying all the worlds they touched with their Beautiful Soul Selves, their incredible Light and their energy imprints. Yes, I did mean, "indemnifying," Celest. Neither Jesus nor Mary confines themselves to one locale; they are spared the endemic constraints that many other Souls must patiently endure as a result of their reincarnational choices. Mary and Jesus were both born into nobility and have always epitomized this highly placed quality. They can assume many guises, depending on the situations at hand.

When it came to pass that the dark energies knew that Mary would be here with Jesus during the lifetime when non-believers' of the true realities claimed Jesus had been crucified, a final thrust, a last ditch effort by the dark to prevent women AND men from knowing who Mary truly was, was launched in the most brutal, most heinous attack ever endured by her. So many, many, many, of My other Children here were TAUGHT to believe that Mary was a harlot. Even though she was not and never could be. The defamation of her true character was so intense that the longevity of those intentional lies has long outlived many of the entities who first proposed the evil plan. It was deemed to be of such a highly important task to keep her memory alive as a prostitute, thereby negating the FACT that she was indeed the wife of Jesus THE Christ. It also accomplished another purpose; one that was as hideous as the first!

If the women had ever known the truth here on this planet about Mary, they would have striven to emulate her qualities which would have caused them to effectively emulate their own selves as women, as well. And they would have then brought their own children up in the same manner. Women would not be engaged in pornography, drugs, incest or any other UNCIVIL behavior. Men would have clearly understood the role models females here were meant to be for the enrichment of the feminine principle and for all future generations of females on this planet, as well as on other worlds. As a result men themselves would have changed. *Quid pro quo.* Children, you have been believing the great lie for far too long. I simply will not tolerate any longer the continuation of this craftily planned deceit. Another matter you do not know about is what has currently begun here and will always be a major hallmark, a turning point for this planet. Mary is gentleness, she is Light, she is humorous and gracious, yet she does not tolerate man's inhumane treatment to others of mankind. She is not seeking an edict against men for their criminal and immoral behavior towards women. Nor is she seeking it for the women who have run so far amuck. Instead, she and Jesus are handling this matter in a wholesome and serene manner. Up to a point that is. It is not true that women are from Venus and men are from Mars. At least not in the basic tenet which is part of the accrual of life wisdoms that assists in the building process of the Soul foundations throughout their lives. Obviously Planetizens here are from all other planets, but to imply that one is some type of masculine warlike or harsh creation and the other is simply love unabated, is ridiculous.

The masculine energies here as I told you somewhere above in this writing, have been conditioned to believe that they were some type of omnipotent authority over the feminine species. "Conditioning" in this sense is simply "brainwashing." How could men know any better, I ask you now? Certainly there have been millions of males who felt it was not right for women to not attain the same status in life as men. However, between the males' individual upbringings, the harshness of peer pressure and their fears of being ridiculed, men accepted the status quo. Religions themselves were so carefully crafted to pander to the male oneness and continue to relegate females to the lowest stations in life, that males were honestly not able to overcome the illusions. Ultimately all races of females were pushed further downward into an abyss of nothingness. Essentially because male and female have forgotten what they once knew, both genders have become inferior.

Children, can you think of a better, more devious way to mold all generations who have ever lived on this planet and thus cause them to remain in total ignorance? Are you yet beginning to understand what you have been up against? If you need more conclusive PROOF of this then look around you at this world. Remember the usually small ways through thought and deed that you yourselves have contributed to this decay of morality. OK, as all this has continued....*up until now*...to cause the abject defeat and stalemate progression of the God Principle each Soul had innately carried with them to this planet. Your memories **while you have been in mortal form** were effectively erased simply because *you have forgotten to believe.* My mission in the writings of all these books is to cause you to remember while you still are able to.

Each time Mary and Jesus came to the Earth Star planet they did so in order to encourage each male AND female here to retrieve the Soul memories that have been so sorely tainted, so sorely tried and found to be lacking. Although they always have many successes here, what I am about to tell you will soon become an accepted FACT of

Earth Star history. Although the hyped "second coming of Jesus" has been horribly misunderstood, it is and **always** has been the arrivals of the Jesus The Christ Consciousness that you have been long awaiting, over and over again. Not in the manner of yesteryear when so little could be accomplished here by Jesus throughout His many incarnations here, but **NOW.** The Jesus The Christ Consciousness is an all encompassing movement of the greatest of the greatest forms of Divinity extraordinaire, hosting the sum total of all of the energy imprints of all the greatest teachers of this Universe as well as of all other Universes. The Light of this Conscious is unlike anything you can imagine, Children. It is the purest form of unbridled ecstasy, it is the greatest love in all forms and it contains the sweeping effect that touches all hearts, all Souls. It is incandescent yet it is both tangible and intangible. Mary Magdalene **is** the womb of the Jesus The Christ Consciousness. In this manner she has returned along with her beloved Jesus as one unified BEING. She shares the womb with MySelf and with the entirety of the Creation processing as well as the very matrix of Jesus HimSelf.

Jesus and Mary are one, yet they are many. They are exemplary examples of what masculine and feminine principle should be. They share a totality of fully integrated, completely intertwined energies. They are androgynous of course, but just as do all evolved androgynous beings they each have the ability to separate themselves into one male and one female entity as needed. Otherwise when you see one of them, you are seeing both of them, but in only one pure form of brilliant Light! This is the time for this Consciousness to supersede all that has gone here before. This is the time when Jesus and Mary will ascend to their rightful place here touching each and every person here on the planet. You see, even though none of you here know anything about this Sacred matter, as each person is touched by this Greater Consciousness,

39

Mary and Jesus BOTH leave an indelible energy imprint upon the middle of the brow of each of you.

This is the awakening of "the God Principe." In this manner not only are millions of Children here being roused from the long slumber of the unilluminated webs of ignorance, Mary and Jesus are also beginning to awaken all those they can to all true realities. These results will be known by you through your knowing who you are and your own purposes in life, both life here and life everlasting. Children, pay attention to all I am sharing with you: I could have chosen to allow you each to simply fade away from mortality without hearing the truths you have forgotten. But, I did not, so listen while you can. Throughout the reincarnational process each Soul is obligated to assume either male or female genus. This is for either a singular lifetime predicated on learning to live without the conscious homogenous state of androgyny being present in their minds and hearts, or for many, many, lifetimes. This depends on if they have learned all they should, or if the final preference for one gender over another supersedes the need to repeat yet again one gender choice over another.

Essentially this means that all males today have had life experiences as males and as females. Obviously this is also true of all females. The female of today may have been a male for the previous two lifetimes. The male of today could have been a female for the last ten lifetimes. Children, what I am also telling you one and all, is that Mary and Jesus have given to each Soul ever born the energy imprint of both their selves. Because you each carry this imprint, if you are male today then you are a dormant female. If you are female today, you are a dormant male. And so on and so on. So, how does it feel Children, to know that not only have you been demeaning the other gender at one time or another, but essentially by doing so you have been also demeaning yourself? I suppose this could give a whole new meaning to, *"the acorn does not fall far from the tree."* As Mary and Jesus continue to journey on with the stupendous Consciousness that Creates new worlds, many people shall fall simply because they can not live life without illusions. Mary and Jesus are busily removing the veils to see how many of those types of people are ready to receive the imprint yet once again. Millions of Children here WILL carry the Consciousness mark, the Sacred energy imprint. Others shall not. The others shall carry the mark of the beast, in one form or another. You will know them by their Light, or by their loss of illumination. **I do.**

There will no longer be either a patriarchy or a matriarchy. Pay attention please to the new term; after all you will all have to LIVE it. And no, it will not change. The new term is "co-crearchy." These are the ones who will live here as true human beings. No substitutes accepted!

Before I continue on I feel it would behoove Me to give you a classic example of how so many codes are hidden in plain sight. I will use My Celest-Self for this demonstration, simply because one of her experiences certainly emphasizes what you should be looking for. A few years ago a client she had been working with for several years called her to tell her he had a dream about her. Now mind you, he never met her in person nor had he ever seen any pictures of her. He told her that he had a dream that she was standing a few feet away from him. He was able to see her complete image. He said she was extremely tall, I believe he used the term, "unnaturally tall," and that her image seemed to be carefully and completely split down the middle from the top of her head to the bottom of her feet. Yet she was one person. He told her that one-half of her was male and the other half was female and both halves dressed accordingly. He did say that the male half of her had a mustache, well HALF a mustache and how strange that looked.

41

He then said he attributed the dream to having drank a bit too much ale the night before and left it at that. Celest never did explain to him what it was that he was seeing and this man never bothered to figure out the code. Let Me see if any of you can figure it out! Codes are everywhere Children; but if you do not bother to understand them then you are missing out on a great and exciting part of life. Some people have said that I speak in parables, yet the truth is I speak in codes. There is nary a page in any of these books where codes are not present. They are geared to be of assistance to you one and all as you journey deeply into the Jesus THE Christ Consciousness. *The realm that time forgot.*

In the beginning when all of you who are now here wearing human guise were but a gleam in the Creators eye, it was foreseen that moral decadence and a profligacy of words from the false prophets would eventually ensue. Why would this happen? People made it inevitable. In order for a Soul, or in this case a very large contingent of Souls originating from many different worlds with varied backgrounds, personal goals, ambitions and ideals to come together as one Spiritually homogeneous group, it was known Universally that there would be challenges and confrontations on all levels of reality. The issue would always be whatever the present and dominant state of consciousness of any Earthly civilization was. "Consciousness" you remember exists because it can, because it must. As with everything in life, it is dependent on one form or another of what it is nurtured with the most. It also has fortunateness; this energy is reliant on how it is perceived, whether it is to be a challenge that one aspires to understand and overcome, or if it inadvertently sets up a conflict in the minds of so many people. There are so many value systems, differing perspectives and diversity of alternate realties that must be taken into consideration before an unwavering clarity of vision and even at times a surreal sense of purpose may be found. Each of you has out of necessity been guided, lured when necessary, to experience all these emotions throughout your many incarnations. The trouble really ensued when some of you began truly **enjoying** the overwhelming surge of a "foreign" energy that can be received as a result of being thrust into roles that were reeking of control.

You all should know by now that control is just an illusion and that it never has really existed. In order to challenge yourself, in order for many of you to understand what it is like to confront the beast and not give in to its temptations, but still learn what it means to jump headfirst into this arena, many of you chose to dance with the devil. I never encouraged you to do this. So it came to pass that the dance of the macabre that was to last but a millisecond, turned ghastly when the captive fell in love with the captor and then bedded down with the enemy. Now you all know how well that one usually turns out. So many people disregard all common sense when it comes to affairs afflicting the heart. The people then toss aside their ability to know better and surrender themselves to a moment of pleasure and to the enticing thrill of the hunt. This is when civility once honored and revered again gave way to uncivil behavior.

My dear Children, it matters naught if you feel you are a righteous person with strict moral codes and creeds you adhere to, if you do so only out of service to self. The *silent scream* that began here but a few short years back has become deafening, the innocents are crying out for justice and equality and rightfully so. The deprived people want their slice of the pie; can you fault them for this? I remind you that many of them may have been abused and downtrodden, *however* do not forget that for millions of people here, it was their choice to remain as they have become. Uncivil or not all of you have stood idly by while this pandemic reached epic proportions. As with any disease it must be eliminated from the source. The source in this sense is the people of this world. Remember what I have told you in the past, the dark has no power without you. You feed it with your fears, your insecurities and your *poor me* attitudes. Here is another perspective: You have all had ample time and sufficient reasons to break the patterns of your lives. MANY OF YOU have been judgmental of others without bothering to consider that perhaps you yourselves and others like you, may well be the problem, not the ones you are judging.

The times of the kings are over. I am telling you all now that every person on Earth is equal. Spread the word. Would it help you if I told you that you were all puny, petty and insignificant in the greater scheme of things? Would it make you angry? Well, maybe it should, however I will not state this as a fact because it is not true. However it does not change the fact that many people believe this of themselves and of others. Sometimes I shake My head in wonderment, trying to decide how to get a reaction from My Earthly Children. Have your senses become so dulled that you are willing to accept anything that is heaped on you? You are not beggars; you are Gods and Goddesses, for goodness sakes. Grow up; proclaim your right to be, reclaim your right to have a good life, a life worth living. Do so without recklessly taking and taking and taking from others and you will be much better off than you are. If you feel My sorrow then perhaps the eternal flame I birthed you all with burns on still. I take no pleasure in chastising any of you; however the neuroticism many of you still treasure has left Me no choice.

Civility must be taught once again.

This planet as you are now all becoming well aware is fighting back. The question is, what will you now do? Will you continue on as so many of your predecessors have done and continue to try to defy the winds of change so that all will remain the same? The "same" in this sense is stagnation; it is whirling headfirst into oblivion. How do I impress upon you that you must honor and respect what presently divides you from other people here? This melding of the species within the human races can work; I know it has already occurred within the continuum. All that you need to do is to get there from here. Visualize a large bag, toss into it everything that you do not agree with, the issues that others may hold dear. Fill it up and then toss it out the window. Now create a new bag, one that you will fill with all that you love, admire and respect. As you insert each new element examine it for purity, originality and make sure it can withstand the test of time. See the wonders you have placed within your bags, trace back their origins, connect the dots and try to visualize the grand design. Nurture these items with love as you would love a child and then set them free into the wind. Add to this bag as new thoughts and inspirations come to you. Set them free as well so they ripen and evolve. Look back once in a while to take stock of all you have deemed that is worthy to be freed. All that you have set into motion will continue until their time ends, their cycles are finished. I would say that if you did do your job well, your rewards should be many. Shake the trees, rustle the grasses that lie in your path, see what is hiding from you in plain sight. Understand your differences by acknowledging that each person has a purpose. It is not your business to understand what their purposes are. The truth is all of you have looked away during the times of great need that this planet has had and willfully ignored the needs of others of your races. How long must I remind you of what you should already know? I caution you, when the feelings swell inside of your mind and heart and you then must decide to take an affirmative stand for what is right, do so peacefully or all your efforts will have been in vain. The entire world has been suffering great pain; do not inadvertently add to what has been the predominant condition.

How can any of you sit idly by while a Child of mine is being vilified? How can any of you who see yourselves as evolved or evolving, be willing to sit idly by as millions suffers from hunger or disease? I suggest to you, that you have isolated yourself to such a degree from others of your kind that you feel nothing unless it affects you personally. Many of those who have now stepped beyond the boundaries of illusion are waking up from the misanthropic stupor they had allowed to take place. How many of you see the rite of passage periods, those times when boy becomes man, girl becomes woman and understand how this rite has accentuated many hateful qualities as well as many good intentions? Once true innocence is lost aggression, depression and introverted types of tendencies and total loss of civility may begin. Innocence once lost is hard to regain. I have often wondered why anyone would take away such an important aspect of what it means to be truly human. There must be balance; duality has had its time and now a new era has begun. It will not be an era of man nor of woman.

Today I urge all of you who are left standing to heed My words of caution. Do not do unto others as you would have them do unto you; do unto others as you would have Me do unto you. If you still believe that I am wrathful and walk softly carrying a big spear then you have just sealed your fate for eons to come. If you believe that I have always had all your best interests at heart and that I am kind, caring and that I live that Spiritual creed, then that is waiting for you. As I said, not all of you were keen on being here this time around, yet I ask all of you to understand that you were more needed now than at perhaps any other time in human history. What is left undone in this current timeline will have to be addressed in the future. So I encourage all of you to take a deep breath, look inside, find whatever your character flaws are and address them once and for all. We can no longer afford to spend eons fixing something that could be accomplished in just a short time. I have always had patience with all generations of people on this world. That time *however,* is at an end. No, I will not become wrathful and seek revenge. That is not My way and I sincerely hope that it is not *yours*.

The time of the war birds is rapidly coming to an end. So Children, then there will be no one other than yourselves on whom you can hold responsible for your "condition." Acceptance of all that may be still wrong with the lives of many of you will be your personal responsibility. What will you do? Even I do not know that. I can guess with a pretty good degree of accuracy the probability of your actions and decisions being healthy Creative ones. What I see right now in the hearts of most men and yes, most women too, is that they will continue to choose the least controversial avenue for them to sustain or fulfill their needs and desires. I see that it will indeed take a few more generations of humans to be birthed before the generational teachings have altered to an enlightened, well-informed state of higher consciousness. It is the few among you who will close the rift between all lands. It is the few who **are** making a difference here on the front lines. Yet it is the few who are now wonderfully influencing the new joiners of the collective consciousness. The lines still get thinner each and every day and some people find they do not have what it takes to hold the candle steadfastly in the winds of change for all others who will be attracted to its light. Beacons are those who have learned to bend rather than bow. The nonexistence of civility in all cultures in this world has caused the many to bow when they should have stood up for what they believed in. There is not a culture that has not been contaminated by the stench of the darkness that is entrenched in the bowels of every facet of society.

Even your aid programs have been corrupted. There is no charity to be found between animal and man. There is little to be found anywhere on the **world *of man***. Everywhere I look however I do see some light emerging from those who have broken free of their bonds. These

47

Souls need and deserve reinforcement; are you the one who will offer it to them? There is nothing you can do for the ones who find little use for truth. Conspiracies and personal agendas hold their attention, at least for a little longer now. Soon they too will discover that their secret agendas, whatever they may be, will no longer sustain them. They will be consumed by their conspiracies because they are intellectually binding. **This** world will no longer feed their curiosity even as limited as it is and they **will leave** in search of new lands. Whatever they find there in their **new lands** and what they bring with them will create their reality for some time to come. The truth is many will not know that they are not in familiar territory any longer. They will be the ones who will be amplifying all that they were drawn to in this world, that is...... *before she changed.*

Smile a little smile each and every day. Trust in yourself to be the best that you can be. Be ever mindful of the little ones that can not fend for themselves. See the wealth of possibilities that lie before you. Civility is not an art; it is not something that you aspire to. You either consider it to be an exceptionally important aspect of your life or you do not. I can not teach you how to live your life without prejudice, this you must do on your own. Many of My Earthbound Children know this before they descend into this world. Yes, I did say "descend," thankfully that term as it applies to this world's many inhabitants will no longer be applicable. For as long as I have known all of you, your antics and lack of steadfastness when you are pushed in to an area that is devoid of any form of civility, does still amaze Me. Each of you knows how to swim yet many still feel as if they can not. Why is this? Of course I already know the answer but since this is My Book, I will use the forum as I see fit. I left much of this up to you, the human races, and when push came to shove you botched it many times, sometimes through no fault of your own. You see, what few yet realize is that each of you since earliest sojourns to this planet have been fighting an uphill battle. You have fought your way valiantly up the mountain only to find that there was another waiting for you. Throughout the valleys that most of you can equate to as down time, you have been still further confronted by others. You dared not confront the waves of discontentment that ebbed about you. You all have looked at one time or another at the Earth Star journey as a one-on-one battle that is waged in order for you to confront your personal demons. Few have rallied to the true meaning behind the term "benign." It is true that Earth of the past has been a teaching planet, one that tested your strengths and unequivocally defined to you your weaknesses. The most practical of the weaknesses that you were confronted with was finding the need, the desire to work for the betterment of all mankind. Many of the Children of this world will never know how much they have missed out on. They still yet have not grasped the reason for working as a unified group. You want to know how to advance on your Spiritual quest for enlightenment? I will tell you that you can not do it alone. This is usually a group effort. Alone you can create the most magnificent of tapestries. Together; you breathe depth, life and imperial luminescence into the scene.

I spoke earlier of a vision that Celestial had about huge areas of the landscapes all over the world that had been hollowed out, "shoveled out" is the term she used I believe. (Referring to the previous God Book.) This is also what we have had to do to keep this planet from imploding. So many of the mannerisms and body language as well as many words, that each of you uses that have no purpose beyond feeding the beast, have multiplied the problems of this world. Uncivil behavior is on My list as number one. Look at the words "civil" and Uncivil" for a moment. Take a look at how these relate to the presence of organized chaos and disorganized chaos. Can you see the correlation between the two?

49

All around you there are undeniable signs of people rising up to lay siege to the beast in its lair. I ask you, are they doing as they should? Children, there can be no peace found on the other side of violence. There can be nothing worth having if it relies on violence or guns. Many people who do so do it out of desperation, yet others do so because they are incited by other people. Their civil disobedience comes with a cost. I told you before, do not become martyrs or all has been for naught. My Children, My dear Children, how do you imagine this world will change for the better if the same practices which failed before are used once again? How can you see the way through the tunnel if you cause the tunnel to collapse before the end can be seen? There is nothing I would not do for any of you; I am your father, your mother, your brother, your best friend. But I will not sit idly by and watch you waste your last chance of meeting My Son because you are using violence and taking inappropriate actions. ALSO, this world can not survive a long drawn-out battle again. Nor should she. My Children, you have come so far to let it all be undone. Walk softly and turn up your light, bright, brighter, brightest.

For the first time in your current history, the politicians, the dictators of old, are being confronted for all that they have caused to happen. Did this happen by accident? I would suggest to you that it is the combined efforts of the Creation process as a whole that comes to your rescue. They have looked into the cauldron where the long hidden secrets are being kept. They are releasing this information to the world.

Many of you desire to congregate in much larger groups of like-minded individuals. I ask you to reconsider this decision. The Light encoding that each of you carries must be dispersed. If you are all in one area how will this be of any benefit to others? You will be guided to areas that will provide all that you need. Trust in this. My word is My bond. If you try, as in times past, to force an issue before it has reached its maturity, it will backfire on you. If this happens the uncivil behavior of the masses of this world will be the least of your problems. I believe I have said enough for now.

In Love and Eternal gratitude to

The Holy Grail... God

Codex 3

I Speak on War

God... Well, here we are engaged now on one of My least favorite topics, yet one that is of incredible importance to those who are desirous of aspiring to a new way of life. I feel in all fairness I should give you all a warning now. *Truth is always hazardous to your perceptions of reality.* This codex will be a no-holds-barred writing. If you believe this is too much for you to handle, then by all means leave this book now. The people who leave would be the very ones who probably need truth the most. However, if you decide you can not cope with what I am about to discuss, then I can do nothing more for you.

War is an aphrodisiac for the mentally challenged and Spiritually deprived. In other words it IS their drug of choice. It feeds; it stimulates that primitive side of themselves that so many Earthlings still have yet to find a way to control. The tie between acts of war and the use of drugs has been well documented. Drugs themselves have long been a part of every culture; some are beneficial and were originally intended to be so. I gave you vast fields of poppies and look what you did to them. Most drugs however offer an addictive placebo, one that is a thinly disguised veneer *over reality* which allows people who are not confident of their own wellbeing to find an escape **from** reality. Reality in a very real sense is what each of you makes of it. You can define it or it can define you, the choice is always the <u>definitive</u> factor. For MySelf, I prefer the hard to dispute truth. Let Us get down to the nuts and bolts of it... if something is broken then let Us find a way to fix it together. Then there can be no little white lies based on deformed illusions that people can hide behind. Each

Soul has to make a choice. It is to either hide from the truth or face it head on. Ultimately, all people of all races must have the faith in themselves to be able to **ride out the storm** when illusions *disguised as the truth,* are placed in front of them.

I can see by some of your expressions that you may still be teetering on which path to follow. I tell you now it is much easier to confront your demons with a clear mind and an unrestricted heart. David himself, used to have a coffee cup which stated rather matter-of-factly, that "drinking does not solve my problems, *but* it does put them on hold until tomorrow." Thankfully he retired that coffee cup long, long ago. The reason I bring this up as a small example is that so many people prefer putting important decisions off until the last possible moment. This is procrastination, it is a crutch, it is a disability and this My dear ones, simply will not be allowed in the New Dimension.

War has long been the ***poison*** of choice for those who wished to keep others in a downtrodden position while simultaneously elevating their own illusionary position. No longer will this be allowed either. This type of energy, *remember that thought is energy,* does not exist, it could not possibly exist, in the higher dimensions. Yes, there are battles being fought on many different fronts throughout each and every galaxy, throughout every Universe and all the corresponding new Multiverses. Each Multiverse regardless of how long it has been in existence has its own protectors. We, the other Luminescents and I, prefer to call them "Peacekeepers" or simply bringers of peace. Just because I said they are peaceful does not in any way imply that they have not been well trained. Among the Warrior Class are some of the best teachers to glide through the Multiverses. Out of necessity these bringers of peace have always been around and ready to prevent, circumvent and forcibly when necessary, dissuade the dark legions' intentions of ensnaring otherwise peaceful populaces. You yourself have armadas of these wondrous Souls protecting you as you embark upon your Earth Star walks. They protect and defend the Earth Star at all times. On your home front there in the practical world, this is a different story. This is where personal responsibility must come into play. Each of you must out of necessity learn to protect yourself. The legions minion's, mere puppets as they may be, prefer to work from the protection that the shadows provide and it is up to you to defend yourself and to eventually ferret them from their hiding places.

Material greed combined with looting natural resources without consideration for the environmental impact, is and will continue to be one of the downfalls of this current human civilization. There is nothing wrong with wanting nice things, a comfortable home to live in and plenty of food to eat. The question that lies in wait is, "how long will you be willing to give **a pound of flesh**, how long will you be willing to turn a blind eye to the injustices of this world to have what you need?" Is one pound OF FLESH ok, what if they ask for more? When is enough, enough? The powers *you have allowed to be,* used your insatiable desire for more of everything, compounded with your insecurities and fears and your naivety to control and manipulate you. These are the same ones who tout themselves as being creative, the very ones who invented nuclear bombs and unequivocally caused you much heartache through the onslaught of disease. The *powers that be* do not now and never have had your best interests at heart; many of you are now learning this the hard way. They use your weaknesses against you and easily transfix the minds of so many of you as a means of furthering their ambitious goals of world domination. Filling their coffers with money and resources is just a means to an end for them. The more they have means the less you will have and the more powerful they will be. In times past two things happened. Those with less were more self-sufficient, something I might add you have lost along the way. The flip side to this was that the less you had made you more dependent upon them to have what you needed to survive. Now the tides have changed, those with little are arising to challenge the system. A challenge I might add, that is long overdue. Wars have been fought for less.

Can you think of a better way to enslave the populace of a planet then to pit one country against another country, one person against another person? Simply put, by doing little to defend your own interests you chose the easier way out and made their jobs much simpler. Rather than **rock the boat** many of you chose to fight their battles for them, all in the name of God and Country I might add. Tell Me, where was I when I summoned the trumpet calling for all of you to bear arms against one another? *I was not there, for I did not say it!* For that matter, where have all of you been when I issued the call to put a stop to this madness? This noncommittal attitude so many of you have, as well as the wrongfully committed beliefs of others, was and still is the catalyst that has effortlessly propelled the rest of your civilizations further down into *the rabbit hole.* No, there is no blue pill or green pill for you to swallow that will whisk you back up out of that hole into the realms of knowingness where righteousness, equality for all and truth reigns supreme. This is something each of you must strive for, you must aspire to and you must do on your own. I MySelf am reminiscing about the "sugar pills" that doctors on your planet offered to children and adults alike, who like most hypochondriacs have imaginary illnesses. They would create these illnesses for themselves as a means of shirking some area of their personal lives, areas that they did not want to take responsibility for. Yes, as you all well know there are the evasive dodgers among you who still to this day are proficient at avoiding any form of commitment, NIRVANA forbid, they should choose to take a stand. This is war of a different kind; it is war **of** and **for** control of the mind, your most vulnerable point.

The mind, it is erroneously believed, is the last frontier to conquer. Far be it for Me to jump right in and set the record straight. However, *since you asked*, the mind is simply a tool supplied with the body you were born into. It is but one of many of the tools you carry with you that you must maintain. It does not control you unless you allow it. In the deep recesses of the mind lie the roots of all your fears and insecurities. It is up to you to extract them, one by one if necessary. It is here where those who strive to *empower themselves*, by keeping you in a constant state of unbalance through the improper utilization of fear, try to implant their insidious subliminal messages. Once implantation is successful they can with ultimate ease control every aspect of your lives. They can control your purchasing preferences and guide you in choosing to abuse yourself in fundamentally flawed, basic first and second dimensional primitive and deadly indulgences.

If you want to know when and where the final battle will be fought for the human species' **right to exist,** it is here within the minds which control the hearts of those who have lost their Soul connection to themselves. This war will not be fought with bullets or bombs or idle threats, it will not be fought over food stores or planetary reserves. It will be fought in the bowels of the intellect, an area that you alone have always had the keys to unlock and bid or forbid the **shadow surfers'** entrance. Shadow surfers are the ones who effortlessly glide in through the cracks of the damaged psyche. Once they have entered with little effort on their parts I might add, they set up the combative confrontations between the Soul *who knows best*, the mind *that knows only what you have taught it* and the intellect *that you have **covertly** trained to protect you.*

The Illuminati in their cunning pursuits devised and implemented the most sadistic of plans. It was to make each of you, once they were assured that you were docile and controllable, to become needy and ultimately dependent on them for cures to what ails you. They set up their storefronts cleverly designed with glitter and glaze to hide their paltry, noxious tools of their trade. First they designed all forms of disease from which they birthed *the need* for doctors who were trained by them, to peddle their remedies and recommendations. Then came the pharmaceutical companies whose sole intention was to keep you dependent upon them. All the while both sides of this double-edged sword was taking a bite out of your humanity and easing the way for all they peddled that caused the unrest in the physical bodies. As an added bonus the sellers of these pollutants tarnished the works of Mother Nature herself, so that you can no longer find anything pure and untarnished. What makes this battle even more deceitful is that once they have you *on the hook,* they can then extricate from you anything they desire. These demon riders are the same ones, their descendents of course, that orchestrated the original need for the use of coin. You My dear Children, were placed between a rock and hard spot with nowhere to turn but up, sadly... few of you remembered how to climb.

Now let Us get to the crux of the issue here, what is it that war does, what is its purpose? Is it the suffering and pain that is associated with war? Is it solely for the acquisition of land, resources and monetary and strategic gain? I would suggest to you that these are byproducts of one and the same. The intent behind most wars is to set up an imbalance. Tell Me dear Children of Mine, what is the one concept or principle that ultimately causes each of you to segregate yourselves from one another? No, I will not give you the answer; each of you should know this one by now. Suffice it to say that this one key element which exists within the hearts, minds and intellects of all of you, is the one thing that not only causes you so much pain but it will also keep you from becoming a unified race of beings. If that happens you can not come together as ONE. Have you ever engaged in a verbal battle, an exchange of harsh words, with someone over whose idea was better? Of course you have. It is time to retrain your minds and **table** all forms of confrontations. Come together and toss about ideas, inspirations and alternatives to the way things have been. The collective of your thoughts will spring forth as the concepts and principles that will define the tomorrows of the human race. Without the need for *the art of war* I might add.

Why is it that you battle what you describe as evil? Is it because you do not like the odor or the color it displays? Is it because somewhere, at sometime, someone told you that you should? Are you sure that evil itself exists because you KNOW this in your Soul, or did someone just tell you it does and you believed them? None of you should ever have to witness the atrocities that I have. That having been said, I can tell you there is not a one of you who has not felt that callous evil caress upon your face. The worst acts of violence go on behind closed doors, where thankfully none of you can see. However there is always someone else who **knows**, someone else who always **sees**. There is nothing that is "hidden thought" that is not known. The sooner everyone accepts this fact the better off all life will be. I for one will be glad when all these "cloak and dagger" facades have run their course. What goes on behind closed doors is meant to be private; *as long as the discussions remain* as productive reformation plans that are also amiable to all people, I will allow it to continue.

Today the Children of this world are being indoctrinated into the art of warfare almost from birth. Parents engage in this, siblings mimic it, why should the new Children being born in this world not do the same? The answer is: because so many of you seem not to know any better. Basically, too many of you see no wrong in this debacle. Generations after generations have passed their ideologies and bad habits down to all subsequent generations who have then carried on this disgusting tradition. The instruments of religions and of old-fashioned ideals have seen to that. ***The sins of your forefathers are not yours to bear,*** so please, stop that cyclic behavior now. In the days long past, it was the male in <u>most</u> cases who was the hunter and provider. The males were the ones who dictated how things were meant to be. In the earliest of days of your recent history, it was decided that living as a "civilized race" meant that the gladiators would settle their disagreements on the field of battle. It also meant that the men who were participants in this abominable SPORT exercised their free expression to kill at large. You see how well that one went. Tell Me dear ones, where is the honor in inflicting pain on one another? Which brings Me to another of My pet peeves: tell Me, where is the honor in battling an animal in the archaic entertainment of "bullfighting?" I can tell you quite honestly that the battles you each face on a daily basis by confronting the "real Beast," are the ones that should be occupying your minds, instead of playing trivial pursuit or watching dogs race around a track.

There is hardly a confrontation that has taken place in times past, as well as those in present times, that does not have religious overtones to fuel the fires of discontent. "In the name of Allah, or God wills it," are two of the most commonly used reasons. I must seriously disagree; **cockamamie** may well be the word I would choose to sum that one up. The training ground for all the shadow warriors who align as a unified force known as "Legion," battle their way into the homes and the schools. Any sport that teaches people to maim or commit an even worse act of violence is unacceptable. While these socially accepted forms of sports MAY teach a person endurance, the side effects can be extremely devastating to the fragile physical vehicle. It was never designed to endure these types of abuse. I understand the need for all of you to be outdoorsy and adventurous and to maintain good physical strength and yes, flexibility is extremely important. If I were free to choose for each of you some venue that would stimulate the heart, mind, body and most importantly the Spirit, I might lean towards the noninvasive practices of martial arts or Tai Chi. When it is learned well and practiced correctly that is. These are the types of exercises that are used to instill and maintain focus and bring more people in touch with the body and Spirit. The great teachers in these fields teach discipline and respect for ALL Life. These are My suggestions, although I am well aware that it is not everybody's cup of tea. Now, if you are wondering why am I speaking of all this, I shall explain.

The human body can be trained to withstand great amounts of pain and torture; it is the **mind** that is most delicate. If you remove the mind from the equation then you have the perfect pseudo human to carry out the will of the few. This will ultimately impact on the many. I spoke earlier of the battle for the mind and its ultimate importance on the future of humanity. If you combine the training and unconscious acceptance of indoctrination elements that are commonplace in this world, you can see how easily peoples' minds can be manipulated without their even knowing this is happening. Take for example video games, the movie industries and all the violence that is portrayed.

Video games, violence **disguised as entertainment**, in all its myriad forms was implemented with one purpose in mind. This purpose was to dull and eventually block the "caring" sensors within the conscious minds. This effectively cuts off all connection to the Spiritual part of each of you, *unless* you recognize what is happening and then take appropriate action. The well-balanced human being can view these forms of entertainment specifically to keep themselves better informed of the affairs of their fellow Earthlings. Reading is fundamental, but the sum total of a person CAN be defined by what is read. Being aware is extremely important; burying your head in the sand and refusing to acknowledge that there are grave injustices going on all around you, is contributing to the problem.

There are very few industries that practice equality and this must come to an end while there is still time to do so. So many of you ask Me to bring peace into the world, yet so many people are indecisive about what is it that they personally can do to assist in this process. Take a look around you; there is not a direction you can take, not a stone you can look under, where you can not see something that is corrupt, abusive or invasive. If something, anything by any manner directs its bias towards one segment of the population, then it is *warlike* and is also promoting class distinction. If your lack of tolerance towards another's belief systems is in any way degrading toward another, then that too is an act of aggression. If you can not find acceptance, if you can not remain passionately detached and be open to civilized means of discussions pertinent to how to view and deal with any situation that comes before you, then you too are not part of the solution. You are in effect contributing to the moral decay. I have told you before that the multicultural diversity that exists here in this world is and always has been a testing ground for the eventual advancement of all uniquely diverse races of beings. It is up to you to learn to get along with one another, I can not do this for you, nor can I **will you** to do it either. Until such time as you allow the differences that define you and your beliefs to UNITE and strengthen your bonds with one another, there *will be no peace* to be found here.

It was the human races that taught animals something that I had never intended. Many times they intentionally bred the animals of this world to become the predators they are today. Like the Children of today and yesterday the animal kingdoms learn by example. The infringement by humans on the animals' natural habitat has forced many of them out of necessity to become aggressors in order to survive. They, like the humans of today, are now battling among themselves for the last scraps left on the proverbial table. Do you want to know when the real feeding frenzy will begin? I shall give you a clue. When you notice water becoming even scarcer than it already is and the crops and livestock no longer thriving, then you will know that the pendulum has swung the other way..... for a time.

Most people view war as a confrontation derived from an irresolvable disagreement among many Souls. There is always someone who is the instigator, someone who is throwing in coal to further fire the frenzy. Isolate and remove this element and your warlike tendencies will fade into the dusk. My hope this day is that I have added some clarity to the erroneous ways so many of you have of viewing your differences. Battles are being fought in the ethers above you; many a good Soul has given their life in your defense, as I have stated on more than one occasion. Do not dishonor them or the memories of them, by not changing your ways. <u>Settle your differences now and all of this can come swiftly to an end</u>. Until there is balance within **each** individual, until homes can reclaim and regain their status as a safe haven for all who reside within, until such time as each of you can look at each other and feel as if you are looking at your own self, there will be no peace to be had on this planet.

OK now, now that I have touched on some aspects that I wanted you to hear of first, I will now proceed to other parts of war. I know in My Soul that this is the most providential gridline intersection to further address this matter. Children, perhaps this is the time to focus your thoughts completely on what I still have to say. I am not saying it will be pretty or that it will be easy for all to digest, but **TRUTH IN THIS MATTER** never is. Wars are a convoluted processing of the merging of thought and matter. Because of this wars truly began after early humankind first came to this planet. Granted they too arrived here sans memories of what to expect, however because they were the first most primitive of races here, they relied basically on their savage self-instinct needs to survive. At any cost. There were many people here in one sense but geographically they, **YOU,** existed as small bands of people who totally lacked literacy. The intellect back then was still too new to be of either great assistance or great hindrance.

If you remember I have already told you that the early Illuminati leaders were primed to inveigle mankind with their own energies here on the Earth Star planet from the very moment the first humans arrived. Then you can imagine, I hope, how difficult those times were for the first people. Although there were of course many, many, hundreds of My Star Keeper Children from other worlds, other Multiverses here to assist in the early day establishment of the primitive tiny colonies of new world settlers, it still did not take too very long for the infiltration process of the Illuminati to take place. You see, unbeknownst to the earliest of humankind, the dark energies invaded their thoughts first and their bodies second. Although these settlers did follow the stars' alignment through sheer curiosity at first, they later began to believe that certain movements of the sun and moon were some type of bad spell, something they could not accurately put into thought except that it scared them. Even during the times when they used a simple type of sign language they still had minds that were a very fertile place, a breeding ground for the dark.

This was because their minds were in a sense, "empty." They had not advanced into a type of civilized groupings of colonies yet, so they had nothing to fill their minds except their day to day and night to night excursions. I ask you Children, how could they compare anything with anything, if their minds housed nothing to compare anything to? No, this is not a trick question, but it is the only way I can think of to give you a prime example of how a void within the mind can not interact, can not interface with something if there is nothing there. I did however make a point of telling you that their minds were fertile, untried, untested, but fertile nonetheless. Just as in all other aspects of fertility, it is a common ground where much can be planted or IMPLANTED, as the case may be. Fear, was a common reaction back then to unknown conditions, unknowable circumstances and the great lack of total understanding of who they were and how they should live. It was as My Children from other worlds taught them how to use the basic survival instincts as a means of bettering their life conditions that the two-way war broke out in force. My Star Keeper forces were continuously under attack by the dark lords who knew full well that the early races here would be just the tools they needed in order to control the newly settled world.

Although those dark sources were able to thrust and parry at will, our Star Keepers could not force any type of action on the people here without the peoples' consent. So, because of the lack of literacy and the limited simple sign language, it became major impediments for our off-world teachers and peace keepers to confront. Telepathy really could not be used, however the use of simple light symbols so elementally basic that they would be at least seen by humans as something peaceful, rather than offensive or threatening did help to an extent.

Over time however as the newly Earthbound Children began to respond to gentle and persuasive beckonings by our own good Souls, the dark energies began to carefully explore the fertility of the human mind. Remember now, the mind was essentially empty as far as logic was concerned. Although the people did respond in a very childlike manner to simple gestures and to different colorations of light. Yes, of course Soul Voice was present, even back then. It always is. It was as the dark ones spread a cloak of uneasiness, edginess and restlessness that it then became the causation for other things to happen. This further caused the natural curiosity factor that each person has, to wander more freely into dark mind spaces. This is where the lesser children were implanting hostile FEELINGS. You see, it is in this area that even today, or perhaps I should more correctly say, "especially today," the emotions can and do run the gamut of experiencing all sensations of all feelings, on all levels of consciousness, even simple thoughts. Now to make a long story short, here is what else happened back then as a result of these situations.

The battle that waged here then for many eons was over the right of the newly formed free people to live and learn simple lifestyles while evolving at a slow, sometimes erratic pace, while being pitted against the bloodlines of the Illuminati who were intent on planting **their seed**. The human races' free expression rapidly dwindled. This was in great part because of the inhibitions they had MENTALLY. The dark streamers insidiously continued to implant the still childlike human races with intense feelings of hostility and blood lust. Our forces had to withdraw and observe at a distance all that was occurring here. Each individual Child of course had their own guides and Mentors watching carefully over them. *However,* as in all cases when a new civilization has been birthed, sufficient time must be permitted for the new life forms to explore their own abilities; regardless of how limited they may be at any specific time in their "emancipated state." This emancipation is the carefully conceived ability to formulate feelings and understanding of right and wrong, regardless of how primitive a civilization may be. The early humans waged blood wars against other human tribes they encountered. It was senseless slaughter that was only partially caused by their self-preservation instinct. The rest was caused by the continuous acts of the inflaming of their emotions and fragile minds by the shadow beings that lurked in the darkest of the now dark recesses of the human mind. The Creator, the Creation Processing and I had previously specifically seeded the God Principle into the minds of each human being. This was the "enabler" of the God Connection.

Obviously it was already a part of the matrix of the Soul. Therefore, it had to be left up to Soul to attempt to navigate through the troubled waters of the mind. **The God Connection** is not a trivial mass of formulated thought. It is a CORD that connects the human mind to the Soul and to the heart and simultaneously extends upwards to the true realm of Creation. It was by the continuous bombardment of the dark streamers that the God Principle began to be relegated to such a dim Light. It began to be displaced by the black formative powers of non-creation. The first humans here began to lose their way. In no time at all the humans who had been successfully seeded by the Illuminati ruthlessly took over as the undisputed leaders of their colonies.

The wars that had been waged against all other human colonies in all other parts of this world then continued to expand unabated. In time the Illuminati overlords themselves descended here wearing human forms and mated with early mankind. They did so as a contingency plan; for they knew that our Star Keepers from other worlds had already seeded humans with their own interplanetary genetic material, simply because early humans WERE of the stars! So, you had humans' bearing Children whose bloodlines were directly linked to their original home planets and that planet's race and you had humans who had been tricked or brutalized into mating with the Illuminati, in order to continue the Illuminate bloodline here on the Earth Star planet. Do not be fooled readers, that dark bloodline is still very much still here and reproducing at will. Those times that later epitomized the true loss of innocence on this planet, also became known here as **The war that began all wars.**

As people here progressed into a more civilized state but were for the most part still illiterate, they did birth the early leaders of both the Illuminati and the more mature Souls of the Light. The Souls who bore the greatest amount of Light however did not have very long life spans. They were effectively mowed down by the murderous rage mankind had either inherited from the dark, or had LEARNED from the dark. So, the Souls whose very missions were to be of service to humanity through early teachings and imprinting less evolved Souls here with the Light energy signatures, simply insisted on rebirthing again and again and again. They cared not in the least about the insane actions that would be launched against them again just as it had happened before. Their purpose was to fulfill their tasks and they would continue to do so for as long as it took. In all races on this planet Soul Voices became so muted back then, that it seemed that there were very few Voices calling out from the darkness. As I look back over this torrid period of Earth history I can not help but wonder how it came to be that so many people of all races today truly forgot ALL of these events. *I did not cause this to happen. Soul did not cause this recognition to cease to be.* I do know that people remember only certain aspects of their history, only the ones they are TAUGHT to remember here. Even though the history taught is badly flawed. It is as simple as that.

OK, now: let us see if you are following this true trail of tears and bloodlust as you should. Although I always speak in **God Code** to each of you both privately and publically, can you yet grasp the enormity of the situations that have been recreated here time after time after time? People here want so desperately to believe that all things can be altered by ONE SINGLE GOOD THOUGHT that they blithely go about their everyday lives not understanding that **nothing**

here is as it seems. Icons permeate your belief systems, each purporting to either "be of God" or "be symbolic of a particular race or culture." In the first place you have no true understanding of symbolism! Symbolism does not require any icons. Symbolism is but another form of CODES. Ironically the people of each race here who brag the most about helping other races are the ones who are the most parsimonious in their Spirituality. Why? You either know the answer or you do not. If you do not, then perhaps you should.

The God Principle that was originally intended to house the God Connection, thereby assisting in negating odoriferous types of superficially implanted practical world dilemmas, can cause an individual or a group of people to not merely maintain this connection but to enhance it. In this manner people can draw upon it as needed for their own evolution and the continued ascension of this planet. However, **it has been lost!** This does indeed constitute a dire situation. Without this Principle intact in the hearts and minds and in the forefront of the Soul Self, you lose your birthright. Many will lose it forever. The dark principality of the Illuminati that We call, "the demon energy imprint," has superimposed itself over the Lighted Principality. This is the most horrific, most serious of all wars and you are thrust deeply into this battle **NOW.** No, this war is not for the weak-minded, yet it is the weak-minded who have wrought such havoc here. The wars, both declared and undeclared, are engaged in a different type of duplicity now. They are all cutting more and more deeply into the psyches and obliterating the known presence of the Soul. The brainwashing techniques that have been so deleteriously successful with all the human races here are NOW racing to an unstoppable climax. This will continue to result in the deaths of millions and millions of Earthbound Children here who refuse to recant. They refuse to begin a new way of life and to live the way they should.

Has anyone wondered why so many military forces in all countries are so intent on consistently bolstering their armed forces with the use of more and more money and more weapons of mass destruction? Are you aware YET that there are far greater weapons of mass destruction that have been covertly made and hidden from public eye for absolutely the worst of reasons? Had it not been for the **"Guidance System"** of our Star Keeper forces, many races would have already been blasted off this planet and Terra herself would have suffered irreparable damage. Bloodlines tell the story here. Although the progenitors of the Illuminati are long gone now, their descendants have been living long and ruthlessly wealthy lives as your political figures and your religious ICONS to name but a few. Military units are highly impersonal; this is how they are intentionally trained to be.

Men and women who are in the service have their identities removed. They are treated harshly and impersonally under the thinly disguised mask of learning to be detached enough to identify the perceived enemy and take wrathful action against them. However, what really happens is that they are being taught to lose their humanity. No, this is not a contradiction in terms. It is merely another brainwashing tactic that I have observed being RECREATED over the centuries. So many lies and so much covert action have led you all astray with your PRESUMPTION of guilt against other races. You have all acted very foolishly in this matter, preferring to believe that who you have been told is the enemy, really is. BUT in truth Children, it was never this way. It has all been a dreadful sham, a ploy to pit you against one another and cost you your lives, your sanity and the final eradication of the God Principle.

Countries here enter into secret agreements with other countries to begin wars presumably based on potential or active aggression by other countries. Children, I have watched, listened and felt the absolute insanity of these manmade actions. All is predicated on specific factors that are seen to be the best way to not only bring more and more profits to the warring countries, but to keep the minds of the populaces further enslaved to fear. To expedite this writing I am simply going to use the term "President," instead of breaking it all down to King, Queen Prime Minister, etc. Each President of each country believes that he or she is in total control of the populace, of the country overall. This belief wanes quickly however. This of course does not include the people who have retained office through violent acts of mayhem and murder for 30 or 40 years or so. In fact however behind each President, the ones I spoke of earlier that is, lies the shadow governments, those who have risen to power in the shadow land and are here to try to continue playing out their hands of control and the final decimation of what is known as "the human Spirit."

It has always been these shadow governments that have pulled the true strings of power behind the presumed leaders of the countries. Although today a goodly number of them are still part of the infamous Bilderberg Empire, they all have their own underlings who continue to thwart any actions that a good leader tries to enact. You say that countries are all bankrupt; yes, in fact they are. However that is not YET the case with the infamous cartel power mongers. However, I can honestly say that even they are now beginning to feel a monetary crunch unlike any they experienced before. *Who are the Bilderberg group?* They are the ones who through their perceived right of descendancy have for many, many, generations been awarded great wealth through CARNIVOROUS means. Many are the elite in the banking industries, all the pharmaceutical industries worldwide and military families and Presidents and their spouses both past and present. They are corporate people in every sense of the word. This has been accomplished as part of a secret pact to maintain control over all governments. It has been through the outrageous acts of levying threats against the lives of leaders' families and promises of outright ruin in the leaders' chosen political fields that good men and women surrender in abject defeat to the children of a lesser god. Assassinations of political figures bent on "doing good" are always the last resort for keeping other leaders in line. Many absolutely hellacious and cleverly designed plans born in the dark closets of the descendants' minds and the humans they are aligned with here, were responsible for many atrocious acts such as "911."

They were able to accomplish much by counting on the foolishness and conditioning of many humans here who simply accept what they THNK they see and what they are TOLD by those in governments, who claim they know what actually happened. Most Earthbound Children do this because they are too afraid to consider the implications of "what if....it was their own government. What would they do?" In fact however there was but one government responsible for 911. This government had long been seeking a way to cause war to be waged against another country, but one that needed to have the backing of the actual culprits' populace. Wars are not "incidentally planned," nor are they based on last minute considerations. They are well-planned, far in advance of the actual scheduled combat date.

A few leaders, who dwell in faraway lands but remain true to their passion for truth, are usually overlooked by MOST of the dark agents. My Dali Lama-self is one of these very few whose way of life and consideration for others has never been compromised by him. Although his belief system of Spirituality is a path that he must follow in accordance with his chosen path in life, he still has managed to withstand the forces of the dark agendas by staying true to his path. There are many inconsistent and erroneous beliefs in the faith he is part of, but in no way should that demean this great Soul.

Shadow governments however, *"were born in sin and continue within."* They strike at the heart of every government by working *within* the governments and hide in plain sight. Their emissaries are many; yet in the present Earth time of today, they are actually beginning to feel fear and uncertainly about maintaining their status quo of keeping the races of this world under their thumb. It will not be for several more years yet before these shadow governments are all crushed beneath the WHEELS of justice. However, *the wheels-they are "aturning!"* More and more of these heinous people in all countries are now being confronted by the very politicians and religious leaders **they set into place.** The ones now confronting them have developed a greater fear of the umbrage of the people than they have of these Illuminati descendents. Children, duplicity in all of its devious forms is beginning to be unveiled. This is an event of unheralded proportions, yet it was decreed long, long, ago, that THIS would be the very time for Us to STRIKE BACK.

Military protocols must change AND THEY WILL...I assure you of this as well. The secret collusion between the dark Star Keepers from other worlds who worked in conjunction with the early Illuminati is already a DEAD issue. And please stop your minds from flitting to, "oh, ALL the grays are responsible for this." Do not speak of things you YET know nothing about. Part of what is occurring here now is that leaders of countries, who were intended to be the right person in the right place at the right time, are receiving more than ever before extraordinary high levels of protection by OUR Star Keeper forces. This is to not only ensure the continuation of their lives, but to also permit them to enact some good changes here rather than the ones that have previously been proscribed by the Bilderberg group and their LEGIONS of death. Yes, I am well aware that there are minds reading all that I am saying and thinking, *"oh no! God is a conspiracy theorist!"* I tell you one and all NO, I am not. I do not deal with theory, I KNOW what I KNOW which is far more than you do.

In eternal service to "right defeats might." *God*

Codex 4

Angels

God... Ok now Children, in case you have not yet realized this, this book in particular is intended to deal with many subjects that may cause normally serene people to feel a bit squeamish. No, I am not on a "squeamish" mission; I am as I always am dealing with issues that you now need to be better schooled about. I do not want any of you to walk into your new lives here without having properly assimilated information relative to true Earth history. History that is, which exists *on all levels*. For instance, "Fallen Angels" is but a badly used metaphor. However it is a term that I KNOW you all have heard and one that you THINK you know about. Hmm, "thinking" and "knowing" can be worlds apart, you **know**. You have all heard the fables and seen some really obnoxiously bad movies about this subject. I think it would be proper of Me to ask you to ask yourselves at this point, how much you believe and why? Is it because of any religious leanings you may have that you still carry as baggage? Is it because you need a scapegoat to persuade you that there have been gross injustices committed against you by beings that once stood by My side, thereby causing you to feel better about yourselves? Is it that essentially you can not see any personal responsibility needed to be accepted by you that is relative to this world's conditions, because after all, *the fallen angels did it?* Or could it be your need to have an answer handy to how much you believe and why, "just in case" I may ask you to accept responsibility for your own actions in this matter?

The very term "Angels" is misunderstood to a serious degree. Angels are highly evolved Beings for the most part that is, who reside in what is termed the "Angelic Realm."

74

The realm is multidimensional and exists as but one part of many Multiverses. Each Universe has always had Angels that have been Created long, long, ago for the specific purpose of working with the Soul of each life form, regardless of where that life form lives or which planetary constellation it is from. During the early times of the Creation Processing venture, it was of course well-known that all life must be respected for the very fact that it **IS** life. Because of this innate understanding that We all had, the Creator decided that spatial Beings should not only be Created to assist all incoming Souls who arrive in Nirvana, but to also assist in the Creative process of bringing new Souls into Light Bodies, regardless of the maturity status of the Soul.

The Light Bodies themselves simply reflect all aspects of a Soul. So it is that if a Soul has always been a shining example of the illumination cycles and stages and has always sought the good, then that Soul enters into a Light Body that may differ from another's Light Body. Less mature Souls obviously enter into the Light Body that is a reflective stage, one that in time can progress to a higher form of Light Body. Of course on Earth it is different. Each stage of the Light Body Process complements the entirety of an individual Soul. Souls in the higher dimensions enter Light Bodies at specific times predicated upon the totality of the lives well-lived and the rewards inherent that are bestowed upon Souls who are returning to Source. I will speak more on that part later.

So Children, certain beams of Light each housing a Soul were encased in an even more luminous dressing of Light that was brilliant beyond compare. You see Children, when a Soul has given birth of itself TO itself, or in some cases TO itself of itself, all Souls AT THAT NANOSECOND have the free expression to decide how best to be in service to all aspects of Divinity. They also decide how best to establish themselves through the subtle embellishment of Light and Soul Voice with a monad that is an aspect of the Creator's own Soul Light. During the early times of Creation, the Creator chose to select specific beams of Light and then to carefully give them certain aspects of the Highest Forms of the Divine. To some of these beams He gave total expansion of thought and thought-links that could and would connect each of these beams to all forms of Greater Consciousness. This is a spectacular Consciousness, greater even than the Super Consciousness Awareness Factor. This other form of Consciousness was not new by any means. The Creator HimSelf is a gigantic Light Show in His own right and He possesses every form of Consciousnesses, many of which you do not experience here on this planet.

By the very act of sharing this special gift with these Light Beams it was understood that the more beings they would work with and teach through "signal transference," the more rapidly Souls of any level would be able to rise to a more refined and dedicated aspect of themselves. Yes, these monads I speak of are quite diaphanous and contain incredible strength. *However, they are not microcosms of reality, they are MACROCOSMS.* They defy any simple language that I could use to explain their appearance. Here is what I can describe to you though: These monads are fluid by nature in ONE sense, they are mutable and linger throughout the ethers as what you would probably think of as an advanced "not of the world" kaleidoscope.

Their mutations of coloration rapidly change as the timbre and tonal qualities of each move at times swiftly, at times slowly, into an ever-changing shifting of patterns of Light and music. I can not properly explain this harmonious, melodic music to you, Children. You do not have the understanding of this type of matter that is **non**-matter, non-material. No, in the strictest sense of the term, it is not intangible. The tangibility is all encompassing, all pervasive, all enduring. The Source of the Creative

Processing is the Creator. So it was a simple task to bring these "bearers of wisdom and luminescence" into a manifold existence. One that is eternal. These angels actually derived their group naming from the term, "of pureness." That is in essence what these beings are. Since We do not use any chronological ages for Ourselves or for others of the Divine, I can not say how old any angel is. I can tell you that they have all been "around the block" many, many, times. Some are of the same spatial age state as the Creator, while others are only a mere few millennia old. Although they are all teachers extraordinaire, each of the groupings does have their own clusters. These clusters are predicated upon the chosen or designated missions each angel may have.

If the Soul of an angel chooses to always remain for instance, in the citadel of learning, the citadel where all Souls enter at one time or another for more advanced teachings then, *so it is.* If a cluster of angels that is so very advanced is asked by the Creator to forestall any desire to journey to another different realm and instead to be of service to the human races on Earth, then *so it shall be.* All dimensional realities are overseen by many large bevies of angelic beings whose combined life force is one of pure dedication to higher learning and the limitless expansion of mind-thought performed through right actions. As singular entities rather than part of a cluster, they still have access to all of the Akashic records housing all knowledge that has ever been. In this manner one angel may pursue and expand upon established or new "stellar recognition" paths and other sundry avenues through the process of disclosure. It is through this process that an angel gathers more expanded versions of wisdom and then proceeds to share this knowledge. This is accomplished by the disclosing of certain information to other Souls who are not part of the angelic realm. These Souls the angels are sharing information with are intent on following paths that are available to them only here in the higher dimensions. It is a choice they have made to remain here and teach others rather than be Earthbound or bound to a different planet. *Consciousness* is a never-ending part of the Creation process.

Therefore Children, all of the angelic realm may be privy to certain states of consciousness never known by any of you while you are in mortal form. Although certain elevated states are known only as exalted states of proxy, all Souls MAY eventually travel the long path that arcs through the Light of ALL Lights and successfully attain the states of "consciousnesses in exaltation." It is "proxy" because in a very real way it is <u>a mirror</u> that can and should always reflect the true nature of the energies. It does not mean that a being IS a proxy. OK, each Soul who has ever been is assigned an angel; many Children here refer to these angels as "guardian angels." Some angels choose which Souls to remain eternally aligned with while others choose which Souls to remain with only for a specific time. At times, and only at times, those Souls who have the permanent alliance of an angel MAY at some future instance choose to transform into angels themselves, Remember please, I said, "MAY."

The qualities that angels exhibit are of the greatest forms of peacefulness, total tranquility and utter understanding of their own individual life choices and the necessity of their having been brought into the state of manifested beings. Their individual energies are always expanding because they live lives of infinity. In this manner they can always continue to evolve, not that they would ever choose otherwise for themselves. Yes, angels are a prevailing force in every world, every Universe. You can always know when you are in the presence of an angel because of the extraordinary glow that infuses the core of their very being and extends itself outward to encompass everything, whether it is solid matter or not, for incredible distances. Angels also bring with them a "HUSH," a quiet so intense that it is quite reminiscent of the ones that Jesus and Mary bring with them. Angels have merely to extend any point of their long reaching Light into any direction and touch the heart, mind and Souls of any living being. It is not that angels FEEL compassion, they ARE compassion. This is also true of the most gratifying love that they exude; love the likes of which you can not even begin to imagine.

Angels demystify myths and whisper the truths of those matters to all Earthbound Souls. Angels always work in complete tandem with the core of the Soul of each and every being. Soul and angel-an untouchable, unstoppable Creation. IF Soul flounders or finds itself engulfed in the quicksand of depraved indifference because of the inappropriate actions of a person, or because of the unflinchingly dark thoughts of the personality that Soul has aligned itself with, angels aid in encouraging Souls to remain as indifferent as is possible to those terrible onslaughts. I will not reveal HOW they accomplish this; you have no need to know about this now. *We will discuss this when you are home.* There are many levels, many stages that each angel must tread as each ascends the steps of higher forms, higher stations of immortality. There are far more levels of "angel status" than you are aware of. I will not go into all those levels at this time.

However, angels on all levels do indeed respond to any and all clarion calls that you issue. I do suggest you remember that angel business is a serious business. Although they possess the most incredible, most awesome sound, almost like millions of bells gently tinkling when they are expressing their humorous side, they are always seeking better ways, all noninvasive manners of helping each Child of Mine and each Child of all the other Luminescents to move progressively forward. They aid in assisting all Children EVERYWHERE who are seeking even more refined evolutionary ways to assist themselves.

They do so WHILE still working in an ultra dynamically charged fashion to assist through mind and MIND-THOUGHT whatever planet the Soul is living on. Guardian angels do in fact "guard and protect," whoever their charge may be. However clusters of Earthbound Souls for example, are also overseen by a "Guardian Being" who also is an angel, but is one who is of a greater elevated consciousness status. This is true of all clusters of Souls everywhere whether they are Earthbound or not, you all have one. Yes, even all of Our peaceful planets and galaxies that are moving forward at their own pace, but without warfare, are still assigned a Guardian Being. I have tried in the past to get you all to understand that Our help is limitless. Your individual angel protector, those you call guardian angels, are a "first response" team during life and death experiences.

OK, understand now that even though you have many Spirit Guides and a Master Teacher guarding you as much as you let them that is, the angels are also still present throughout your entire lifespan. Oftentimes the angels aided by Guides and Star Keepers from other worlds rush in to snatch a person from the jaws of death. That of course is predicated on individual Soul Agreements and the personal and planetary destiny of the person. There are so many varieties of angels though. There are healing angels, teaching angels, angels who keep careful watch over medical institutions and so forth. They are your companions and your life Guides in real time. They and the Spirit Guides extend welcoming hands to all good Souls that are on the brink of physical death. However, they also suggest to many, MANY, Souls who are preparing to die, those who are straddling the precipice between life and death but whose timeline has not arrived yet, that they should return to their mortal life until such time as *they are called to return home.*

80

Do angels walk the Earth? Yes, but of course they do! Again, all depends on their particular assignments and also on whatever the Creation Processing has decreed where angels' help is required. So many of you Earthbound Children have been in contact with or had encounters with those of the angelic realm but you do not know this. They appear as if by magic here and leave the same way. Sometimes I see them touching vast fields of wasteland that had at one time been fertile and pristine, until the human races corrupted it. When **the angels touch** it reestablishes fertility. BUT normally it must remain in a dormant state until such time that a gridline intersection establishes itself which allows for the new and slow growth the angels had precipitated. I mentioned earlier, "signal transference." This is a highly placed energy that encapsulates a modicum of energy each angel has and is successfully passed to another being, in this case to many of the human races here. This is a LINK; an extension of Light matter that is coordinated to remain with the angel and yet with the individual as well. This is a line of communication through telepathy and through imaging and is also a modulated current that directly links the angel wisdom to the heart, mind and Soul of an individual. Yes, the transference is as real as you are.

Think of it as yet another part of an energy imprint. EXCEPT that this one is a continuous supply of highly placed energies designated to assist the receiving human being through the wondrous display of manifold knowledge sent through the current of energy displacement. In this way energies that have now been considered to be no longer necessary or perhaps no longer needed by the receiver, are subtly replaced with a more finely tuned streamer. BUT this streamer is of a higher vibration which exists at an accelerated frequency. No, Children, this is not a trivial matter. If it were I would not be discussing this with you, now would I? There are many levels and forms of Light Bodies that CAN and MAY exist here on the Earth

81

Star planet. When a piece of clothing has finally become worn-out, then it is time to replace it with something newer and possibly better. In this manner you have transferred what you once had by relegating it to the "no longer of use" bin. This is a rather simplistic example of energy transference, however it is the most logical example I can give you. Light Bodies can only exist when the former life beliefs, lifestyles and the lesser grade of Light cells housed within the molecular system are no longer a relevant part of a human's life. In a previous book I already explained to you how and why Light is inducted into the human body and how the cells in the body receive the infusion. If you do not remember what I told you then I suggest you go back and reread the book. I am not going to repeat it.

OK, each person here, regardless of which race they are part of, regardless of their Soul age, CAN and MAY receive this energy transference. This transference is perfectly aligned with the SLOW steps that a Light Body must undertake before a person can actually be said to be replete with the new cellular body. Light Bodies are not given to anyone haphazardly. This process is a methodical "inching up" of atoms and neurons necessary to sustain the physical vehicle, while carefully embellishing the newly established DNA changes without causing undue distress. In this manner the Light Body must undergo many stages before it can be considered complete. *NO,* people here who are still blind to the newly arriving dimensional changes CAN NOT develop a Light Body. Those people who are one-dimensional, two-dimensional and three-dimensional humans, WILL NOT. The dimensions they are "a shifting" and the fourth dimension is being carried on the winds of change. This means that without the necessary vibrational input, lower-based forms of dimensional understanding will perish. This is also why those called "fallen angels" can not exist in a Light Body.

When all the angels were first called in to assist in SEEDING Terra, so long, long, ago, some of the angels ignored their own innate understanding of what they should not do here and became entrapped in the illusion of time. It was understood that the linear would need to take place here for a long period; however it was also understood that none of the beings assisting in the Creation process here should become ensnared by anything that even hinted of a linear conflict or constraint. No, not all of the angels who were here then were evolved. Remember, I told you that even each of their lives must be one of a continuous reaching upward for greater spans of illumination. An anomaly took place here; one that has had far-reaching implications. Some of the less mature angels became so intrigued by all they could help to create, that when the call was issued for all of the angels to return to their own realm, some simply did not choose to go. Some chose to walk this planet awaiting the arrivals of the first human races here. YES, angels are pure innocents, yet even an angel who was too naïve could be inveigled by the dark streamers IF the angels in question were exposed too long to the darkness of the ones who have NO illumination.

Again and again We called them to return, but of course their own free expression is what they followed. I and others have all told you Children repeatedly, "Light can not exist in the dark and the dark can not exist in the Light." *Think about it.* So it came to pass that angels who remained behind divided into groups. There were those who chose to create new beginnings for themselves on this world but lacked any FIRST HAND experience on how to go about doing this. There were those who decided to remain here to see what it would really be like to live as a mortal without actually being mortal. A goodly number of these angels were swiftly taken over by the arriving dark legions. None of you should have any trouble in understanding this. After all, you may not be angels but you are gods and goddesses and look how far YOU have fallen "from grace." In but a short span of linear existence the angels' Lights became more and more subdued and erratic until such time that except for seeing their etheric bodies rather faintly, it was difficult to see them at all. No, there never was any great battle between angels vying for supremacy here. They truly believed that remaining behind here they would somehow or other be of assistance. "Dark angels" did not ever truly exist. That is but yet another well-planned myth created by mankind with the aid of the dark streamers.

An angel could fall into the dark and in many ways become OF the dark, but that did not make them dark angels. They were taught here by the dark energies to exercise their creative prowess by aligning with the dark streamers and to follow the direction they were given. In all fairness those angels were badly used by the dark overlords. They were lied to and they believed the lies because *they had never experienced a lie before.* Children, remember the dark can and does pose as anything it wants to. By wearing various guises it can and **HAS** destroyed many civilizations of Planetizens here! However, those angels were never forgotten by any of Divinity. A door was always left open for them if they decided to return home and undergo a purification process. Many of them did. Others chose not to and learned many painful lessons about what really happens to human beings AND TO OTHERS when exposed to the dankness of the non-illuminated. I am pleased to tell you that a few of the angels who remained here decided to play the beast's game against the beast but to play it better.

These few I am speaking of retained just enough awareness to know that they had been badly tricked, yet they refused to return home. They stayed here to learn as much as they could about how the beast would continue to play its terrible game against the human races. They were appalled when they fully realized to what levels of depravity the dark would stoop to in order to fulfill its mission of destroying and conquering. Although it was never Our intent that all this would take place, We were able to see through the eyes of these angels and listen through mind-link as they signaled all they had learned to the angels at home. Perhaps, when all is said and done, the angels who remained behind learned of life in a far different way than they would have in their own realm. I said, *"Different,"* not *"better."* Angels who had been completely taken over by the dark did of course do the bidding of those overlords. Although the angels were not mortal when they arrived here, they entered into a world that had rapidly become a place of sheer constriction of thought, so they lost their innocence. In time, these angels did pass over and return home. No one can live as a mortal in thought, word and deed and still retain their immortality on this current plane. This is as true today as it was then.

No, none were chastised for what they had unwittingly become. All were granted the time necessary to choose to regain their Soul status or choose not to. Some did and some did. Angels have learned a great deal from observing human races here and by working as diligently as possible under the conditions of duress here, of how best to aid Planetizens while still evolving themselves. However, I believe We all learned a valuable lesson thanks to the angels who made grievous mistakes in judgment.

I did mention that Souls who return to Source enter into Light Bodies. You have to understand that this type of Light Body is vastly more different than the ones you may be given here while transitioning from the third-dimension and entering into the time of the Golden NOW. NOW is the never-ending experience of always entering into more definitive forms of herself and newly forming more and more cycles of herself. Yes, in a broad sense she is fourth-dimensional and on up the rungs of the ladder to even higher dimensions than you are aware of. So it is that the Light Bodies you will wear here would simply be a variation of the ones you will wear when you return to Source. Within the Source there are no physical limitations that must be considered. Everything you are as Soul denotes the variations and the level or status of the Light Body you will have. It is certainly not that one Body is better than another; it is simply that many will be more advanced than others. Yet throughout each incarnation period you have the ability to alter the next Light Body you will become into an even finer expression of yourself. This can continue for many millennia before a Soul has achieved a state of rapturous alignment with the totality of the Creation Processing, which is the highest level you can attain. At that point you will decide whether to remain on that level or integrate your Soul with My own and function with Me as one unified, indivisible entity. A few of you however, may be asked to join the ranks of the Angelic realms instead. Regardless of all this, you will be immortal.

Also, no matter what you decide there are always other options and opportunities that will reveal themselves to you. Each individual, whether human or not that walks upon the Earth is susceptible to the environment around them. This means that as you evolve the environment evolves in accordance with the amount of Light that you are sharing with it at any one time. Yes, it is possible to "touch" someone with your Light essence and have that portion of your Light become a part of their own Light. This is why I have encouraged all of you not to hide your Light under a bushel. Spread it evenly by all your endeavors to be Light and share Light. The Angels know all that you do and they too will share with you the energy streamers that will most benefit you at any one time. Sooner or later the Light always prevails; it is only a matter of spatial timing. The result of spreading knowledge is seen as the seeds you plant in your travels. In this manner you will not only be doing My work, you will be doing that of the Angelic realm as well. You have all heard rumors or myths of beings that lived for hundreds of years while here on Earth. Yes, this is true, although many of those that are written about in your fables were indeed those from the Angelic realm. I encouraged many of them to take part in the training of the earlier human beings. They knew this task would be fraught with difficulties and still they chose to remain.

There is more that can be learned from any one experience than any of you realize in your present state of awareness. The Angels had to learn this as well. I have spoken to you repeatedly about the need to experience, experience and experience even more, all aspects of life. This is how you learn it is by trial and error. This is how you expand your consciousness and this is how you alert others who are off world Guides and mentors who will guard and protect the upcoming generations of humans. To walk the mortal walk is a test in and of itself. Many of the Angelic realms learned this the hard way. It is easy to be trapped in illusion, it is hard to look out from inside the veils and grasp a thread of truth that will set your Spirit free. Many of you walk upon the Earth Star and have no conscious remembrances of who you really are, David can attest to this one. He is a Light being that many of you would refer to as, "out of this world." For reasons of his own he has chosen not to remember all that he really knows. This is an admirable trait not a foolhardy one. The more he can achieve in the state of conscious awareness during this lifetime, the brighter his own Light will shine. This newly acquired Light will be added to the whole of his previously attained Light bodies. These are from all his other sojourns to the various realms he has been sent to, throughout his time as a Soul. No, I do not expect he will achieve Angel status anytime soon, he is fine portraying himself as an Angel in training for now, just as all of you may want to. Celestial, now that is a different story.

The Angelic realm always has room for one more angel, what they do not have room for is for those who are not willing to go the extra mile in defense of others who are not as fortunate as they themselves may be. Walk the path of the illuminated, be more than you are and stay the course I have set you upon, the course that is the emergence of the true human being. Who knows, there may be an Angel waiting for you just around the next bend. I am not going to speak of the Archangels in this codex; I will leave that up to your imagination. What you need to know is what I have already shared with you. Those who are wise will think about and intuit the other information I have shared with you. There are many truths for you to discover if you seek them in earnest. Take what you have deciphered, combine this with what others have taught you through their own unique forms of teachings of what is relevant information and write it down for others to benefit from. As the New Book of Revelations is written there will be volumes of other "illuminations" that will come into form for all the generations who will follow. There is never too much information to absorb, it is knowing how much information to absorb at any one moment that is the key to understanding.

Humans more often than not try to assimilate all the information in one sitting. They **may** see the overall picture; they **may** also lose the imprints that are important to their further education. Sooner or later you who have read My words will go back and revisit the information and you will be seeing and reading it with new eyes. Then the Light encodings that your Spirit Guides and others are sending you will be received by you with greater value. This is what many of you have been asking for, "evolvement," and now you should be gaining a better understanding of what this entails. It is not an instantaneous process; it is a continual process that once started can not be stopped by any other than you, yourself.

In the movies "Angels and Demons" and "The Da Vinci Code." I watched to see how many of you knew when the truth was not necessarily what was being presented. These movies were prime examples of what a mixture of truth and fantasy can look like. Yes, the genetic bloodlines of My Jesus and Mary self continues on. Why shouldn't they? Many of the earliest seeders of this world were from the Angelic Realm during the times they assumed mortal form.

I am telling you that at any given moment there are more Divine Beings in service to this world of Mine than any of you have ever imagined. The Angelic Realms, The Masters, My Star keeper Children on other worlds and all those other wonderful beings who you are presently being *reintroduced to,* have been with you for as long as you have been. From My vantage point I see all their Soul signatures glowing as the true Light beings they are and shining as brilliantly as a Sun in a sky. May your Light join them as well.

In loving and Angelic service... *God*

Codex 5

Soul Partnerships

God... In every relationship there are verbal as well as nonverbal contracts that are either implied, agreed upon verbally, or written. You as humans utilize these throughout the duration of your natural lives. From the time you are born an agreement is made about what your given name is to be for the duration of your life, later on there may be modifications through the union of marriage or business associations. In fact in any professional or personal relationship there are other contracts. Initially these started as verbal agreements in some countries sealed with the time-honored practice of shaking hands. Other cultures did so by taking blood oaths, others used the exchange of goods to seal a deal and the list goes on. What you should all know by now is these same types of agreements, without the barbaric need for *bleeding* any part of the body of course, are completed before any Soul is approved for admission into any culture or society, whether a person is a human or not. Some of the bonds I wish to speak of today have to do with the agreements made between those of the opposite sex as well as those who are of the same sex. No, I am not going to debate with you gay versus heterosexual. I believe both Celest and David and Blue Star the Pleiadian did a very adequate job of clarifying this issue with their writings on this subject in some of their postings.

There comes a time in every person's lifetime when they will be faced with the choice of either honoring the agreements they originally set into motion long before incarnating here on Earth, or they will choose to break or alter the agreement to pursue other ventures. Or quite possibly they may choose to remain in a type of holding pattern until other opportunities present themselves. Thankfully for all of you *who have ever been in human form* there have out of necessity been alternate plans set into motion to maintain the flow of an individual's lifetime. These new agreements may not have been your Soul's first, most preferable choice; however they are viable options that you agreed to well in advance. I ask you now **not** to look back over your life and begin the process of second-guessing yourself. This would be counterproductive in this regard and the odds are that you would not be able to tell exactly where, when, or even **if** a fork in the road of a new direction in your life had occurred. What is important is that many of you are doing the best with what you have to work with at this time. I can also tell you that many of you are not. I can also assure you that most people have to the best or worst of their abilities performed as they saw fit.

The trouble with agreements begins when one or more people choose to alter the original covenant. It is then that one or perhaps both people may feel badly used. This can cause a setback for a time until they arrive at a reckoning between themselves. In a perfect world everyone would hold up their end of their commitments. However, this is not a perfect world as I have said before, not yet anyway, and so people's feelings get hurt. Many of you have realized this already and instigated preemptive measures to counteract the negative emotions associated with the disappointment factor. Hopefully, more people will get a grasp on their common sense soon, in this manner you are acknowledging that no one can hurt you unless you let them. Your feelings and emotions belong to you and you alone. You can choose to feel sorry for yourself until such time as you come to terms with the disappointment, or you can carry it with you for the duration of this lifetime and ultimately force yourself to have to deal with this issue in your next upcoming life experiences. This is what is known as "karma." Karma can be considered either good or bad depending on perspectives and circumstances. I prefer to refer to what is commonly accepted as bad as *not so good,* for there are no bad choices, just errors in judgment. It is when the *self perceived* errors in judgment are not addressed and dealt with to the satisfaction of the Soul inhabiting the body, that they then must be dealt with in an upcoming lifetime. As I said, each person MAY have the good types of karma and obviously the not so good, it is up to the individual to differentiate between the two and take appropriate action.

I spoke earlier of the relationship that exists between Jesus and Mary; as I said this was a unique circumstance that brought the two of them together again. This does not always happen to everyone and even under the best of circumstances free expression comes into play. Especially when it comes to the bonding of two or more Souls for a moment, a lifetime or eternity. I can tell you that when a separation between Souls occurs there is always a link that continues on between the parties involved. This will never change. Each person who comes into close personal contact with another whether it is to a minute span of time or to a greater degree leaves an impact upon the one or both who were the "encounterees." This is the indelible imprint that all of you have and you give or leave it with others whom you have interacted with. Time can not erase these encodings that become an internal and eternal part of any Soul's essence. Remember, it is the sum of the parts that makes up the whole. Good or not so good, each encounter, each inspiring moment or revelation of thought you have had, continuously defines who you are, here in the present. Which aspects of yourself you chose to enhance defines who you are or will eventually become. Also who or WHAT you may attract.

Soul partnerships happen for a great many reasons, many of these reasons you may be aware of on a practical level. Everyone who has ever lived on Earth has entered into many of these agreements, so consequently they are being role-played in every moment, in every country, every day. I am speaking of the most serious of contractional agreements, the ones each of you makes on a daily basis. If your word is your bond then you are the type of person who tries to live up to the words as best you can, *for as long as it is in your best interest to do so.* This type of attitude in certain people sets them apart from much of the rest of the human population at this time. Each kind gesture, a fulfillment of an oath anyone gives freely to another, is what separates this type of individual from the people of the earlier human races. The reason I said that this type of endeavor separates the few from the many of this current civilization, is that there are still entirely too many of your fellow humans who are self-centered. Before they will do anything to benefit another, they want to know what is in it for them. This is not a partnership; this is an independent entity acting in support of the continuation of the "me, me, me" generations that have been coddled by the technological breakthroughs of the last two hundred years. This has made them complacent in fulfilling important aspects of their Soul Contracts. The much sought after, highly revered and irrationally pampered partnership that exists between man*kind* and machine has blinded two-thirds of the Now generation to the real reason they are here. This two-thirds majority, including the political puppeteers of today will not survive the changing of the guard that is underway. They can not become the **Caretakers** of humanity's tomorrows. They will not blossom in the welcoming embrace of My Golden NOW. This future that awaits those who survive the changing of the guard is a partnership of a different kind. To those who work with the planet, the planet will give back to them and bless each and every one of them with all they need to survive, thrive and evolve. The good deeds of the few will manifest the blueprint that will be followed by all the Children of Earth's future. This is a partnership, a type of marriage that is and will be supported by all parties involved. Can you say the same about the majority of your fellow humans at this time?

Let us look at some aspects of Soul partnering that have gone on that many of you are unaware of. The reason I bring this up is that the focal point of many people's views are still based solely upon what they can see and feel, in other words the tangible. This is familiar territory for them; it does not require them to look beyond themselves and this is easier although very limiting and Spiritually inept. These types of individuals are cheating themselves out of many of the important aspects of life that Soul desires to be exposed to. OK, so by now everyone should know that there exists an undeniable link, a bond that exists in all aspects of the physical world. All of you should also know that everything ever manifested in the Creation process has a lesser or greater degree of sentience. Sentience itself will have Soul partners.

The Earth was formed and planned with great discernment before introducing all the elements here that would be eventually offered to her physical being. A type of supercharged "engine," which is the planet's core was Created that would give this planet gravity. This core propelled her into motion so that she would turn and interact with her own solar system and have seasons that change. Then it was decided what type of terrain to put upon her surface while taking into consideration all that would be required of it. Water was introduced as one of the necessary ingredients to allow life to burst forth once the seeding process had begun. These are all partnerships that are done at Soul level. One without the other would not necessarily work. Take the grass and trees for example. There must be a foundation in order for one to build upon the other. There must be soil and water, nutrients must come from somewhere to supply the plant life with all that they need to grow. The soil of this world is naturally supplied with all pertinent nutrients through the delicate balance of the diversity of the mineral, animal and plant life. All good farmers know that their fields must be fertilized. This is essentially what each aspect of the Creation process does for the other. The ground brings in the roots when the elements of air and water are introduced. The roots spring into plants, trees and so forth. The trees then reciprocate by providing a degree of protection and sustainability to the soil by offering shade and erosion control. The trees also give back to the Earth herself the oxygen, the nitrogen and all the other elements that make the ground fertile. The animal life forms survive upon what is now naturally reproducing all over this world. They eat the fruit of the bushes and trees, the seeds are dropped onto the ground and the entire process of regeneration continues on harmoniously. The system is flawless. The unknown element is mankind. Humans like to change things, clean them and modify them to suit their own needs. More often than not they create disorganized chaos simply out of ignorance or shortsightedness. Although many more times then I can count it has been intentional. This Creation Process is flawed at this moment of human history, because the *perceived* dominant species on this world, mankind, is altering the flow. This is done without taking into consideration the impact these alterations are having on the rest of the ecosystem. The system that so many other life forms are dependent upon.

This then starts the process of the breakdown of communication between Souls of different life statuses. All life is dependent upon other life to give the individual elements a degree of stability. This entire Universe is in Soul Partnership with the Sun. The Sun provides stability, heat and the magnetic pull that keeps all the planets in synchronistic orbit. If one planet were to fail or fall, it would ultimately change the orbital patterns of the other worlds within the Sun's reach of influence. You see? OK, for those who need it broken down further let Me see what I can do. The Earth's core and magnetic poles stabilize her, thus she spins and continues to be able to Create and sustain life. She, this planet, was put into synchronistic orbit around the Sun so that there would be a continuation of the seasons of the year, thus maintaining all life. In order to sustain the life that was to be part of her this world needed a shell or shield to protect her from the worlds orbiting the Universe around her. All factors are taken into consideration when setting a new planet into orbit in and around other planets, otherwise they would all collide. This is where delicate planning needs to take place and everyone involved has a voice in the decision-making process.

I can not stress enough to you the peril the human races almost placed this Universe in, as well as all the other Universes. This could have been a catastrophic consequence caused by not taking responsibility for the welfare of this planet. If Earth was to fail, the shockwaves would have inundated every other Universe, this could not have been allowed to happen. This is why My other Children and I have said to all of mankind repeatedly, "the planet will survive with or without you." The Soul partnership between Terra and all of mankind was not upheld by one of the parties involved. Can you guess which one? That is why two-thirds of this world's population is now on the endangered species list. It never had to be this way; I would have preferred it to be otherwise. When the Creator gifted you with free expression it was decided that the only way this was to work was by allowing reincarnation so that errors of judgment could be corrected at one time or another, you all know this. The problem ensued when this process took much longer than this world had left to give you.

There was a violation of what remained of the Soul agreement between those of you who refused to change and this planet that was bent on change. So what you now know of as a final attempt to change humanity for the better in order to allow their continual survival, was centered upon their ability as individuals to live up to their half of the Soul agreement that was originally set into motion. My dear Children, you can see by the state of upheaval that is ongoing in the world here in the present time, that the lines have separated. There are those who would stand for truth founded on principle and the right for all life forms to coexist harmoniously and there are those who have not and probably will not in this lifetime.

Terra made an agreement with every life form here on Earth and I can assure you that she has honored that agreement in full many times over, despite what she knew to be in her best interests. In My eyes, all life forms are equal and I am not speaking solely of the human being. The human race can die out and have all of its Soul partnerships dissolved and yet life will go on. I urge you to rekindle those relationships you have allowed to wane. Get out from behind your computer or whatever else it is you do and go out and spend a day with nature. Have your eyes open and absorb the beauty and the elegance of her design that so many take for granted. Within the blink of an eye all of it could be gone and you would have wasted the greatest opportunity to be part of something greater than yourself.

Now I can not tell you in exact detail what lies ahead for the entirety of the human races that survive, except to tell you that I see the newly developed Collective consciousness of this world elevating itself to higher and higher levels. This will be the new development of Soul partnerships between people and the Earth. This will take time dear Children. In every lifetime however many people find their twin flames or Soul companions through a trial and error process similar to what you have experienced living life here as a human being. Except of course for those partnerships that have been predestined. There are not many who currently walk on the Earth Star who have found their Soul mates, however this was by grand design.

From the time that a newly birthed Soul arrives at a state of awareness, there is an immediate recognition of the one new Soul with all those who took part in the birthing process. Each Soul knows of their encodings because it is their purpose to know. There is that magical cord that exists that connects you directly to Myself, yet there are similar cords that tie each of you to others of your Soul Cluster. Then there are the definitive lines that connect each of you to the main OverSoul Cluster where all the other Soul Clusters exist. The pairing of Souls does not happen only with the individual cluster, nor are they always brought **into form** through interactions with larger groupings. Each of you as directed by the Creator has the right to choose your eternal partners. Many partnerships are made and maintained long enough for the one or both of the independent entities to grow and expand from their connectedness. As Souls mature more and become much wiser their needs change just as yours do as you pass though the state of puberty into adulthood. Along the way you will come in contact with many people you will partner with for many varied reasons. Some partner for the purpose of providing for one another, others simply for comfort and reassurance. No one likes to be alone, but it is the mature Souls who are the ones who live comfortably in the state of aloneness. They patiently wait for the time to arrive when they can begin to interact with another who is at the same level of sentience as they are. The alone times are by grand design. They give each of you the time necessary to find yourself. Use these moments wisely, for they may well be your saving grace. Use the time for retrospection and introspection and learn to isolate your strengths and weaknesses. When the time is right you will partner with someone who will hopefully strive to reinforce the connection between you. This will bring both of you to a higher level of understanding and you will have a greater appreciation of all that you are truly blessed with. Understanding the blessedness of having life, being able to live a life fraught with challenges but also with excitement, love and laugher and a sense of purpose, is in great part what I wish for all of you.

Many Soul partnerships also occur between people yes, but what about the partnerships that occur between Earthbound Children and those in the higher dimensions? I realize none of you think about this in these terms; however they are true events nonetheless. Each of you, each life form that was ever Created has a familial relationship with Spirit Guides, Master Teachers, off world families, The Masters, Angels and all other entities in the higher dimensions. YES, these are Soul partnerships I am speaking of. YES, they are vitally important to you. If they were not I would not have broached this subject, now would I? A Soul has an immediate connection with these beings on an independent level. This means that this magical cord does not EVER separate you from one another; instead it enhances each part of this grouping for eternity. In the most graphic way possible for Me to explain this: you are your Soul but you also SHARE an aspect of your Soul with each of these other very special beings AND they share an aspect of their OWN Souls with you! Do not even tell Me, "Oh, I knew that," because on a conscious level no, you did not. In the most intimate parts of your own individual Soul LIVE **many Souls.** Yes, you are One Soul but you are MANY. Although each Soul is part of the main OverSoul Cluster, you are each in a way still an OverSoul yourself, of yourself and of other Souls.

Souls who must function here wearing mortal form are continually signaling back through the matrix of themselves vital information that is immediately transferred to these other parts of themselves. No bit of information is ever squelched. Even random thoughts have *a purpose.* Although in this book I have been speaking to you repetitively about encodings, not many of you have made the association between encodings and **Codes**. I would really like to see you improve on that part in your consciousness realizations. You should all better understand now how it is that Angels and all others of divinity share each thought you have, each moment of your personal discoveries about yourself, each, "aha! Now I understand" moments. OK Children, every coin has a flipside, so here is the other part. So many of My Children here on the planet, especially those who have studied metaphysical content, even though I must say there is a good bit of that content that I do not approve of, have long tried to understand how it can be that their sentience seems to expand at times and yet be in a standstill position at other times. Here is what I can now explain to you. You see, I am only explaining this through My own written words. It has NEVER been common knowledge. Each of the beings I spoke with you about who are other aspects of yourselves continuously transmits information relative to whatever your current train of thought is. Whatever you NEED to know about in greater detail is sent to you. This of course depends to a degree on how much you truly WANT to know and how much truth you can handle at any given time. All these beings that you share a cumulative Soul aspect of yourselves with and they with you are on the same level of sentience, the same level of maturity as are you. Therefore, it is only as you yourself either evolve more on an <u>individual</u> basis or in many cases devolve, that the changing of the guard takes place. These events are overseen and set into immediate movement by **The Holy Grail.**

It is incumbent on every aspect of SOUL to always enhance itself through the process of instant regeneration which is carefully regulated by the Creation Process. This means that as a Soul wearing the garment of mortality for instance, valiantly pursues its own solidarity of mind links with all other aspects of itself, even if this is purely on a

Super Conscious level only, a spontaneous change occurs. This alteration is one of major impact on all aspects of Soul. That very nanosecond of spatial timelessness signals in the IMMEDIATE replacing of aspects of Soul that had been a part of the Soul living in mortality. This is an instant replacement on a Soul aspect to Soul aspect, which brings the greater, more refined, more evolved entities from higher dimensions to form a "new conclave" of Soul to Soul-Over Soul. So it is that an Angel for example, who may have been an aspect of your Soul for the last 10 years, is suddenly replaced with another Angel who has achieved the same or slightly greater degree of Soul maturity than you now have. Although there are many variables in this process, the core, the matrix of yourself immediately undergoes a splendiferous new and more strengthened union between yourself and your "new selves."

No, you are never out of contact with those former beings that had been with you. From the moment of your original birthing those aspects of yourselves were even then on the level that you were on. Each of these aspects attaches a type of filament to each Soul they are now co-joined with. Each of these filaments lead directly to the Tapestry of Life and each remains with you for all eternity. When one aspect of yourself is replaced with another greater aspect of yourself, the former ones maintain their filament with you as well. Throughout your many lifetimes, regardless of where you will spend them, your individual appearance apart from the sheer luminescence of you as Soul, you are seen as a being covered with multitudinous tightly woven rainbow streamers. This is part of the evolvement of all life. It is and always has been the growing and expanding through SHARED experiences and the ability to move forward and share those experiences with other incoming Souls that is an all inclusive ASPECT of you as Soul. In this manner all of you who have ever been will always impact on other Souls in ALL dimensions. *And you thought you were alone!*

The aspects who are with you at any given moment learn in great measure not only what you are learning here, but they can better understand how and why life here and learning anything of good substance on the planet can be so convoluted. Many of these aspects are heard to think such thoughts as, "why in the world would he believe such nonsense," or "Boy, it took her long enough but I think she has it now." This is all part of the Grand Design: learning must never cease to be, teaching must always be in motion. Your very own sentience IS yours but NOT yours alone. Sentience is also a great teacher, however here on this planet it has to a great degree been stymied by the people who indulge in drugs or the overuse of alcohol. In those cases the people usually remain in a "standstill" state until they alter their lifestyles. If any beneficial changes do not ensue, then of course the other aspects of a Soul either remain as they were, or change places with less evolved beings. When I have told you all in the past, **the future is up to you,** I was not kidding. So Children, do you think you have been learning more about yourself or less about yourself as a result of this once secret information I am sharing with you all? Obviously I know the answer I would like you to give Me. By the way, I remarked to Celest that perhaps people should really make an attempt to learn God Talk and to learn the CODES and she replied a tad sarcastically I would say, *"Gee, you think?"*

In loving service to all aspects of MySelf... *God*

Codex 6

Fanaticism and Ideology

God... Children, it is troubling to see so many fine examples of humans of all races caught in the webs of misunderstandings with one another. It is even more troubling to know that these people misunderstand their very own selves as well. If you can not understand your own self, then I ask you, how can you understand anyone else? Long ago Celest told you all that I always speak in *God Code.* Yes, in fact I do. However, even if I would choose to speak in the simplest forms of English and in the simplest forms of all other languages, it would still make it too easy for many of you to not bother to see beyond the concept of written or spoken words. That would accomplish nothing. It is why I decided so many millennia ago, to always speak in codes that are carefully triggered to react with certain coding that you each possess. This should actually work beautifully, **except** that too many people think and speak in logical terms, thereby missing the whole point. They never see beyond the CODE CURVE. I did not set you in place here wanting you to all sit back and become purely logical beings. Yes, there is a need for logic, AT TIMES, but do try not to overemphasize it please. The topics I have chosen for this particular codex are particularly important because of the causal impact they have had and will continue to have on you each as human beings. You are all now living in a continuous state of causal events. Some are beyond your control while others MAY be controlled by each of you if you understand the effect these events can have on others.

One of the major blind spots that so many people with disheveled thinking patterns have is their fanatic grasp on their beliefs. Therefore it is their own beliefs that do

CAUSE the EFFECTS that CAUSE Earthbound Children here so much distress. People of any race whose minds are so set in stone that even the intellect itself can not separate truth from fiction, are the leading causes of disharmony and disenchantment on a Soul level and on a practical world level. Fanatics are MADE not BORN. Although they can be separated into different categories, each category has a subcategory, so I see no point in discussing all of those parts. Essentially, when fanatics are made, it is the result of manmade beliefs combined with either excessively bound ego tendencies or low self-esteem that causes a person to think, feel and act radically. This belies the need for real truth. Radicalism is only productive in the manner that it breeds even more of same thought energies. I did not say they were good energies. Same thought energies would be a sub-category. Extremism in any manner is simply highly unhealthy and spreads itself like the contagious virus of the mind and Spirit that it is, to every facet of life. Wars depend to a great degree on the insurgency of a fanatical individual and his or her followers. Fanatics do however have their own unspoken code. They live as "do or die" individuals who are intent on converting all others to their own beliefs.

Fanatic energy is a twisted coil of disruptive thoughts that sidle into the human mind and then corrupt the heart as well. These people are uncompromising and have their own best interests at heart. Hidden deep, deep in the farthest recesses of their minds, dwells the most terrible lust for power......AT ALL COSTS. This is why so many of them are drawn like a moth to the flame to politics and religions. Their minds were long ago compromised and this begot the loss of honor. They became enslaved to a hunger and thirst that simply can not be satiated. They are not benign people at all; if anything they can be deadly. They develop in early childhood a conniving way to use people to their own best advantage. That is an early training ground of sorts. The more they refine that ability the easier it becomes for them to "deflower" the virginity of another person's human Spirit. When they are able to they usually try to join the military of whatever country they live in. In this way they can feed their unrelenting need to harm and kill other people. The military simply teaches them how best to get away with it. Obviously I do not expect My words to be fondly thought of by people in the military. However, *it is what it is*. Only the most stable of men and women can survive the life of a military person, even though they too will bear emotional scars as a result.

So how do you think that a fanatic would behave if deprived of whatever power source it has learned to rely on? The answer is simple Children; look around you at all the ranting and ravings that you have heard about that issue from many of the mid-eastern races, for example. They are coming from people whose thoughts are of vengeance and control. OK, understand now that the more and longer they rant and rave two things happen spontaneously. #One-they attract others who share the same disruptive mind thought who attract still others of the same types of people. #Two-people who simply dismiss a fanatic as someone "delusional or just plain crazy," makes a major mistake. To simply dismiss these individuals in this manner is no different than walking through a dark alley surrounded by rattlesnakes. *Sooner or later they are going to get you.* Extremists depend on the lackadaisical attitude of non-extremists in order for the fanatic's weapons of choice, **ignorance and the states of entropy,** to be successful in the long run. You see Children; fanaticism is a learned response which causes these individuals to cull others from different stratums of class distinctions, whether they are lower-class, middle-class or upper-class people, who suddenly find themselves willing to "join the cause." Whatever the stated cause is, it is always just smoke and mirrors masking the true deadly intent of these people.

Fanatics are not all well-read people; some are not very intelligent and must rely on physical prowess in order to impress other people. BUT, they share a symbiotic relationship, one that is based on luring people who are living lives without purpose and all too willingly then begin following those who HAVE a purpose. Even when or perhaps I should say "especially when," the people who are floundering are in dire need of **something to believe in**. Fanatics are great actors; they know how to bend a person's mind and on occasion they can **WILL** them to do the extremist's bidding without the person even questioning why. An important part of any fanatic's dogma is insisting that all people in their units act in unanimity but within the confines of the beliefs the leaders have. In this way just one person can affect millions of other people through a type of "mental contagion." The wiliest of these groups are the ones who have cultivated the art of living and working among healthy uncontaminated people who are for the most part idealists. This is how they can work within a system, by successfully causing havoc and yet remain undetected while they formulate their plans for overthrowing governments and establishing their own rules. Children, please understand; these people are not parasitic. They are far worse than that. They are magnets in a real sense that emit powerful and odorous energies of decay and function by living lives of hate. They do not need to FEED on anyone. They simply CONVERT them or cause them to suddenly "disappear."

It is particularly difficult to observe the manner in which they raise their own children. The children are bred to be completely subservient to the males in their families and are **born in hate.** Females are for the most part disregarded and used rather badly. However, females are needed to maintain the breeding machine. This births the larger numbers of males considered "all necessary elements" required to continuously enlarge the sheer numbers of these people. Seldom ever is a male youth of any age known to rebel against the terribly harsh upbringing and continual brainwashing that each male child is subjected to. These children are raised barbarically and trained to lose their humanity. And they do! It is **essential that you each learn to understand the mind of the fanatic.** You can not fight against things that you know nothing about. Make no mistake Children; this is a deadly fight for the mind and for the human Spirit. When fanatics reach the darkest level of depravity they very literally fall **INTO** the deepest, darkest recesses of their own minds. This is a death trap. At that point there is no hope left for them. None.

OK, idealists are on the opposite end of the spectrum. Some of these people have such highly imaged principles of which ideals should rule the world that they lose sight of the main fact. This fact that they do not understand is that idealism without a PRACTICAL world view, without a true understanding, that the practical outlook and the Creative ability each of them has must merge-must function as one unified entity. It does not make any sense to simply voice your ideals if there is no foundation beneath them. Some idealists live sheltered lives, therefore how can they possibly know what should be done and what should not be? Please do not lose track of the fact that some idealists, far too many actually, want to create a perfect world in imperfect civilizations. This will never happen. Too many of these determined people have tunnel vision and lack the wherewithal to understand that idealism DOES have its proper place, but can only exist within the mind, within the dream, if it is not correctly implemented into EVERY society, AT THE RIGHT TIME. Most idealists tend to pooh-pooh fanatics. Of course this ultimately empowers the fanatics, you see. This is not in any way any different from the fact that there really are Earthbound Children here who absolutely do not believe that evil exists in any form. They do not understand that the more they refuse to accept

107

a truth-based situation, the larger it grows. The more powerful it becomes.

Ideology itself is a philosophy based on principles of thought presumed by the practitioners to state what is and what is not best for the people of this world. However, not many considerations are given to the fact that not all people want to share a belief simply because it is stated by other people who **may** not share a commonality of thought. Do you understand? If idealists could just remove their sunglasses and accept that NO, nothing here is really as it seems, and that YES, by bringing people together who all share solid same principles of thought, rather than in any haphazard way of gathering fractured mind thoughts, YES, great change could occur in a blink of My eye. I am sorry to say that a large proportion of idealists have agendas in mind that would ultimately place them in positions of power <u>that they are not yet ready for.</u> The perfect idealist would be a male or female who has walked many avenues in life, who has lived on both sides of the tracks. A person who knows how to experience the **practical** world while still maintaining a firm grasp on the reality of the Spiritual world, would be a true pragmatist, an idealist with a firm foundation beneath their feet and above their heads. Too many here who had been following and still continue to do so, the teachings based on strictly "something is either black or white," are now doing so at their own risk. There has not been any real cumulative effort to live and work with all others regardless of whether or not the other people are seeking a world of idealism. Children, pay close attention to all that I am telling you. I say <u>nothing</u> without a purpose! *True idealism, the epitome of perfection, is NOT to be found on this Earth. Not yet, anyway.*

Too many idealists share a commonality however with the fanatics. More than one anomaly, actually. Neither has a firm grasp on truth AS IT IS. Now that I have managed to shock many of you, I shall continue on. Truth should never be vilified; it should be honored and respected, not symbolically but "actually." Truth can be a harsh taskmaster for those who refuse to accept and understand it. **Truth is the result of being right and speaking right and serves up consequences for those who refuse to do so. It is the opposite of being wrong.** I have no doubt what I just stated will give you all a great deal to mull over. I will wait and see how many of you really understand what I just said. I will give you a hint; *look beyond the obvious.*

As people around the world are rising up and being challenged for their individual and collective beliefs now, many situations will REALLY heat up as fanatics and idealists clash over and over and over again. These collisions were inevitable. Neither side really understands the other or tries to; yet each side believes they are right. These collisions between them will continue and will be the cause of an even greater rift between those who know and understand truth but are open to seeing the other side of the coin without compromising themselves and those who do not and will not. Now I will share with you all an ironic twist to this volatile situation. Neither of these groups truly understands change nor do they realize what they are actually doing. *People who fight against change do not realize that they are CREATING change.* The more protracted their disagreements with one another become, the more they will be reinforcing each others openly stated beliefs and standards while ADDING even more distrust and dislike into the picture. They will be unwittingly changing even others' thoughts about themselves. Many people who have not wanted to be aligned with one side or the other will now proceed to choose a side. While this occurs still other people will decide that whichever group they had once believed, once followed, is no longer speaking the words that the people once resonated with.

Children; this is part of the timeline you are all now in. You will hear many spurious remarks made by one group targeting the other. Many names will become sullied; many people of dubious character will attempt to make the most of these collisions. Please, try not to become involved in their dramas. OK, even out of this debacle shall be born great good. The more that freethinking people of all races exercise their ability to question agendas; to look for any illusions hiding behind spoken words, the more these freethinkers will mature, will evolve and yet still be able to work within the parameters of the practical world as well, *while* CREATING *and ENHANCING great changes.*

As this year of 2011 rolls over into the next year, you will be witnessing acts of barbarism as each side tries their darnedest to convert each other to join their individual camps. Isolated pockets of protesters will then attempt to reach out to the masses in order to find a way to quell the violence and indifferences that will rise in the heat of this battle. Each side again will believe that they are the only ones who have the right to claim righteousness and this will ultimately prove them wrong. I have seen this happen too many times before on other worlds when a great turning point in mass consciousness takes place. This is when the true separation of the gold from the lead occurs. There must be those who are capable of separating those who are capable of bringing the Spiritual element into a pragmatic society from those who are not. This is when the scales of justice are more evenly centered. Each person must be willing to accept the fact that MANY of their views will not always be the most beneficial or Spiritually correct for everyone.

I shall give you an example of when the fanatic and the idealist has managed to focus on the same issue while at the same time both believing they had each arrived at the right conclusions. The date 9/11. It is not just a number; it was cleverly designed and instituted as an unconscious symbol denoting fear thus promoting uncertainty and further doubt within the minds of others. "911" is no longer seen as a number, it is a panic button. Idealists and fanatics on all levels used the carnage of this day to promote their ill-conceived beliefs. All sides came together after this chronological date to extract vengeance for something that they believed had happened. At this time I see that it will take approximately three future generations of human beings to properly remove this numeric sequence from their reflective minds. There is nothing in this world that churns fear that is disguised as anger, than to strike fear into the hearts of minds of otherwise goodhearted, nonviolent people. Can any of you reading this tell Me that you were not personally affected to one degree or another by the tragedy of this event?

Conspiracy theorists abounded as the tide washed out all the evidence of the crimes committed that day. But as I have always tried to remind you, someone somewhere always sees the truth behind the event. Seeing *is* recording. What is covertly swept under the rug will eventually resurface once the rug is removed. Idealists and fanatics both love to debunk the conspiracist whose logic has no firm backing. It will be an interesting day when they are taken seriously in the eyes of the many, not just those who are considered to be introverts. While this is one way of achieving a means to an end it is most certainly not the most productive thing they could be doing. The theorists, idealists and fanatics alike all have one thing in common and it is the one thing each must deal with on a personal level before they too will sever the repetitiousness of pattern making. They must lose their tunnel vision. Nobody can afford to wear blinders any longer. What is right in front of you is not necessarily as important as what is going on all around you. In other words, the properly focused peripheral can bring illumination to what I call "the Houdini effect." It is misdirection supported by illusion. In these instances what the eyes see the mind misinterprets because the full spectrum was cleverly disguised by the illusion.

Would it surprise you to hear Me say that there have not been any religious wars fought on this planet? Let Me explain this. If it is true that the true fanatics cleverly disguise their self-proclaimed missions by secreting their true motives from the people they are inducing to do their bidding, then is it not possible that most if not all wars have simply been fought to feed the lust of the power-hungry and egotistical people of this world? What if for the sake of argument I was to say that the religious aspect of war only entered the equation through the puppets themselves and were enhanced by the outcry of "for God and Country."

I envisioned the human being as a soldier of God. Not in the literal sense, rather as the one who would bring a balance instead of the differences that have segregated each of your ancestral races from the earliest of days. I thought that if each of you had the firsthand experience of living each other's truths then you would be able to join together as one united yet independent race. I know this vision is coming true, it may just take a little longer than even I had dared to hope. When the time comes and you all finally get tired of finding fault in others then you will be the mirror reflecting My presence here on Earth.

Universal truths will now begin to be revealed. The ripest of the tiniest of emotions, the most innocent of thoughts can be the catalyst for awareness and cause you all to rise above the insanity that is ongoing all around you. In all the succeeding moments of this current timeline you are in, specifically as it relates to My voice being heard once again on this world, you will become privy to knowledge that has never been a part of the Earth Star realm. I am hopeful that by introducing this information to you that you will further understand why each of you are so vitally important to the survival of this Universe. I will speak more on this at a later time *and you will know it when you read it.* For now I want you to know that idealists as well as fanatics are not birthed as such, they have been brought up that way through the influencing of all of the ancestors that they had.

To be truly human is to know the truth when it is presented to you. Up until now you have only been given slight and rare glimmers of truth by the mass produced materials that have been presented to all of you through your earliest teachings. There has been a control factor that has tried in earnest to keep all of you from EVER finding out about your individual importance. The cleverest among you have grasped hold of pieces of the grand design. Then through the assimilation of this information have moved on to the next sequential step in drawing in other parts of what you really needed to know. The roots of evil began to take hold on this world long before many of you first arrived. To cause confusion and beguile you into remaining docile and controllable has always been the obvious plan. There are very few among the many here who has not to some degree or another contributed to the almost inevitable dissolution of the true nature of the human races. There are events going on behind the scenes that will forever change the way life exists here on My beloved Terra. If you have not yet dropped all the baggage you carry in your minds then you will have a very difficult time adjusting to the new frequencies of this world. As I said earlier, if you do not assimilate enough Light particles into the cells of your body, your physical form will not be able to survive the changes. You must learn to live outside your mind and listen to your TRUE self in order to really see what is going on. I can not tell you how to do this; you must experience it all on our own. The definition of the NOW is absolute. Starting NOW is the first step. See if you can manage to escape linear time for longer and longer periods each day. Then you will understand the importance of living in the timelessness of the NOW.

There is now a movement ongoing to bring the people of this world to a greater understanding of all that has had to out of necessity occur before a greater awareness of what constitutes the makeup of life could be further understood. I know that there are a great many of you who are actively pursuing the missions you signed up for. What I wish to bring attention to are those who believe so strongly in what they are doing that in fact they are slowing the pace of evolvement for the rest of the people.

In loving service to misunderstood truth.....*God*

Codex 7

The Four Horsemen of the Global Conspiracy

God... OK, I believe that it is time to discuss another part of the Earth Star history that has eluded you for so long. I have spent a great deal of My time speaking with each and all of you about issues that I <u>know</u> are of paramount importance. My mission with this writing of Mine is not about spreading sunshine and roses among you. It is about hidden truths and the loss of your realities. I can see no better method of hopefully removing some of your indoctrination than by further counterbalancing it with untainted truth. Children, I realize far better than you think I do that some topics I choose may be unpalatable to you simply because I speak about issues that are difficult for you to bear. However, the very fact that much truth needs to be understood here should at the very least compensate you for your discomfort. I feel that laying truth in front of you, even if I must do so in a forceful straightforward manner is what I need to do.

I am obligated to inform you all that only NOW, in this present timing, am I permitted to reveal certain well kept secrets; those that have been intentionally withheld from all of you. I will expound more upon this later on in this codex.

I recently spoke with you about fanaticism, that was My way of telling you what you needed to hear while at the same time laying the groundwork for this particular codex. Fanatics of all nationalities have long been the tried and true testing ground used to channel much misinformation to all people. This must be accomplished while the fanatical people are still functioning as USUALLY unwitting agents, to act as provocateurs in the desperate game of the race to control space, landmasses, and all waterways, everything relative to this planet. You see Children; those same people here who have for centuries upon centuries been the unseen rulers of this world will stop at nothing to "have what they have while amassing even more."

Races can be contaminated by the thoughts and actions of those who are either the leaders of the lands, the leaders of religious movements or the leaders of certain groups of self-serving political movements. It is all a mind-game in the initial stages. This then slowly but surely always progresses into a die-hard movement that relegates each race here to subhuman status. The shadow riders then herd each race to be in exactly the life circumstances these leaders want them to be in. The original four races of human beings here were quietly led to intermingle and interact with one another, BUT on levels of deception that had been predetermined by the shadow riders. This was of course in direct opposition to all that We had planned here for the human Children of all races. So it is that in your today times you are all being subjected to a massive onslaught of irrational thinking fueled by the shadow riders who have been quietly for the most part, using to their advantage your deepest uncertainties and turning them into magnified fears. You are actually living now in a gridline intersection that had been planned to bring in *The Order of the One World.*

This was not a planned event that is "just starting to be birthed." It is in fact an event that was first begun when early mankind was just beginning to become a bit more literate. Although that was still back in the sign language times. The more the earliest of the Illuminati learned of the SEEMINGLY unlimited resources here, the vast areas of the waterways and the truly massive proportions of what today is considered to be precious minerals that lay deep beneath the crust of the Earth, the hungrier they became to lay claim to all Terra had to offer. Of course behind the plan was yet another plan that I will speak of in a bit. It had been decided by them that Terra would be the perfect place to ravish all flourishing resources, but they had need of the human races as well. Although they were loath to have the people on this planet learn any form of spoken word, they eventually decided that the best way to continue to maneuver themselves into outright positions of power would be to work from the **inside** of the human races, while cunningly controlling them from the **outside** as well.

I have already spoken of the early mating that took place between the Illuminati disguised as human and the human races themselves. Intelligent humans at that time were NOT a requisite. OK Children do you yet see how the necessary element of breeding within the races has played such a paramount role in how it came to pass that so many Illuminati descendents live among you? They literally created an epicenter of destruction. One that was carefully calculated and geared to ensnare each race on the planet. Even more so, this was to infiltrate the Spirit on ALL levels of life of each Planetizen who had arrived here from so many other worlds. This resulted in literally **forcing** the people to curtail any desire they had to merge with individuals from the other worlds, thereby successfully forestalling Our desire, Our plan, to have all the races integrate on ALL levels.

Children, do not be disheartened because I must speak of these matters. Many of you have for too long lived in blissful ignorance. Too long have you been carefully tutored to live lives of abject apathy with dismal and dubious desires to learn truth. You tell Me that you have a true desire to forever shed the fetters, the bonds of deceit that have held you, these shackles that have enslaved you to moral and Spiritual decadence. Well, I am doing MY part and I fully expect you to do yours by reading and listening to what I am saying to you. Then comes the hard part......*you must understand it all*. NO, I am not going to address any karmic implications here or the addendums of any Soul contract. Please stay focused and become fully aware of how all that has transpired here on the Earth Star planet is affecting you NOW. I am offering you each the optimum truth and its ever-present reality. Only in this manner can you even hope to assist Us in *changing your futures*. Not to be willing and able to assist Us would be a grievous error in judgment.

So it came to be that every generation that was ever born here was immediately placed under the thumb of the shadow riders. Every male and female at that point was carefully and craftily scrutinized to determine which ones would serve on the front lines, which would be "the beasts of burden" and which would be assigned to be consorts to other individuals. Those who had the lowest perceived mentality became the beasts of labor. Those who could easily be indoctrinated to become harsh, undisciplined, coldhearted killers became the earliest soldiers of sorts, those who would maim and kill at will. These individuals, who were all men of course, were easily brought up to live lives of bloodlust. The males and the consorts that were selected as the ones to "rule" all races were of low moral character, not too intelligent, but willing to follow the shadow riders' bidding and they were descendents of the first overlords here. Leaders were NOT born, *they were made*. Also please remember that SOME of these shadow riders were walk-ins from the dark world. So it was that all four of the interstellar races here were corrupted. It required no time at all to have the peasant types work the fields, mine for precious metals and be conscripted into the militia when seen necessary. Understand now, during these times life spans here were very short for the most part. This was in great reason why females became simply breeding machines.

During these times there were many people born to all races who were sent here specifically as the Souls who were needed to be on Earth in an attempt to counteract these malicious doings. They did so while living quiet lives and marrying others who had NOT been totally corrupted. In this manner seed was once again spread here, BUT it was for the advancement of the human races, not for the total annihilation of the God Connection. Yes, these Earthbound Children were few in number then, but look around you today and you can see how well this plan did work. Of course it was a slow, tedious and dangerous task, but there must always be a beginning to something before anything can arrive at a satisfactory conclusion. It was very provident for all four races here that WE could also depend on our walk-ins to fine-tune the slow advances that were made and to procreate more good people here. *This is the way it has always been.*

It was during the early leadership roles that were enacted here that the diabolical plan of creating and instilling *religion* into the human races came to be. The prevailing mind-thought of the shadow riders was one that was decreed by their LEADER, it was that in order to properly infuse the minds of the people with the intent and desire for total segregation from all other races, there had to be a CONTROL FACTOR. One that could not be broken. Initially it had been planned that there would only be a ONE WORLD RELIGION. However it was quickly changed to become several different religions. BUT, each had to initiate beliefs that would obsessively force austerity on the people while maintaining a chokehold on the peoples' abilities to think for themselves. By the inability of people not being able to think for themselves the shadow riders AND THEIR LEADER believed that the people could NOT live AS the God Connection. Children, you must understand all the confusion that ensued here. Even OUR own born-ins here were struggling to understand how it was that a person should respect and honor a god that was said to punish and was said to send people to hell. The people were taught to believe in a god who had total control over all, to believe in a god who was greater than they themselves were and to believe in a god who was _outside_ of themselves. Even back then people did not know that "hell" was nothing but a perfectly contrived fabrication, a myth. All those many generations of people were forced into religion without any knowledge at all of the diabolical implementation and carefully laid out construction of religions created by the Illuminati and their children. What people then lacked in their own links to the God Connection, they more than made up for in their unwillingness to know the truth. _Sound familiar?_

The ingenious plan of the shadow riders was to use religions to further control not only the mind but the very **Spirituality** of the races. This unfortunately was easily accomplished. OK now, here is where the direct connection between religions and the control factor took on a whole new attitude. It was considered to be imperative that the people never know about a matter that would have given a whole new meaning to their lives. The Illuminati knew full well that the diversity of life on all other planets also included the ultimate state of androgyny. Furthermore, they were well aware that all the people here of all races **WERE** to not only evolve here and to LIVE the God Connection, but that it had been well-planned in advance by Us, that eventually all of you would have the opportunity to live lives as androgynous beings while still mortal. This Children, is the state you could be living in at this time, this year, this life experience, IF you had been able to evolve rather than devolve.

This was why religions HAD to exclude any talk of reincarnation or androgyny. This was part of the order they received from the LEADER.

Then of course the control factor was during those times simultaneously creating and installing a movement known today as *Politics.* The people themselves knew nothing about what was really ongoing behind the shadow curtains. The ubiquitous Illuminati and their never far from reach descendents made sure of that. It was planned that a vast collective of men in every country would form an established ruling body loosely based on whatever values and dedicated principles the secret junta lurking deep within the shadows decreed. *HOWEVER,* it was further agreed that each of these allegedly governing bodies would be diametrically opposed to one another. The reason was to maintain mass confusion not only between the people of each country, thereby successfully further segregating them one from the other, but between other countries as well. Peace was not an option; far too much was to be gained by *WAR.* Politics would feed religions which would feed war. Do you yet understand the seriousness and the consequences of all the beliefs you once had?

Politics birthed **Wars** and **Religions**. The offshoots of all of these were the moneychangers, the bankers and their subsidiaries and they DO exist in all parts of this world. The policymakers had to ensure that the human races would be assaulted on all sides in a contiguous manner. The one faction was to rule the minds and actions of the entire populace of this world, while the other was to rule and defeat the human Spirit. It was seen by the shadow riders to be a win-win situation for them. However, even though these were the leading causes for the fracturing of the psyches of most of the people of this world, there still remained some concerns for the free expression people had that at times did seem to rise to the occasion.

Children, there have always been carefully planted instigators and black-hearted people among all groups of goodhearted people; among all worthy organizations, among all those who tire of the burden, tire of the heavy

121

yoke they are wearing. Why do you think that especially today during civil riots and the outpouring of fear and anger over the food shortages, that there always seem to be certain individuals who suddenly can turn peaceful collectives of people into screaming mobs? Far too many of My Earthbound Planetizens have too easily dismissed the existence of the shadow riders. Too many people have seen the upswings and downswings of economies here as "something that occurs as cyclic periods." *Those beliefs are exactly what the shadow riders count on.* Who or WHAT do you now think is responsible for mainstream people believing that way? I assure you all; it was not I. Religions fractured into offshoots of main religions because some people felt differently about the dictums of the already established religions than did others. However, that was just a small part of the true situation. *Remember what I said about instigators and black-hearted people.* The more that other new religions were founded, the more the splintering effect of brother against brother, spouse against spouse, child against child, increased. <u>This was all carefully planned.</u> Are you paying attention yet? Are you seeing what I am showing you yet? I hope so, for you are now in the time when the many Souls that are lost may include your own. I have had the great pleasure of knowing many fine and dedicated men and women who have been part of religious movements. They chose to do this for many personal reasons. Yet not even they were strong enough to thwart the dark riders hidden in the shadows of religions.

The political scenes really have not changed much here since their actual inception. The names change but the agendas remain the same. In many ways it is but a perversion of the game of monopoly, only using humans of course. There has never been a leader of a country, of a province, of an institute, who has not been at the mercy of the shadow government. Leaders are really only figureheads which allow the people to believe in something. They give people false hope, although many leaders really do start out with the peoples' best interests at heart. It requires no time at all for them to find out in very shocking ways that they can only do the bidding of the secret governments. They understand all too well that it is not worth their lives or the lives of their loved ones to attempt to put their fingers in the dyke. They can change nothing. It always comes down to this: *only the people themselves can CREATE great change.*

Children, what I am about to tell you all now is germane to you if you will be among the individuals who survive the greatest holocaust ever enacted on this planet. I ask for your focused attention and I ask you to read every word I say for as many times as you need to, if that is what it will take for you to understand certain perilously close encounters that you were INTENDED to experience, these are ones that were not planned by Me. If you can see, hear and clearly understand what I am about to speak of then you will be able to **cope** with the truth, rather than being rudely pushed into the reality that has long been truth. *This is where truth must stand on its own.*

When the Illuminati first arrived here and began their saturation campaign of betraying the early peoples' trust by enslaving them, they devised a principle that would have far-reaching effects on all mortals. The Illuminati believed that the principle they developed would last until the end of what **they** thought would be the existence of the human races. Children, you all need to understand that contrary to what many of you believe evil does not "just happen." **IT** plans for its own continuation as a massive energy by designing plans for long, long, long, into the future. The Illuminati leaders knew as I have mentioned in the past, that the Jesus THE Christ Consciousness would interfere greatly with their own plans for **total world domination;** *the order of the one world.* They also knew that a spatial period would ensue here when the Golden NOW would of necessity coexist with this

Consciousness in order to fulfill what they had known would be the turning of the tides here in the now present times. *How did they know of all this so far in advance?* They too know how to intuit when they need to know of probable outcomes that will manifest as a direct result of their own actions. They were for a very long time gleeful about how they planned to control this world; how they planned so cunningly to control the human races here and how easily this would all come about. However in time they were able to see by simply looking into the future millennia, that many people stood to become disenchanted with their lives, they also saw that the human Spirit would again and again and again, rise above the manipulations ongoing here. They also foresaw that our walk-ins and born-ins alike would help to turn the tide against the Illuminati factions. It was then that they immediately decided on specific measures that needed to be taken here. They chose **a** time period here, one that required a great leap into the depths of their own evil. AT THAT DESIGNATED TIME PERIOD HERE, they would establish a one world society developed by the shadow governments at the behest of the main shadow government. Children, you are now <u>living</u> in that time period. This is the time NOW when *the black beast* has raised its evil head in the Middle East.

It is the black beast who so craftily formed the religions, the wars and politics. However he also knew that over time he could recreate a control network; one that he had foreseen would be necessary in order to rule every important part of the future. He could rule, he could dictate the very lives and train the thoughts of all that new generations here would need or desire. I did tell you he designed everything he could to assure the downfall of the human races here. It was only through the careful implementation of the monetary system that he exposed a serious Achilles Heel that all the races share. He was "in ecstasy" and continuous states of rapture when he discovered that both monetary excesses and monetary deprivations of humans was the sure way subconsciously force the people into submission rather than rebellion. Try to think of a picture of the world; a picture where you are viewing the world from a distance. Now keeping that image in your mind, imagine a gigantic firmly woven NET that encases this world. *This* Planetizens is what you are ensnared in. The black beast excitedly formulated the conglomerate he calls "The event," which was the money lenders, the later formed banking systems, wars and religions and politics, so that ONE unit became THE focused, dedicated system to bring down the human races. There is in fact but a small group of people today who are actually the financial empire grouping. ALL banks, whether they know this or not, are brokered and subversively tied into the main unit and all the banks are owned by this unit. The agreement has always been that the unit would support politics, wars and religions FINANCIALLY, but those other aspects of evil had to support one another. Do you see? And yes, the paper trail leads back to the Middle East. BUT remember, the tentacles are in each country regardless of the country's size.

OK now, the cradle of the Illuminati has long been in the Middle East; this does not in any way imply that all the males and females there are part of this nefarious grouping. They are as victimized as are you. Millions upon millions of them since the beginning of time here have been slaughtered in the name of religion and politics. But then again, *religion is politics!* Millennia ago, that area was a different type of landmass, far greater in structure than it is today. You see Children; all landmasses have altered dynamically, far more so than any of your scientists, biologists, anthropologists or geologists are aware of. In Terra's beginning times what you think of today as the Middle East was many, many, many times larger and far more sprawled out for many thousands of miles, yet was

125

not land-connected with any other country. The oceans, seas and bays were all different then as well. Longitude and latitude was different than you know it now to be. It was by far the largest of what you would call a "continent" today. Strategically it was placed so well that other smaller landmasses that adjoined some larger ones were in direct proximity to where the Middle East really was. It was the pivotal reason why the originating secret government BASES were established there. It was to this place that many indigenous people were brought after they had been captured by the shadow riders. These captured people had initially been part of the first mass groups of people who were assigned by Us to live on the other new landmasses. There was at that time ONE major dark LORD who was believed by the shadow riders to be immortal. They believed this because he told them so. Understand of course speech was through telepathy and IMAGINGS. OK now, this ruling dark LORD scornfully decried any thoughts by others back then who did not really want to acquire more land. This was because the first BLACK BEAST here had a great need to spread his tentacles of hate and death through all landmasses here.

In seemingly no time at all he had managed to amass Earthizens from all the 4 races. No, the BLACK BEAST is not immortal; he does however have a very long lifespan. He has spawned many descendents of his own, all for the express purpose of ensuring that his legacy, his immoral decrees would continue on to the end of the time of this world. Of course he did not take into consideration that over millennia this planet would shift again and again and again. So, the horrific state of affairs continued unabatedly as he ruled the first assembly of the governing body on this planet. He planted the fear of himself into every living Soul he had ruler-ship of. It was as the landmasses changed that he decided to place many of his own tentacles, some who were in the form of humans but not REALLY human, on every newly merging landmass. He cunningly decided that he could still rule this world *by being in every country and still retain his chosen domain in the Middle East, all at the same time.* Children, it was in this highly convoluted manner that he was able to be "here, there and everywhere." The black beast delegated responsibility and some authority to many of his stewards. In this manner they used a direct mind-link communication as a means to relay important information about each new country and the people who were being controlled, back to the beast.

Understand this too please, in a manner of speaking the Middle East was so ideally located that it was the ideal point for the Illuminati to disembark because of certain planetary alignments within THIS solar system. That may not mean anything to you now, but it was of pivotal importance back then. One strategically placed hub, a center for the command to maintain a watchful eye on the entire world was the desired result. This then Children, remains even today the bastion, the main fortress of the Illuminati stronghold. Children, people there have very little for the most part. Millennia ago they had even less. The less people have the easier it is to keep them downtrodden, to keep them in chains of ignorance. And the easier it is to convert people to believe in dying for the cause, for dying in the name of their god. It is what it is! Please also remember that it is much easier to corrupt a person and to destroy a civilization by offering them lives of great wealth. There is also little resistance if the dark ones offer them lives of unrestrained power if they simply follow the trail of the politicians. The people then embrace the unrestrained powers of war amid their dedication to their religion and are kept in the dark about the black beast. The people do not really WANT to know anyway.

I also wish to mention that major manipulations of weather on this planet have been conducted by the secret governments. I am using the plural form of "governments" simply because of all the carefully placed leaders of these governments who have been covertly and advantageously placed all over this world. However, there is only one great black beast that rules all. Yes Children, even well-intentioned scientists have been convinced through shear connivance to follow the rules and manipulate the weather. Neither Terra nor We ourselves manipulate weather; we merely alter some patterns in concordance with Terra's wishes to birth the new Earth. However, the manipulations I was speaking of are in direct conflict with the soon-to-be new changes in some areas and the "now occurring" Earth weather and topography changes.

OK, I mentioned that I would speak on the other matter, the other part of the plan behind the plan of the Illuminati. The longer the shadow riders laid claim to this planet and all of her people, the more they intensified the other part of their agendas. You have no real understanding of the vast numbers of galaxies, of worlds within worlds and of parallel existences, so I can not expect you to see this as "known information." However, they are all very real anyway and most have been in existence far longer than you have! The Earth Star planet and her solar system complete a certain configuration on an interplanetary level that is relevant to the stability and continued existence of all these other worlds. I will give you the most simplistic example I can think of. Perhaps it will help you. Imagine perfectly rounded oranges all placed within a circle with the exact same distance between them. Now look within this circle and you see other oranges in other circles that flank one another. Each circle holds corresponding circles of oranges, even though many of the oranges are of various sizes. This is in effect a rough example of how other Universes, those that are parallel Universes and those that are not, are aligned in superior synchronistic fashion to function as individual entities that EACH have their own solar systems as well. All these solar systems rely in one manner or another ON each other and on the fluidity of all other new Universes and worlds that will come into Creation. Bear in mind that there are vast numbers of worlds that are part of each Universe and that the very galaxies themselves are resplendent in their gossamer array of billions and billions of stars and suns and moons. Now think about the Earth Star planet.

She dear Children is in an alignment that even your most intelligent, most gifted scientists are unaware of....YET. Although everything that impacts on one or more planets CAN and DOES affect other worlds, Earth is in such a key position that **to totally control this world would result in totally controlling all other Universes!** This long sentence now perfectly describes **a** part of the secret doctrine of the Illuminati: "Take over this world AND all her people and then cause the utter destruction of all other worlds, all other Universes other than their own." Essentially, this means that none of you would ever have been born, because you would never have existed. *Removing the present removes the past.* You would never have known love or joy or levels of happiness. You would never have known the ecstasy of life eternal, or the tears and pain that some challenges can give. You would never have had any loved ones, for you would cease to exist. The Creation Processing itself would cease to be, as would the Creator. All Luminescents, *all* of Divinity must always continue to evolve, all must continue to expand each one's various levels of consciousnesses in order **to be.** The Illuminati have been ravishing this planet by using humans to do the work. Of course they know of the intrinsic and TRUE technological importance that ALL crystals have. Because they are well-honed mindbenders, it was simplicity itself for them to cause even more confusion here by placing vast wealth ratios upon all natural resources. The Crystals serve many important functions for Terra; although I will not go into this now, suffice it to say that without the carefully cultivated growth of massive amounts of crystals beneath the Earth surface, Terra could

<u>not</u> exist. I would like you all to remember that diamonds ARE crystals too.

OK, I spoke with you at the beginning of this codex about why a crucial timeline here was decided to be the one when I could speak more freely with you about long held secrets. It was well-nigh 20 years ago in Earth time that is, that the Illuminati accelerated their campaign of mass confusion here. *They had a crucial purpose in doing so.* They began by stirring the cauldron of the long misunderstood Mayan calendar. That 20 year period was needed in order to successful train the minds of the people here to retain an almost obsessive mind-state about the Maya. Well, are you learning the God Code yet? Are you able to see any connection here at all to the havoc that has taken place especially over the last twenty years? I think I prefer not to hold My breath and wait for the correct answers to surface in many minds. The Illuminati overlords began leaving here at an <u>accelerated</u> speed around 2005-2008. Their initial mass exodus coincided in great part with the arrival of a colossal mother ship that came here in October of 2007. The fact that not only did she arrive here, thousands of My Star Keeper Children from other worlds who were aboard her at the time, remained here as a massive unified force who are still here today and working with all goodhearted Souls. They are doing this while "shoring up the perimeter" in preparation for 2012.

Some of the overlords left here because they finally realized that the Jesus THE Christ Consciousness could not be stopped. Others did so because they began losing a bit more control over the races here. There were other reasons too, but the main point is that as they left they made sure that the lower echelon of their groups remained behind to do whatever they could to impede the peoples' progressive states of mind-thoughts and to try to hinder the work of the Star Keepers here. 2010 had been the calendar year here decided by the Illuminati as the correct time to launch the worst and possibly the last assault against what was understood to be the newly formed collective consciousness. The shadow riders still here caused many attempts that were harshly invasive to take place that pitted countries against countries in an even more diabolical fashion. However it was the combined consciousness of the Star Keepers, those of the Spirit world and millions of Earthbound Children themselves, who prevented the worst of these events from taking place. You all have My deepest gratitude. You see 2012 had been the selected year here for **the final eradication of the human races.** Terra then would have found herself in the throes of being the unwilling satellite used as a launching pad to destroy all other Universes, cause Creation to cease to be and render total control to **the black beast.** Children, are you yet understanding why the mass disorganized chaos surrounding the topic of 2012 came to be? *It is the dedication to fanaticism and deceit that revolves around 2012. THIS is what the beast had hungrily planned as the time for it to count coup.* This is why 2012 is but the BEGINNING of a beginning of a new time. *Not the "end of times."*

I know that My Emissary Blue Star the Pleiadian and many others have for years been warning you about the Illuminati and telling all of you the truth about them, while HOPING you would all listen and learn. However, not even they were permitted to reveal to you, not even one time, all that I am revealing today. No, not even My Celest-Self or My David-Self was permitted to do so. It had been decreed by the Creator and agreed to by all the Luminescents, that only I should be the one to tell you about this and only at this time. Please do not fault any of these Souls for not telling you. It was imperative that they NOT do so. David handled the veil of "permission not granted" very well. Celest, well, lets just say she muttered a lot.

131

Children, your very lives, your Souls have been spared. Your Creation development will continue. The Order of the One World shall not happen. *But* do you better understand WHY great numbers of people are forbidden to enter into the Golden NOW? I do not believe I ask much of any of you. I am however NOW asking for your understanding. How else can you be progressive? Never give up what you believe in; to be a true Light Worker, a true Light Weaver, to be a true peace keeper, you must be a **warrior** as well. Let Me see if you understand what I just said.

Now that you are learning more about how you have been cleverly deceived it is up to you to pass this information on to others who are like you. The process of education must never again be allowed to stop, be impeded or remain stagnant for even a moment. A *hush in the continuum* has long reaching effects, remember this well. I am happy that there are many Souls just waiting for the chance to come back to this world once the cruelty and harshness of your present reality has been lifted.

Do you now understand how the Illuminati strategically positioned themselves in order to be *visible* but without being *seen*? Do you now know or are you beginning to see all that must still be done? Many battles are now being won by Us but the war is far from over yet. As the beast becomes more visible in the Middle-East there will be confrontation after confrontation between other Middle-Eastern countries to reclaim control over what each believes they have lost. These will be desperate attempts and ultimately futile. Unfortunately the many innocent Souls who have lost their way in the *wilderness of time*, will be caught in the crossfire. The sordid minds of those who curry favor with the dark overlords are still convinced that they must have total control over this world. Children I assure you this will not be allowed to happen. The dogs of war are barking. If you want to know who will be behind the push for war then look to the people who have the most to lose. As I have stated before retaining and maintaining a position of power is a strong incentive. Politicians and world leaders will again and again sound the cry for war, citing religious differences and protection of the homeland. Do not be fooled.

Please be aware that each succeeding generation of Souls who incarnate here will begin the overwhelming task of participating in the reformation process long after all those who could not hold themselves in *the eye of the storm* have been removed from this world. It is they, the upcoming generations, who must dedicate themselves to service to all others... not to self. For now however We have a very small window of time when all that has been damaged must be repaired. You can not begin to imagine how much you and your unwavering commitment for renewal will be needed. Suffice it to say that it requires your total focus and dedication, but it must be *in concert* with the efforts of all My Children from the Spirit world, as well as the Star Keepers who have been training, preparing, for this moment for a very long time.

Because the Illuminati have always known far better than any of you **did** of the importance of the Earth Star planet, there will continue to be well-executed incursions in other countries. Those of you who remain here especially for the next 12-15 years must have the strength of mind to see through the lies and to see the truth of the situations. In the months to come there will also be attempts to coerce the people of Earth into engaging in a new world war. This should not really surprise any of you. Whether the independent countries will commit to this will depend largely upon the people that reside within each particular landmass. As of now the races of people are so downtrodden that they do not have the will to carry on yet another war. Even as I speak of this there are revolts going on within the militaries of the governments. These people no longer see the sense or the benefit of further incursions and altercations. It is also the people themselves of every country who have had enough of war, poverty and disease. They have had enough of endless corruption and the separation of people caused by the castes of society.

Now let Me bring to your attention another facet of this engagement between the Light and the **one** *who is* **many.** This will affect you whether you stay on Earth or return to your home worlds, so please pay attention. We are in the time period when We who are the guardians of each Universe have decided to bring the battle home and into the lair of the beast. This will involve civilizations from all worlds *including* Earth. This engagement will be long and drawn-out. Both sides are geared for this battle. It is on the less evolved worlds, those few places where Souls are sent who have yet to reclaim their humanity and also on the dark world of the shadow realm, that the shadow riders will seek reinforcements for their much depleted ranks. What We consider to be "much depleted" in numbers would still seem to you to be a staggering amount of their forces. They rationalize that those who were incorrigible here on Earth will easily be so once again. Legion's forces have always been fortified by the thoughts, actions and nefarious deeds of those who continue to live a life of extremism, please always remember that as you observe this last great battle. And observe it, you shall. This final battle will be fought on many fronts simultaneously. What all of you need to remember is that time and distance have absolutely no relevance when it comes to the ability to reach out and *touch* someone. All realms, all levels of consciousness are threatened by the continued existence of these, the last of the shadow riders. Therefore it has been decided to encourage those Souls who have been only marginally tainted and ask them if they are now ready to rejoin the Light of all Lights. If they truly have a desire now to recant and rejoin their brethren, then family will most assuredly assist them in the healing process. It has also been decided to escalate the process of *returning* others to Nirvana. These are the ones who are not willing to change, not willing to explore whether the possibility exists of a better way of being.

As to the global conspiracy: The diabolical horsemen believed that during the present time when the Jesus THE Christ consciousness has been slowly arriving here, that they would still have ample time to continue to control the outcome of this world's financial and social collapse just as they had done so many times in the past. They calculated that the disorganized chaos that resulted from these collapses would be enough for them to continue to retain their hold on the human races. They had their plans. As I have told you We initiated far-reaching plans of our own to countermand theirs. Bringing truth and awareness to the people is a major part of these plans. This is another reason why the information in these books is so critically important. It is paramount now for you all to know of things that are occurring and those events that shall.

As I have told you previously the fatal intent behind this war is for the acquisition of <u>the minds and Souls of all human races</u>. I am underscoring this statement because I do not want any of you to forget this. To forget could be fatal; it could be your undoing. The black beast will sweep in from the four winds, the four directions, using all the puppets that he has acquired throughout this lifetime and try to rally all countries, all people with one final thrust as a means to parley his situation into the acceptance and desire of the people of this world for him to become the main overseer here. Many people will fall; many more however will not. I must warn you that there are countless numbers of people who will become casualties of this war.

Children, please respond to ALL that I am revealing to you by having clarity in your minds and KNOW that I must let the world know about this NOW. There is <u>no</u> time left. As to the identity of this black beast who walks, talks and lives as a human man, at least he has been living as a human now for the last 3 millennia, his name should never even be whispered. He is evil incarnate and danger unlimited. As of the date of the writing of this codex, (* October 22, 2011) he is still alive and rapidly approaching his "own end times." *No man or woman here can destroy him*. I <u>can</u> and I <u>shall.</u> My own way and in My own NOW moment. No, never expect the black beast to be repentant. He does not even understand what that means. So, Children, you have **war, religions, politics and the black beast.** At least for now you should arrive at an understanding of WHAT We are all fighting.

In loving service to *MY TIME...God*

Codex 8

A Snapshot for Eternity

God... Among the many things that you are unaware of while you wear the dress of mortality is the fact that during your "away" times, those times when you sleep and are then "traveling" and working "abroad" and during the transitory states when you are preparing to leave either Nirvana or your own home planet, are the times that *pictures say a thousand words.* At the risk of sounding repetitive I have told you all before and I have explained in great detail that *you are never alone.* However, there is much more to this issue than you think. I must of necessity share information with you in certain increments, never in cursory ways. OK Children, I must tell you how amusing I find it to hear so many of you thinking that you never dream, while others simply insist that dreams are but **logical** assumptions that are **psychological** in nature. I think I must speak with My Freud Child about that. Yes, you do all in fact dream. I did not say you remember all the dreams. *That would be highly illogical.* Prior to your scheduled departures from other realms to either the Earth Star planet or to another world, you are each sent many imagings which have been predetermined to be the ones to best assist you during your upcoming journeys. All of course depends on what life experience you have either chosen for yourself or I have chosen for you. Be that as it may, I always ensure that you have all the proper tools.

Those Souls who have selected a solitary lifestyle, desiring neither spouse, lover nor best friend, would necessarily have the imagings that are more impersonal in one sense, but are concentrated on planetary events as the required focal point of their life experience. No, these people are not all recluses; they simply decided to avoid all the hustle and bustle of mainstream people and study more diligently all the goings-on that take place for example on

137

this planet. So of course their personal imagings would be set into motion in a dedicated fashion that is equal to their intent as well as to their capability to learn as much as possible. The imagings they receive are also a type of "motion detector." Since the planning stages for this journey as well as all others are already in activated format, it is crucial that those individuals are able to always be attuned to the vibration of the imagings they carry within their minds. These are the specific vibrations that will unerringly lead them to be in the right place at the right time. Very, very often, people will experience a sense of what they call "déjà vu" simply because what is occurring to them at the minute is recognized on Soul level for the imaging it truly is. So, Souls who are traveling to Earth have an abundance of imagings intended to assist them in maintaining a healthy although sometimes hectic lifestyle here.

Regardless of what their chosen professions will be here they each carry the imagings of what they may expect and who they many encounter professionally. This is of course one small aspect of individual Soul agreements that will play out. All parties in Soul agreements carry a TYPE of corresponding imagings that interact with the other Soul agreements of those they have mutually agreed to either spend quality time with here, or perhaps just for nanoseconds of reality that you sometimes refer to as, "ships passing in the night." It does not matter what level of quantum time issues have been agreed upon. What does matter is that they are each carried out to the best of the abilities of the participants. Children, please understand that this does not **ever** cease while you are in mortality. All possible and probable venues have been taken into account. Yes, this also includes the possibilities that CAN exist if one or more of the linked participants changes course. An old friend of My Celest-self always refers to these imagings as her "ding-ding-ding" frequency which alerts her to the immediacy of incoming imagings. Of course human nature being what it is, there have always been millions and millions of My Earthbound Children, who walk through many life experiences completely unaware consciously of the imagings. They are usually the ones to always be heard to say, *"Oh, I have such a boring life!"* If they only KNEW what they **know.**

Throughout your mortality certain time periods <u>during</u> all your sleep states are the ones selected for imagings consistently and constantly appearing within the mind's eye. In this manner the individual is unconsciously preparing for the day, their next encounter with someone from their own Soul cluster or from another cluster. This happens on the frequency that was established prior to descent here. This also occurs during times of meditation or when the mind is actually in a "do not disturb" mode. Although YES, frequencies always alter as a person evolves, this does not in any way interfere with imaging progression. All beings from all other realms that are aligned with an individual are adepts in a sense; they easily transmit NEW imagings predicated on the individual's responses to the previous ones and the evolutionary progress of that person. You may not be living in a perfect world by any stretch of the imagination but your imagings are perfection themselves.

OK, as to the people who do not even know that change is crucial to them and to this world, let Me give you a woefully classic example of how a person's thought patterns can influence their imagings. A fairly intelligent but mentally and Spiritually bogged down person recently emailed Celest and David and said, *"what's wrong with liking living in the third-dimension? Where would we be if we did not have it? I see nothing wrong with it!"* David just shook his head sadly while Celest....well, lets just say that gentleman should count himself very fortunate that she did not email him back! She just loves the "delete button."

This man is indicative of the huge numbers of people who do not understand the necessity of change **because they do not want to.** What happens here as a result of their refusal to understand, is that he and all others like him, will never in this lifetime even be in the queue for consideration to be living here in the upcoming future time. His imagings and the imagings of all those people who are like him will remain solidly planted in the linear. This means that they can not live outside of linear time. Nor will their imagings ever reflect that they can. They made their choice. OK, do you remember that I have repeatedly pointed out that many, many people will perish here because they are unable to live in the higher frequency, the higher vibration of the NOW? *Are you beginning to understand this better yet? Are you able to see the impossibility of the situation?* I can only hope that you can.

Children, whether or not you accept what I am about to tell you as truth is a moot point; however I am telling you that during deep sleep states well over half of you literally travel to and from other planets, other realms of learning. For some of you I always insist that you are sent to a special realm designated as the regeneration area. This is to enhance you when you are in physical form again and you can also regenerate Spiritually if you are involved in any intense Spiritual work during your awake times. Each of you is carefully monitored at all times whether you are asleep or awake. This is to ensure that you maintain whatever level of good heath you are capable of and that your frequency is always operative. When poor heath situations occur here it can dull your sentience to one degree or another. When this occurs your imagings are intentionally slowed down to prevent you from being overtaxed. When you have re-stabilized the imagings progressions accelerate once again. Those who are not traveling to and from other planets or realms are usually the Children I feel are not capable enough to move that progressively. I prefer that they are kept here until such

140

time they complete a bit more practical life training on a one-on-one basis. This way I know that they are ready for their next sequential step on the spiral staircase that leads to immortality.

Now here is yet another piece of information you did not know about. *You are each constantly sending imagings back to US.* Every single thing you do, every single thing you see, hear, feel and ALL your own thoughts are imaged back to us. This is a direct line of communication that We give the highest priority to. It is in this manner that We further feel all parts of your mortality; that We further experience on all levels "the human walk." It is also in this manner that We who are the Luminescents can better prepare all Souls who are coming to Earth from all Our Universes to be more solidified in mind, **mind-thought** and intention. You learn from Us and We learn from you. Do you see?

OK, when you each return "home" for whatever specified period it will be, all your imagings that you sent to Us are viewed by each of you in a type of chronological and Spiritogical composite. THIS Children, is one of the most pivotal self-teaching tools you have. None of you view ANY of these imagings at that time in any capricious fashion. When you have thoroughly absorbed the rather startling nature of these imagings and are in complete control of yourself as Soul, you then are permitted to view IN THE SAME ORDER, all the imagings that were sent to you while you were in mortality. I would like you to imagine that you are looking at a microdot. This microdot as tiny as it is, is the compacted information of both the microcosmic and macrocosmic world OF YOURSELF. Children, THIS is what all your compacted imagings during any one life experience become. This tiny dot then resides within your Soul in a dormant state until, or unless, a timeline arrives when you once again need to refresh A MEMORY from the past. Yes, the past always influences the present in one manner or another.

Obviously the more experiences that you have had anywhere you were "in life," the larger your collection of microdots becomes. **Never** underestimate the power or ability of Soul to cause certain "life enhancements" to resurface AS SOUL SEES FIT. Please bear in mind that the term "enhancement" can be seen as either one for the betterment of a <u>life level</u> OR one that you need to learn from. I rarely see any Soul here that has not had a day go by when imagings they received while in the sleep state were not acted upon the following day or so. Sometimes it can come about as a change of perspective, or a "new thought," or a releasing of an old worn-out routine or life pattern. Other times it is received as new inspirations relative to an idea or issue. It can indeed incorporate the former way of thinking with a new but better way of thinking. Then again many imagings come into manifestation because of a deep desire initiated by your own perspective of a great need to improve yourself or to improve on a matter you are working on. Thinks to one of David's experiences, here is an everyday example of how things come to be. I must say *I just love having Celest and David as My scribes for many reasons. This includes the fact that their lifestyles are so different from others' lives that they make the perfect "subjects" for Me to use as examples at times.* Why should today be any different? Years ago when Celest was building the Blue Star Speaks website, David was totally ignorant of how to use a computer, let alone all the intricately developed computer codes involved in web work. Although he kept backing away from even trying to involve himself in computer work, after a time he asked Celest to teach him so that he could help her. Celest worked with David every day for a couple of weeks and he was very slowly learning the basics first. Then one morning after David awakened from a solid night's sleep, he began yelling, "Honey! I know web work."

He sat down at the computer and lo and behold David was typing quickly and using the advanced methods that Celest had not taught him yet. David is such a charming renaissance man! He told Celest that while he was sleeping he was receiving computer lessons. He could not explain it any more than that. What happened there was that his off-world family was sending him imagings of the lessons. They did so because it had long ago been determined that this timeframe would take place.

Imagings impact on an individual's inspiration; this is also true when a cluster of people gather together to discuss new or better ways to alter certain conditions they are seeing as needing to be changed. Because of the affiliation of the ideals and projections of Soul cluster participants who are in correct alignment with changing not only conditions of a personal nature but planetary as well, one microdot can and does influence all <u>similar or same microdots.</u> This strengthens each microdot while simultaneously influencing on a Super conscious level, the next sequence of microdots to be Created. Each of the series of microdots each person possesses is upgraded as more evolved groupings of themselves when needed to be. These imagings and microdot influences then carryover to become new and at times radical ideas that literally birth new revolutions of thought and matter. Thought always influences matter; I ask you to always be aware of that. Yes, the very non-gravitational force of thought can and does alter the chemical properties of matter. This of course includes the wave-particle duality. In time many of the NEW scientists We will be sending here will have complete understanding of this. Until then however, be content to know that each of you has not only the "linked imagings capacity" to alter conditions here but the **ability** to do so as well. Pre-cognizance is not a requisite for properly using the imagings you receive. However, it certainly does not hurt! OK, on the other side of this coin lies the fact that imagings are also sent to black-hearted people here, the ones who do the bidding of the beast.

The same overseers whose own dark world exists in a vastly different dimension have always been the ones who influence their kindred spirits here. Their imagings are always a repetition of the ones they have always sent. The only true difference is that throughout all the time this planet has existed, the names of the landmasses and the people here have changed. Ergo, the newest names of each of these principalities and of each of the people here are changed from the former ones to the ones being used at any given time. This means that as each Light Worker passes from mortality another who takes their place is then subjected to the same invasive onslaughts of thought and action as the people who passed over had been. In the terms of landmasses here; as each millennium has passed and another ensued, landmasses known by you as "countries" have had their names changed quite frequently. However simply changing the name of a country does not in any way prevent it from becoming raped by those dark imagings carried by the black-hearted people or the Illuminati themselves. I did tell you all, *"thought is everything and everything is thought."* I have also told you all that the dark entities do **not** have the ability to create anything. *They can only recreate.* If you think about this statement long enough, then surely you will have more clarity in your understanding of why so much that has unfolded on this planet for millennia, are always the same events happening, the same problems and the same worldwide conditions.

OK, you understand then how imagings influence other people. The dark imagings serve to keep the darker people here in line; they keep them captivated with fantasies that are falsely laced with soon-to-be positions of power, wealth and revenge for whatever these people as individuals feel they have been denied by other people of any race or

144

culture. This is part of a *culture built on illusions.* In its own perverted way it is a loosely based network of same-minded men and women intent on acquiring all that they can regardless of how they have to do it. There is no real conscience among these people. Children, these people are beyond being sociopathic entities. They rarely see themselves the way they truly are. They rarely acknowledge that they are truly evil. Without the control factor of the imagings that are constantly sent to them, they would then become puppets without strings. However, that is not the case yet. These people view all goodhearted people with contempt. Although they do not live in only one location, they too possess the magnet energy which allows them to attract others who are just like them from anywhere on the planet. Some of them send imagings to one another unconsciously, while others who know how to do so do this consciously are well aware of what they are doing. What they do not know is the true "WHY" they are doing WHAT they are. In fact they would refuse to believe you if you told them. You see, they can not believe you; it would cause the very foundation of their minds to collapse.

Yes, some of them are among the gloom and doom prophets of today. In that manner they try to elicit large amounts of monies from naïve people while chortling to themselves and being braggarts among other groups of "themselves" of how easy it is to dupe people. Yes, they see other people as stupid, yet they see themselves as superior individuals. Imagings Children, it is all about imagings. There is sad irony here though; because the human mind is such a complicated system for filtering and retaining information, it can if the center for imaginative recreating of illusions is hardy enough, become a steel trap for these doomed Souls. Simply stated, many of them begin to truly believe all the lies and deceit they foist on others. These are the ones who have to believe or their minds will shatter. The true shadow riders see these people as expendable rather than as collateral damage. Why should they not?

145

They have always been able to sway, cajole or threaten feebleminded or egotistical people and cause them to do their own bidding. In this manner they have ALWAYS been able to bring as many people of all races into the realm of the dark as they want to. It is imperative to them, because of the gridline intersection you are now living in, to hasten and corrupt all the people of this world whom they can. Since I already explained the WHY in the previous codex, I will trust that you will all remember. Please also understand that the very people who are receiving these dark illusionary imagings are also sending back their own imagings in the same manner that you do, as I explained in a previous paragraph. Yes, it is always essential to the shadow riders to know the strengths and weaknesses of those people they are depending on. This is one major way that the shadow riders are alerted to major attitude changes among the people on this planet.

Let there be no misunderstandings here, none of you is permitted to see others' imagings. I tell you about these imagings and explain the necessity of them as well as explaining to you the other side of the coin. I do so because *NOW is the time for you to know.* Yes, you are permitted to use this information to your advantage. You can begin to be more aware of the sudden maniacal look you notice for just a brief moment in another's eyes. You can start to be more aware of sudden changes in temperament or manner of people you know. You can start to read between the lines when other people speak to you in disdainful or hurtful ways. There are so many telltale signs you can receive if you but pay attention. In this way, yes, you can come to **know** imagings of others. Bear in mind you can tell when imagings are being sent to either Us or to the dark realm by remembering what you have been told and who told you. *If you can not tell the difference between messages, the imagings that are being sent and received, that are of the Light and those that are of the dark by now, then boy, are you in trouble!*

In the past I, as well as others, have made reference to "The Movie." If you remember, this has to do with the overall view of life as it takes place on this world as well as on other worlds and it revolves around the thought processing of each person regardless of the individual or group consciousness levels involved. The movie is much more than just one snapshot; it is in essence a collective of all the individual microdots that have been formed together in a type of composite. They are then categorized and formatted to probe one of many possible as well as probable outcomes of a timeline in history, in which all participants are to play their part. In a very real sense what you have done, what you are about to do, as well as what may come to pass in the future, has already been seen and experienced by you. This is the movie. The imagings are sent to each participant in this movie while each person is in an incarnate state. The people then are receiving them so that they can continue to play their chosen roles and follow the script *they wrote for themselves* to the best of their ability. But each participant DOES have the option to alter their destiny by the very choices they make or *not make* at any given moment. Think of it as a movie with alternate endings. The dark ones are well aware of the movie as well. This is why they try to tap into the **DataStream** by entering into the imaging cycles of those who are not under their control. They do this to get a glimpse of what those opposing them, those who refuse to give into the shadow riders, have in store for their dark kind. This is all I will say about the movie for now. I will leave it up to your keen intuitive imagings to further extract more information about this and how it may affect you in the present NOW moments.

I am wondering now how many of you have picked up on the fact that all imagings for the most part are received by you in the format I have referred to as *"God Code."* If you have, good for you. You are one step closer to becoming

147

optimized versions of the immortal Gods and Goddesses you each are.

OK, there are many of you who have been subjected to an intentionally perverted version of imagings taking place while you are in incarnate form. The use of subliminal messages has been utilized to a much greater degree against the human races since the advent of the current civilizations' technological breakthroughs. Most of it is indeed quite intentional and widely used in the advertising industry as a means of influencing your thoughts and emotions in one manner or another. I am now recalling an encounter that both Celest and David had many years ago when hosting a conference. One of the vendors shared *a secret* with them. This vendor, whose name I will not mention, was an artist. His specific work was displaying his art on fabric such as tee shirts. Deeply embedded within the colors of his shirts and pictures were encoded messages to awaken the Spiritual desire in all those who read the shirts or saw the pictures but were unable to see his hidden messages. What unnerved both Celest and David was the fact that he thought this was somehow funny and that he rationalized in his mind that he was doing something good. Intentionally influencing another in this manner is never a good thing. I will not go into how another, thankfully now absent acquaintance of theirs in the music business was also intentionally inserting subliminal messages in the background of the audio of the music of all the artists he recorded. These types of people will long regret their actions after this current lifetime is over.

At times however, depending upon the people and the need of the Soul to send them images through other means rather then Soul mind to human mind, there are alternative routes that can be taken. It is easy enough to alter matter in the physical realm because all matter is energy. There are many times when an individual needs to be warned or made aware of something while awake. This can be accomplished by utilizing many diverse forms of media. At times We will influence or change the words on billboards, signs or even the reading material at hand for just a brief moment. This is to allow you to subconsciously if not consciously be aware of what We are trying to say to you. This method has been an ongoing event since the beginning of the beginning of the physical body. There is no form of matter that can not be briefly altered if the intent is pure and the desire is strong enough.

Many of you have what people on Earth term "the gift of foresight." This is true. It is also true that many who use their psychic gifts to give *readings*, which is looking into another person's movie, are receiving images from Us to help them to see what is the deciding factor behind what is really influencing those they are working with. This is not a parlor trick. There are people who are quite adept at this. There is not time enough in this codex to go into all those other types of people who proclaim to be psychic, intuitive, who are really doing nothing more than guessing. Many prophetic dreams are a collection or a collage of images gathered by Us from many sources. We also use *the collective* from the movie as well as images We receive from those who work against the shadow riders. In this manner We can formulate a picture or a brief script for the intended receiver of an event. These are usually events that have been moved beyond the realm of possibility into one of a probability nature that is about to occur. Yes, these same images under certain conditions are sent to more than one recipient. Just because there are those who are subservient to the dark side does not in any means diminish the fact that the dark Children are also My Children. Because of this I do receive the images that they send out to their masters as well. In this manner We can combine all the information gathered to form a hypothesis of probabilities about to occur in the present as well as far into what you refer to as **the future, which is nothing more than contiguous formations of NOW moments.**

I would like to share with you some aspects of your optical sensors that you may not yet be aware of. Each waking moment as you gaze about, you are focusing on what is directly in front of you. What few have yet to realize is that everything that is within your visual field is being recorded, not just what you are consciously aware of. If it is within your field of vision it is being documented. What this means is that you may only have conscious awareness of a limited portion of the larger picture, but We see what you do not. The rest of what you do not see is readily available to all those who are viewing your images. This allows Us to clearly see from many different perspectives the entire scope of events on any world, in any time or place. Many of you have learned how to access these dormant imaging memories by revisiting a scene you retained in your mind. Through this process of recollection you can reconstruct a more complete version of what you had seen. Forensic scientists do this quite often. Those that you term remote viewers do this as well. Nothing that goes on anywhere in the Creation Process is viewed as insignificant. There is nothing you do or say, no thoughts that you have ever had that is not completely documented in the eternal memory banks of the Creation Processing, for your recall at a later time. The more people understand the implications of what I have just said, the less inclined they may be to be with the shadow riders.

Now, in case you were wondering yes, all those of the animal kingdom receive images to guide them as well. Not all of these are received solely from Terra herself. And yes, even those of the animal kingdom can and do send images to one another as well. In this manner they can better determine who is friend and who is foe.

If you are now considering how it is possible that thoughts can influence the physical realm, then reexamine what I have shared with you. If you think long and hard enough the light in your mind's eye will begin flickering.

In the not too distant future, as all the remaining survivors of the Earth Star's Golden walk continue to alter their ways of thinking, you will all be privy to even more information that has long been withheld from you. I can see from My vantage point that many good people who will soon be leaving this planet will assume their rightful places as the guardians of the future Earth Star ventures. The information that I am sharing with all of you through these codices of Mine will be even more helpful in setting the foundations for the future teachers. Learn your lessons well, for everything you accrue in knowledge here in the present, will assist you in the future. I have said before that none of you while incarnate is in a state of perfection, so try not to be so hard on yourselves. The more that you look at yourself and how you view everything that has to do with mortality, the more quickly you will adjust to the new "yous" that you are currently in the process of Creating. As I have told you all before, and it bears repeating NOW, what you do here in the present defines what you will be doing in the future. So by all means leap forward like a flower in springtime and become the one you have always dreamed of being. Lose any vanity, seek higher aspirations and We will know when you have crossed the threshold that leads into the upper realms of Divinity. To be true to your self is more than just well-used words. The imagings you MAY receive this night after reading this codex will signify to you where you are on the evolutionary scale. Remember well what you see this night during your dream state and every night for that matter. In the days that follow your dreams all I ask of you is to review what you have seen and then by all means send Me a short simple imaging of what your intent is for the upcoming NOW moments in your lives. History will be written this way and the history will be your own.

I dedicate this writing to all TRUTH photographers everywhere...*God*

Codex 9

A Deterrent to the Preservation of the Realm

God... Ok Children, as I am sure you are aware by now, this book in particular was intended by Me to be a truth check, a book meant to blast through your intentional or unintentional losses of true reality. It is also a highly conceivable way to alter many peoples' apathy and further their understanding of the central core of all past, present and future events. This sense of indifference has been so prevalent among the races of this world that it has successfully entrapped so many of you. For the next 100 years, beginning NOW of course, this world will slowly transition into a different phase of herself, the likes of which have never been seen here before. It will be throughout this entire phase that this world, My Terra Child, will become her own intergalactic **realm.** She will still remain a part of My Universe, she along with the rest of the planets within the Universe of course. A daring and scintillating plan that she has is now being set into activated motion BUT at a slow steady pace. This is the pace required for all that she wants to accomplish. It does indeed take into account the new civilizations that will be Created here on the dust and ashes of the former ones. You see Children, because the soon-to-be true NEW nature of Terra will be unveiled for all Universes to see and rejoice with, I have decided that I should share this information with the races of this world. "Realms" are not Created haphazardly; each realm that has ever existed must contain infrastructures, certain Creative striations above, below and encircling itself and have specific matrixes devoted to the eternal quest for immortality. I have spoken in the past at great length to all of you of the vast realms that exist. Each realm is part of the history of the totality of the world of eternity. The world of eternity is the

153

greatest blending together of all the histories of each world, each Universe.

Although it is not possible for Me to tell you about each realm simply because there are so many, many, many of them, I did dedicate time to speak with you only about specific ones that I felt you would be better able to understand. Because much of this information is still so new to too many of you, I will not go into further detail about the ones you have no need to hear about...yet. Each realm ever Created and those that still shall be, are crucial hubs designated as PORTALS, where each Soul from each Universe MUST at one time or another spend adequate time periods. These time allotments are predicated on the status and state of the individual Soul as well on what future lives portend for each one. This Universe, as well as all other Universes, exists eternally in a stylized state of organized chaos. In this manner nothing can be overlooked because there are specific prioritized actions and reactions that are always in constant motion. The importance of the existence of realms should never be underestimated by any of you. Each and every aspect of a Soul is educated or reeducated when necessary, through the process of being sent to spend additional time on whichever realm offers the needed information. Nothing in Creation can exist without these sequential realm steps being followed.

All of the "realm processing" is initiated when a Soul is newly Created and continues throughout the entire Soul life, until such time that a Soul can finally be inducted into **"The Return to Source Realm."** This requires many, many, millennia for all but a few Souls who have shown by their demeanor and the lives they have lived that they are exceptional. I do not use the term, "exceptional" lightly. This particular state and stage of evolution is not easy to attain, to say the least. Yet, each Soul who has ever been does valiantly pursue all avenues that are open to them in order to attain this final state of "being." This state of being is the ultimate state; for it is here that those Souls who do surpass their own expectations of themselves and arrive at the zenith of their success, are the ones joyfully admitted to this supreme state of exalted being. This period of living in the realm of exultation is not an "age," it is a decimal point of eternity. As long as the Creator exists, so shall this realm. It is here in this realm that the Creator and the Creation Processing dwell in extreme bliss while faithfully and steadfastly governing and watching over all life, in all forms, in all Universes. They each provide the greatest unconditional love and incredible understanding of all that each Soul must undergo on the path to true immortality.

The notable exceptions here are the Souls who are content with their own status quo and do not wish to attain a greater status; they do not wish to be more than they already are. That is fine; I have no problem with their choice, for it is these Soul groupings who are among all the other Soul groupings who choose to teach all newly Created Souls. Obviously they can only teach them so much. No one can teach exponentially if they are not qualified to do so. Besides, new Souls have great need for a while to learn from Souls who have chosen a more limited prospect, a smaller stylized conception of life eternal as a way of living and being. Eventually all these Souls who have chosen to remain as they are provide an enormous wealth of knowledge to the other Souls. This comes about as Souls leave the different citadels and begin their journeys to other worlds, regardless of whether they are long-term or short-term periods for the Souls. These are in fact a type of incubation period for each. Children, not you or any other Soul will ever be permitted to just live any period of your individual or cluster Soul lives through any method other than organized chaos.

This term, "organized chaos," is much maligned on the Earth Star planet. Although in truth it is representative of the slow, steady development of energy birthed into matter

155

in one form or another which is carefully and constantly monitored by the Creation Processing. By Divine Decree this must be so in order that all Souls proceed with the Divine Schematic system for the continuation of the life-force of each Soul. You would be wise to remember this! It is there on other worlds that all they have learned at that point is tested by them. It is not for the purpose of validation of what they have been taught; it is for a type of experimentation. How else can any Soul know or decide for themselves how much experience they each want to have of a different style of life if they do not try it first?

Inevitably all that they have learned through the teachings of others on the various realms is clearly understood by each Soul. So it is that those Souls who have chosen not to continue to move forward have given these other Souls a precious gift. The gift is simplicity itself. Only during the "relocation to other world times," can those early Souls understand WHY there are some Soul groupings from all clusters that have chosen a life of non-experience. Understand now please, none of these Souls who have chosen non-experience are a deterrent to their chosen realm. Each Soul functions in a perfectly executed accord with the energies and methodology of the realm they inhabit. As strange as this may sound to you the Illuminati themselves have contributed a huge proportion of understanding to all Souls who have encountered them in one form or another. Soul KNOWS what pure evil is. Soul KNOWS and has the ability to SEE what evil really looks like. In appearance evil is a massive psychopathic unrestrained body of matter of an accumulation of black-on-black energy that is fluid in nature. It eddies and flows slowly within the densest of the densest matrix of itself. At times it has a thick membrane within its central core that has innumerable amounts of spiny, hairy-like tendrils attached to it. Each of the hairy counterparts can stretch themselves into unlimited lengths and ensnare unwary humans or other beings from other worlds, IF it can. The entire mass of this energy is a colossal glob that has the ability to move parts of itself in all directions, all at the same time. It possesses the stench of dankness and decay. It also has an odor similar but stronger than sulfur.

So you see Earthbound Children, because Soul is already privy to this information prior to any descent to Earth or to another world, it can readily identify this unclean entity. At least that is true prior to incarnating on Earth. On Earth of course Soul does not inform the personality. The personality is the human form and mind it inhabits, of this matter. Soul can and does **warn** its human counterpart, but of course if you are not listening, if you are not paying proper attention...*oh well.* As to why there are many Souls who choose not to evolve to a higher form of themselves, those reasons are of a personal nature. They belong to the Souls themselves. It would not be proper for Me to reveal this information. Just as long as you each understand in this present life experience that they too are fabulous teachers, the rest you will understand with great clarity when you leave your mortal existence. You always do.

Each realm is a portal, as I have said. Each of these portals must be entered for the further purpose of establishing a continuity of Soul to Soul partnership with each of the various Soul clusters and especially with the main OverSoul cluster herself. You each bear various imagings and energies that are a part of each portal you have ever entered. You each bear a certain luminescence that is indigenous to the main OverSoul. You each bear a tangible "over-thread" that literally connects you to each star in your native constellations. I know that not only I but others of My evolved teachers have made reference to the phrase, "you are each a constellation of yourself." Now I must ask you if you ever really understood this before? *Do you now?* I suppose I could also add that "you are each a REALM of your own possibilities." So it is that as you each entered a specific citadel of advanced learning housed by a confluence of some of the most evolved teachers and Avatars from ALL Universes, you were also greeted and taught by advanced teachers in the Crystal City. Here, where the greatest of the greatest of all Souls have dwelled at one period or another, is where so many of you Earthbound Children of today implement your OWN ideas, your OWN inspirations, by adding them to the Tapestry of Eternal Life. It is here within the Crystal City that one of My most beloved elders Tomás, has proved himself to be an outstanding Steward guarding the gates of eternal life. Tomás is an extraordinary teacher, "elder statesman" and principal caretaker of this realm. If you want to enter this realm and be a participant in the Crystal City, you must first get past Tomás. If there is even a minute possibility that he does not feel you are ready yet, then he will not grant you entrance. It is also here where the High Council convenes as We all discuss all the present circumstances existing in all Universes. Everything is always centered on the further development of new more advanced "Soulologies." All Luminescents are present during these conclaves; the Creator, Creation Processing and Jesus and Mary, are also there to lend their love, support and to offer their own suggestions for these continuous implementations of change. As Souls advance, so do the Universes. This of course is also inclusive of the future and continuous development of new Souls yet to be.

There is one more particular realm you need to be aware of now. This is a realm that many of you do not know of consciously yet. In this realm, those who have damned themselves and thus doomed themselves must spend many, many, millennia rehashing on an individual basis, all that they have done. This includes all that was immoral to the EXTREME, illicit, as well as all the distorted manipulated empirically designed illusions that they foisted on others. Also Souls whose loss of morals and virtues contributed to the loss of others' Spirituality and begat unsavory and degrading thoughts and actions to every Soul they have tainted with their malefic energies, must live in this realm. Many of these Souls will languish there for eternity, or until they are once again returned to the reserve pool of yet to be born Souls. The reserve houses Souls whose Lights have been completely eradicated and are at that point considered "to be without life."Many call this realm, "*the Valley of the Screaming Souls.*" Although in truth they do not utter any sounds, the silent screams of their anguish can still be deafening. It is a vibration, a frequency. I have spent great amounts of time explaining to one and all that those who are irreversibly tainted can not, will not, be permitted to occupy space with those who are their exact opposites. These self-doomed Souls are always under Our constant supervision. *At times,* one or more of them truly do experience deep repentance for all that they have become and for all that they have caused to happen to others. Although these instances are very rare, yes, they CAN and MAY occur. Perhaps it is because Planetizens of Earth have such great difficulty in knowing when a person is lying and when that person may be speaking the truth, that it makes it difficult for so many people here to understand that WE have no problem doing so. Nothing is hidden off-world; all Souls are accounted for and those who must face their own accountability for what they have done or TRIED to do, are all well-known by Us.

So it is that when a Soul achieves that hallmark moment, when the Soul has not only come to terms with the outrageous action it has taken, many different "notes" in the Hall of the Harmonics begin to sound. Then that Soul or Souls must deal with the consequences of their own actions. In this manner they have judged themselves and found themselves to be in guilt. THIS *is what judgment day really is for ALL of you.* It is just that it must be handled differently in this other realm. Over a length of timelessness, these Souls who have chosen to return to the fold receive much counseling; long-term epochs must be spent within certain halls within specific portals where the most basic rudimentary teachings must begin. As this occurs the Souls who were once considered to be unfortunate must carry the internal scars they incurred as the results of their former heinous behavior. They experience a dearth of knowledge; all that that they once possessed in knowledge and wisdom, regardless of what their evolutionary status had once been, has been removed from the matrix of their Soul. This is a natural occurrence that simply must take place in order for these Souls to begin anew.

Obviously I am not suggesting that you should have any desire to become part of this realm. However, NOW is the TIME for you to truly understand not only its existence but the reasons why it MUST exist.

OK, Terra is positioned now to be in direct parallel with a vast grouping of constellations and aligned in a new way with other worlds' planetary alignments. This means that as part of her newly developing evolutionary state that is already beginning to unfold, she will eventually become a satellite which is to be a massive embarking and disembarking point for all galaxies that are now beginning to develop critically placed new worlds in conjunction with Terra's new positioning of herself. As an intergalactic entity Terra will be able to harness the energies of supernovas for example and use those energies to birth more parallel worlds of herself and OF other galaxies as well. This is a primary example of how a world can birth new worlds based on her own particular desire and determination to evolve. The soon-to-be former Terra will have new landmasses that are healthy and fertile and will house the new generations of races here. Terra's very core will erupt for just a nanosecond, just long enough to spew new technological finds that will generate clean pure energy. The Middle-Earth races themselves have long been the guardians of Terra's inner self. All that they have been perfecting technologically and environmentally will become part of the Golden NOW.

Children, can you better understand yet why We simply can not and will not allow any dark-hearted people of any races to remain here on Earth? Not even a single blade of grass that carries contamination below the surface within its roots shall remain. As the new realm of herself Terra will house not only the new people who will be the human caretakers, the new gardeners of the new world, they will all interact with all Star Keeper races who will be setting up direct links here to all other worlds and constellations. This means that the plan We have devised will assure Terra's continuation as a primary base and a hub of advanced technology that will benefit all Universes, all races, all living things. As part of her request she has specifically asked to have different citadels built here that will house many advanced thinkers and doers of the scientific worlds from all planets. It will not be a hodgepodge of beings merely congregating for inane discussions. That simply would not do. It will be the individuals who have the most to offer to and FOR all races here and the entirety of races on other worlds who will also from time to time convene here. Terra will become home to new civilizations that will prosper as a direct result of their teachings as will their students. Everything that takes place here will then be in direct concordance with the eternal plan of Creating new and better worlds and inviting newer and more educated forms of "yourselves" to live here and travel at will to other realms. This is the time We have all awaited. This is the time when the Great Gestalt begins the multidimensional task of bringing to fruition *the time of the eternal harvest.* You see Children, this is not a season, it is not an age; it is the NOW.

I do realize how difficult it is for some of your minds to comprehend this endeavor, it is one that may seem to be so massive to you, so darn ALIEN. However, I ask you to consider the fact that your lives on the Earth Star planet have been severely constricted, thus being the *CAUSE* of your tunnel vision. The tunnel vision has been the *EFFECT* you have been *LIVING*. What you do not remember.....among many things while you are in mortal form....is that the Creation of all new worlds must always have certain planets that each function as a fulcrum to assist in setting the other "free-flowing" planets into place. It is really nothing more than a precise form of geometric calibrations that take place in these instances. What makes Terra different however is the alignment she now has that I have spoken about. Be very aware of what I am about to say now please: *IF* Terra had not approached Me and had not sought the ways and means to not merely survive, but to birth of herself **a new realm, a brand new galaxy,** she would have had to implode. Only through the implosion process would all traces of every civilization have ceased to be. Terra was perfectly willing to permit that to happen. She knew full well that without her presence here, a new world somewhat like she herself would have been Created to take her place.

Of course she also knew that this would have eradicated the shadow riders here. As for the black beast, that entity would have left in great haste moments before she imploded. He would then have begun yet another scavenger hunt to collect any lesser evolved beings he could on any world where he could find them. Children, all of Us, We who are the Luminescents of all Universes, simply could not accept that as a viable alternative. Each world in each Universe is a highly complex union of unlimited sentience combined with the massive composite of all Soul energies who have ever befriended those worlds. As such, each world relies a great deal on the thought forms and degrees of evolution that each entity in each world possesses. Those energies FEED the worlds. There are no degrees of separation between those energies and the heartbeat of a world. OK, Terra agreed to write her own

162

NEW history but in a better time with better races of people here. You see, the heartbeat of each world does indeed impact on the heartbeat of the Universe they are part of. It is in fact these heartbeat melodies that denote the pulse of each Universe. Yes, these sounds are also quite resplendent as their own dazzling brilliant selves, in the Hall of the Harmonics. The stronger the heartbeat of each conjoined world, the stronger the Universe and vice versa. This is but one manner of how a Universe succors each of its worlds and how the nourishment all receive, one from the other, assists in the Creation Processing of new, more advanced worlds.

So the Earth Star planet is rapidly assuming a new pace, one that is perfectly matching the new revolutions of her own Creative processing. No, nothing can or will deter Terra from her self-appointed mission. Although she could have refused to listen to Me or to any of the other Luminescents and caused her own self-destruction, her undeniable strength of determination and her unconditional love for all Creation superseded her exhausted and pain riddled Soul. Do you yet better understand why I will not allow anyone or anything to interfere with Terra's Creation process? Do you yet better understand why it is incumbent on Me to continue to refuse entrance into **The Hall of the Souls,** to those who are shallow minded individuals that are hell-bent on other peoples' and other races' destruction? And all this is rationalized by truly the most diabolical self-serving individuals I have ever seen! None of you should try to say that you can not understand all the meanings within the meanings I am sending to you. That would be yet another copout by you. And THAT Children, although I love you all so dearly, **is completely unacceptable to Me.**

OK, the Creation Processing is not a "concept," anymore than am I. You may have a difficult time in truly grasping the enormity of the situation regarding Terra and her new place as her own realm and the Creation of her own galaxy, totally unlike the smaller less refined version she has today. But even so, you SHOULD be able to understand why under no condition will I allow ANYONE to remain here who would be any form of disincentive energy, any form of less than evolving energy to remain here. *It will not happen.*

So what is it that you have to look forward to? You can look beyond today and look to your heart and Soul. Learn children learn, never ever stop learning. A citadel is only as good as what the inhabitants *of the time* make of it and Terra is to become a citadel of herself. She has experienced far more as a result of the *human experience* than even she first imagined and she has much to say on her own behalf. There are great absolutely flawless amounts of knowledge and wisdom that is to be passed on to all that enter her new realm. Like the Crystal City, she will be a place for all the great thinkers of all Universes to converge and share their ideas, inspirations and sage advice as a means of Creating what has not as of yet been thought of. You, if you choose to and when you are ready and worthy, will be welcome to add your voice, your special gifts and talents to the Creative Process as this *"Terraverse"* continues to evolve and expands herself exponentially. Can you yet begin to fathom the possibilities? I MySelf am in awe just thinking about the potential. I have helped to Create countless galaxies and untold numbers of Universes and so many diverse forms of life and still this enterprise takes My breath away. As it should yours. When David first heard of what was to come he wept tears of joy for his beloved Terra. He will return time and time again in the future to be an active participant in the new world that he and so many others like him will help to Create. Ah, the joy of living. If you do not feel honored and blessed beyond any comparison to be here now at this exceptionally life altering timeline in Earth's history, then I pity you. This is Terra's choice, will her choice inspire you to leap beyond

164

logic and reach out to your own destiny? We shall see. All of you were called upon *by Me* to be here and remove all the negative elements from this world. As a reward for all your patience and dedication, I have just unveiled to you the soon-to-be result of some of your efforts. I consider this to be one of the most supreme moments in this Universe's long line of history.

As Terra births her new self in order to begin the Creative Process of introducing new worlds to her realm, there will be limitless possibilities available for all who wish to participate. The line of volunteers is already forming and leads far out and beyond this world. I have watched as your Creative spurts of inspiration have painted masterpieces upon the fabrics and I have watched as you have combined musical notes to form a symphony of sound. Many of these notes are held in high esteem in the Hall of Records. Now imagine how something basic can be expanded upon in the higher dimensions when the concept is applied to Creating new races of beings. The Creation of new forms of life here that have NEVER EXISTED IN A MORE REFINED WAY BEFORE? Does that not cause your heart to swell with anticipation? If this does not make you shiver with joy then I shall have to have My Star Keeper Children confirm that you are indeed still alive and well.

Now I can assure you that all those who had plans of their own for controlling this world are quite upset by this new development and rightly so. As Terra continues to evolve, the Light emitting from her Soul Matrix will be so intense and so vibrantly brilliant, that none who have fallen from Divinity's grace will be able to enter into her realm. This new realm is something that I am extremely proud of. One by one My work will continue to be done. It requires expansion without boundaries or limits to bring this into reality.

Help Me to help you, by you yourself removing all people, places and things from your lives that are impure or unjust. None of those things will be able to survive here in the days ahead, so you may as well begin the process of weaning yourself from all of it now. I am sure you know of what I am speaking. Strive to better yourself because you **can**, not because you feel you must. A feeling of **must** curtails the further enhancing of the embodiment of a Soul's potential and if you **must** do something, then you are doing so for all the wrong reasons. If you knowingly do something that is limiting, that lacks Creative ability, then you are not assisting, you are a deterrent. And since *the art of work* is **to play,** this would not make sense, now would it? Take the high road; it is there where I will meet you to discuss the probabilities of your future. As a wise man once said and I believe it was Me, "past, present and future are flowing contiguously in the timelessness of the Continuum." When you need help, call upon all the other "yous" that are present throughout time. Who better to help you than you, yourself. I will leave you with that thought... for now.

I dedicate this codex to My Golden Terra Child...*God*

Codex 10

The Intent of Surveillance

God... In the defense and preservation of all of the realms We are responsible for, We who are the Creators, Co-Creators and Overseers of each Universe must always be aware of any changes within each and every movement of the realms and Universes. It must be this way in order to maintain balance and order within the Creative process. In so doing We are better able to more easily calculate, predict and apply corrective procedures when it is known that there will be a disturbance or a ripple within the Continuum. OK, what I am saying is very important because each ripple or wave that is set into motion has a corresponding effect on all life. There are innumerable times when each of Us must make decisive choices. We must only do so through a series of sequential steps. The first step is always by consulting the High Councils of each Universe of course, this is to determine whether or not it is in the Universes' best interests to let the changes occur.

We also need to decide whether it will be necessary that We enact countermeasures to alleviate or possibly eliminate a process that has been set into motion. I am speaking of minute changes within certain physical realms where knowledge and respect for Universal Laws is not adhered to. It is within these realms where the unpredictable occurs. Each change, no matter how small, alters the dynamics of any mass of energy surrounding a world, a constellation of stars, or individual quantities of thought patterns. The consequences of the unsupervised alterations of force producing motion could be severe, far beyond anything that could be construed as trivial or "inconsequential." Do not be fooled into believing that a small ripple far away in a galaxy that you do not even know about, does not have some form of effect upon this world and all who reside here. *IF* that ripple is a deterrent to evolution or is a caustically enhanced projectile targeting a realm or a world, then it can not be permitted to continue on its journey. Also, please do not be naive and think that if something does not appear to affect you personally, then it must not be worthy of your attention. I can assure you that there is far more truth to the statement "everything is connected" than you may *yet* realize.

Everything, no matter how seemingly insignificant it may be, must be monitored. All that exists must be constantly observed by someone, somewhere, to maintain balance. For example: Any forms of planetary conjunctions that may be involved in some type of spatial relapse, or could be outpacing the correct alignments that were set into motion, must be attended to. In the times ahead as Terra enters more fully into alignment with the higher frequencies you will become more aware of what I am speaking of. There are monitors surrounding each world; there are some that are stationary while others are always in a constant state of motion, a state of pronounced but stable flux actually. Many of these monitoring systems that beam down to the Earth Star planet are indeed positioned in NIRVANA. After the final changes have manifested themselves, the New Earth Star planet shall rest comfortably in the Golden NOW. That will be when the denseness of this world has become a mere memory and you will be able to see NIRVANA as clearly as you currently see the Sun and Moon in orbit. This is just a small part of what you will be consciously aware of. Each day astronomers from this world are discovering new Stars and Galaxies that were never apparent to them before. Although most stars, galaxies and planets that now appear as "new" to them have always existed. They all just existed on a level and frequency far different from what you were familiar with. Now that this world is coming into alignment with so many other dimensions, there will be

168

much more information that will be revealed to you relative to the further progression of Earth and her races. All of the inhabitants of Earth will be able to avail themselves of this information; it will be a long sought after and pleasant surprise. All of your reactions at that time and all the physical changes to the planet and to all her inhabitants, *as it pertains to this Universe as a whole,* will be consistently monitored. This will be to correctly gauge the sequential **outcomes** of the evolutionary path of this world. In the vast timelessness of the Continuum, We who are not in mortal form can see these changes already. Every moment of each day when someone alters their thoughts or beliefs, this planet in the **future** moments of NOW, alters her appearance. As I have already told you, the future is predicated on the present. This means that **future** history is being rewritten in a new and better way every moment.

As I have previously stated, each of you is imaging the personal and planetary conditions you are conscious of. These are all of the ones that are taking place in every nanosecond of every cyclic day, every day. What you **may** not be aware of is that your mental health as well as your physical health, is monitored somewhere as well. During your resting periods while you are receiving the imagings that I spoke of in a previous Codex, your physical bodies are given full diagnostic checks to keep track of how well they are faring. Your Earth doctors know so very little about true medicine and REAL conditions that exist within the physical vehicle. They only know what they have been taught and simply deal with conjecture most of the time. The highly evolved doctors' off-world however, have access to unlimited information far beyond quantum physics and quantum physiology that is relative to any life form's wellbeing. These are the ones who are the medical specialists We have working on your behalf. No, I will not go into complex information at this time concerning physical disabilities and causes, nor will I once again explain why We can not just simply fix all that ails your bodies. Please try to bear in mind that those who have not had your best interests at heart here, intentionally Created DISEASE. During the night your physical vehicles are scanned and any changes are noted in your personal logs. The logs are much like a diary, only comprehensive and detailed.

My Star Keeper Children in other realms constantly monitor the charts of your individual medical and psychological history. In this manner they can more accurately see who is moving forward, who is absorbing Light particles into their cellular structure and to what degree of difficulty, whether physical, mental or Spiritual, each of you is undergoing as you try to move through this process. This is a rudimentary procedure compared to realigning the axis of a planetary orb, or shifting the trajectory path of a comet or other orbital object that is in danger of colliding with another object. As you now understand more clearly the how and why of the REASONS for the gridline intersection that is occurring during the linear year of 2012, perhaps you can see how the shadow riders and their cohorts have used your fear to obliterate your individuality. They are still trying, but more hastily now, to deviously instill more fear about this date. *End of the world indeed!* Such nonsense!

If you are wondering who else is "watching over you" let Me inform you that there are no limits to WHO of Us is, yet there are very strict codes of ethics We adhere to. No, We are not interfering with your right to freely choose what to believe, what to think or what to do. If We **had** been allowed to, the human race never would have devolved to the state it has. We simply understand better than any of you do, at least while you are in mortality, the importance of being in a constant state of awareness. Yes, at times We are amused by the antics of the surveillance communities here on Earth. Their means are invasive as well as morally questionable, Ours are not. You may refer to Us as "observers." The intelligence gathering communities here on Earth only serve themselves by believing they have to defend their countries' interests. They are "self-servers." This by the way was taught to them by none other than the founding fathers who were intent on force-feeding the *Order of the One World* to all of you. They use their moles, their informants and their machines; We on the other hand are much more sophisticated, nonintrusive and much better informed. Through the eyes and ears of every creature that exists on the Earth Star planet, We can and do keep tabs on everything. Even your beloved pets signal Us when there is an emotional or physical change within the people they are fond of, they also speak with us about the environment they are living in as well. I will speak on more of this later. If the energy fluctuates in an area even one iota, We know about it immediately. There is little that can be said or done that We are not already in awareness of.

Each duty, responsibility or obligation, is delegated to another being in each Universe. Here is a bit of information for all of you about how our systems function. The more you understand this, the better off you will be! *I am very serious about that!* OK, each Soul possesses a monitoring device that is partially embedded within the electromagnetic center, or core, of the individual Soul. So it is that as each Soul from each CLUSTER chooses or IS CHOSEN to be a preceptor for Souls, a preemptive process takes place. This simply means that certain criteria must always take precedent in deciding which Soul on which levels should be participants on specific growth levels and which should be the ones to emphasize the teaching areas. All must occur on whatever the THEN current levels of knowledge the preceptors are themselves on. The monitoring energies are then passed on to Soul after Soul after Soul through the process of learning AND teaching. In this manner as Soul "ages" into different gradients of maturity, the monitoring energies become even more fertile areas for self-exploration, for further self-discovery. If for instance Soul Cluster area 2,879,2378,007 is the cluster that has been chosen to apply the basic principles of eternal life needed to be understood on whatever planet that the cluster is indigenous to, then those principles will have slight variations than they would have for clusters on different planets. That is not to say the rudimentary aspects are different, it is just that each planet lives its life in ways that are the same yet different, from each other planet. The monitoring devices I speak of are bodies of matter of photon type energies bound together by a single pulsating orb, causing a change on variance levels and stages of "slip streamers." This causes the production of massive proportions of Light denoting the levels of the rapidly changing sentience ability of each Soul. This is applicable to both the preceptors and the students. In this manner, all is clearly seen and understood because of the "eye in the sky," that each Soul bears. All Souls understand the need for them to each be able to gauge not only the abilities and perceptions of others, but to properly gauge their own as well. In this fashion it is yet another win-win situation. THIS Children, directly affects the individual Soul's abilities to enhance all forms of their sentience. These systems clearly affect and impact in a glorious fashion, the self-responsibility individual Souls must have and their own willingness to accept positions as self-governing agents acting on the behalf of all.

So if one part of a Soul cluster in any one of the Universes assumes the responsibility of speaking on behalf of the entire cluster, certain protocols must be adhered to. If that part of a Soul cluster accepts the task of sharing responsibility for maintaining the deflecting of meteors for example from any injurious action occurring on let Us say, Venus, then this is a secondary mission that the cluster has adopted. The cluster does so in pursuit of further enhancing its own evolutionary state. No, nothing is left to chance here. All clusters have their own overseer Souls who are of course multidimensional beings, just as all other Souls are. The overseer Souls patiently watch over their charges while still concentrating on other tasks they have chosen. Duties, responsibilities and obligations abound everywhere within each Universe. It is a continuous action and reaction in the supreme state of organized chaos.

These monitoring enhancements clearly denote every slight inflection of Light mass Creating more Light mass within an individual or group cluster's electromagnetic field. In this manner not only do We Ourselves see how each Soul is progressing, but also how the individual progressions are impacting on the clusters overall. OK, when you arrive to the Earth Star planet you arrive here with your own device intact. Soul does not LOSE the device, even if Soul loses itself here. Now do you better understand how easy it is to observe each of you and your continuous emotional, psychological, physical and Spiritual fluxes? When Soul departs the mortal form of a human being, it carries with it all accumulated knowledge, experience and either greater understanding of itself thus having greater expectations of itself, or it carries a void within its matrix. The void underscores the lack of what it had been able to accomplish; the void also carries some disappointment in itself as well. However, once Soul is home again for a little while, that all dissipates and the device merely shows the colorations that the Soul had accrued during its most recent journey.

The Creator oversees everything; the Creator is the **primary** overseer. I oversee everything within My Universe while always remaining constantly aware of what is happening in all the other Luminescents' Universes. And you thought it was tough to keep track of your kids when they are young or balance your checkbook! I am not making light of how difficult the Earth Star Walk can be, but in comparison with the responsibilities some of Us have undertaken, you have it relatively easy. **Everyone** has responsibilities. You as an individual take care of everything that pertains to you in your personal world. The Spirit Guides and other Mentors each of you incarnates with watch over you and monitor your progress. The Masters of each race of mankind also watch over the races both individually and *collectively*. Everyone has a task; all have responsibilities to live up to. The difference between how We view some things here and how you view things are vastly different, to be sure. Earthizens are the only ones who require monetary compensation for the duties they perform; you can thank the Great Deceivers for that one. We aspire to a higher purpose, a Spiritual pursuit of wisdom that comes from dedication to service and enlightenment above all else. In time, so shall most of you.

Everyone who incarnates on the Earth Star sets out with the best of intentions, well, for the most part. It is maintaining the intent that is difficult. Understanding this should bring some degree of clarity of the awesome responsibilities each Soul whether incarnate or not, must have with the chosen or assigned role they are undertaking or in charge of. Please remember, each Luminescent, Angel or other being is a SOUL. Each of Us, you and I, are constantly in a state of surveillance studying everything that has the ability to affect our continuity. It is the degree of intent anyone places on their responsibilities that defines who, as well as what, they will eventually become. To take it one step further and at the same time bring this subject matter closer to home, it is the intent and ability to follow through with the chosen intent that separates the individual from the primordial ooze. This type of ooze is a result of matter that is in a state of devastation. In other words, if people allow themselves to fall into a bottomless abyss because they have no intent to do otherwise then they like the primordial ooze, will eventually become a disorientated, devastated entity. This of itself would be catastrophic to anyone or anything associated with these particular Souls, including their Soul Cluster and OverSoul. So it is that We monitor all forms of life to keep events like this from occurring.

In every nanosecond We can account for the whereabouts and the overall condition of every mote of energy ever brought into existence. In so doing We can correctly determine the evolutionary path of *almost everything* that has ever been Created. We must always take into account any variations from a chosen path that We see and at all times be ready to adjust situations or events to prevent any deviations from course that had previously been calculated for. We do so to reinforce an entity's right of free expression. We do so when We are asked by a being for this help.

In the Continuum nothing is ever lost or destroyed, everything is used or when need be, reabsorbed to be used at a later date. The human race as a whole has for too long treated life casually and has had low regard for the sanctity of all life. This is but one more example of why We must always monitor every race, every culture, every species of life on this world and all other worlds. If We did not then organized chaos would forever give way to the throes of disorganized chaos.

We have been aware for some time as this century continues to unfold that the agencies now referred to in some circles as "big brother" are in a heightened, frantic state of awareness. We caution you to watch your buying habits, anything you do that is out of the norm. How you conduct your affairs will draw undue attention to you as the ugly head of paranoia takes hold over a great many. You can not imagine how much of this paranoia propaganda is intentionally being orchestrated to drive fear and uncertainty into the hearts and minds of otherwise sensible people. The surveillance communities are information gatherers for the strict purpose of singling out dissidents, those people who can and will upset the "natural order" that has prevailed here for so long. While it is important for these agencies to track the masses for obvious reasons, it is also worthy of mention here that the most important reason for the intense monitoring of all personal data that is occurring in the present, is being done to track, or keep tabs on those who are reaching their potential while in human form. Those people of all races who have the potential to cause the greatest threat to the beast's obviously flawed plans for world domination are those of the Light worker communities, *whether they are conscious of the fact that they are Light workers or not.* For too long the beast has had all people under surveillance. Off-world, it has just been waiting for the right opportunity to gain control over all Universes.

Each person is tracked from the moment they are born to the end of life when your physical body ceases to be. The accepted practice of requiring birth certificates, marriage licenses, death certificates and even driving licenses, has involuntarily entered you into "The System." Once IN, it is virtually impossible to extricate yourself from it. Now that the digital age of man has arrived and is in full swing, tracking the whereabouts and the overall mood of the people has been made easier. You see, the shadow governments, through the rising of their intelligence gathering communities, now has the ability to not only track but to predict the probable mood or changes in patterns of everyone within their system. In effect they have the means to...push your buttons. The advent of such programs such as welfare and social security to name a few have not freed the people to pursue life, they have not made it possible for the people to live their lives as they desired. Each program is yet another form of control. Keeping the people passive and dependent on the governments for their subsistence and the people will unerringly do what they are told. As long as there is not a disruption in the services they have come to rely on. This too, like most double-edged swords has a flip side. A literate *yet ignorant* public, is much easier to control than a well-educated, Spiritually balanced, morally incorruptible one is.

I ask you to remain calm in these days of rage, see through the obviously intentional attempts of harassment committed towards you by your fellow human beings and send love and compassion to all those who still dawdle in the dark. You can not be responsible for them; you can however assume responsibility for your own actions. The sound of "To thy own self be true," rings as forcefully now as it did ten thousand millennia ago. Over the upcoming years, as dominion of this world is given to the good, worthy people, these are the people who will not indulge in harm to anyone, begins to take place here, there will be many transformational stages of awakening for all races of people. Hold true to your values; do not become distracted by the delusional banter explicitly portrayed by the conspiracy theorists hell-bent on convincing you of the "end of days times." Stay focused on what is real, hold on to all your dreams, hopes and aspirations for a better tomorrow. The tomorrows may seem tough and unbearable as you forge the true future of mankind, but take solace in the fact that no matter what you have to endure, all your efforts to reclaim your humanity will not be in vain. If you allow anger to rule your mental state over the issue of the secret governments' surveillance, or over any issue for that matter, then you have lost the war before the battle even started. Be My eyes and ears so that I may better continue to assist you in this, the greatest show of humaneness ever performed here on Earth.

OK, all animals here whether wild or domesticated respond to Terra's continuous movements and react by sending through their own monitoring devices more information to all other worlds, as well as to all other of their own species here on Earth. It does not matter if the animals are land bound or water bound, or if they soar in the sky. Animals are not intentionally pernicious, unless they have been conditioned to be. Their Souls may be different than your own, but they have Souls nonetheless. All animals have long been in touch with the Middle-Earth civilizations; these are the groupings of Planetizens who fled deep inside Terra, long, long ago. Of course these ancient ones have the devices as well. These civilizations have been invaluable in their study of each and every tiny change taking place here. Their own scientific teams have no problem at all in identifying each and every bit of distorted energy that is affecting this world. Results of all their own testing is immediately sent to those of Our own teams who also excel in these studies. Although the rumblings of Terra are but natural pressure equations relative to maintaining her core stability on a day to day basis, it has been the malefic manmade eruptions that have caused such havoc above ground.

The interconnectedness which exists between animal, plant, mineral, water, stone and their own home planets of origin, plays an important role in the further FUTURE evolution of each planet, each Universe. Children, there is not even a tiny bit of land or water here that is not being carefully surveyed on a moment to moment basis. This surveying shows a direct juxtaposition, a direct correlation between life as it is today and what it will need "tomorrow." Terra herself of course has the monolithic task of placing all the energy "informants" at her disposal and aligning them in a particular fashion. She does so as she continues to design and further develop more exclusive new landmasses. These are her new landmasses that will rise from the water and displace most of the former ones. She receives through her own surveillance ability, all necessary and newly updated information that will assist her in achieving her goal for herself and her new galaxy. All information is pertinent to this upcoming event. Not many years ago when Terra was fading, her monitoring energies became so weak, so tragically limp, that We sent her a special "agent" that aided her in removing the crippling effects her energies had been beset with. This resulted in providing her with a much needed respite from the type of carnivorous behavior mankind had burdened her with.

Had I not have been able to convince her to remain here and become an even more shining **star** than she had originally been, I would have reluctantly assisted her in ending her pain. And I assure you, it would have ended yours as well! Children, are any of you who are reading this writing beginning to have even a glimmer of understanding of all that I am speaking of? OK, I am hearing, "yes, no and maybe." Perhaps you could all be a bit more concise and expansive in your answers. Let Me see if I can give you an example that you CAN understand. What if you were going to go to a party; you have a certain amount of time to decide what to wear, how you want your hair to look and of course **how you will get there.** Very few if any of you, would want to wear a mishmash of colors and it seems that you have your own styles, or you WANT to look like someone other than who you are. I just never seem to see any of you attending these types of events looking or feeling comfortable unless you believe you are, or someone tells you that "you look great." OK, this means that essentially you have everything in the order you think it should be in for yourself.

In your own vague ways; you have been physically and mentally monitoring yourself and allowing others to do that to you as well. So why Children, should it seem even the tiniest bit strange for you to know that ALL life does this too? Of course their reasons are not as trivial as yours. They do so for their own survival and because it is the right thing to do. Yes, just so you know that We here, all Luminescents, monitor Our individual selves while monitoring one another. As the centuries soon pass and more and more new Universes are Created, there will be more Luminescents needed here to participate as the

Guardians of those worlds and realms. All that WE each know in the Continuum of NOW will better prepare Us to transfer all knowledge into the monitoring systems of the upcoming Luminescents. The Continuum itself is always under surveillance at all times, simply because the Continuum of and by itself, connects all things together here, even though there are other, smaller forms of the Continuum on Earth and other worlds. I think that perhaps I need to explain the Continuum to you in such a fashion that it may help to develop your understanding of it. Of course the Continuum is androgynous, however at times it visibly displays the feminine principles while uniting new conditions and new events. At other times she displays the masculine qualities when needing to deal with existing events and replacing the worn-out ones with new editions. However nothing is ever lost or discarded in the Continuum, even those events and principalities that are no longer viable to use. The origins, memories and all events, life forms and spatial significance of each is still housed there.

In fact, she is a Creation of the Creator and a mind-link of a Force which predated My own Creation. The Force of which I speak is a convoluted ionic mass that has always been a part of what you term "space." Although space is really a nonexistent term because it denotes a "nothingness zone," I will use that one for now since that is what most of you understand. The Force is a fluid, mutable grouping of excess matter that all stars, all planets, all galaxies exude. Although they are infinitely small they group together because of their own magnetic courses and their own electromagnetic systems. I suppose you could think of this form of exudation the way you would if a dog or cat became wet and then shook themselves to expel the water droplets. It is these "droplets" that first form the initial stages of condensed matter that is usually simply referred to as "Star matter." The magnetism of each one immediately progresses to coalesce with other same matter. However,

180

this is a never ending event. By the way, all planets are Stars as well. Stars may increase their size, although this requires thousands upon thousands of years to do so. Each Star has a lifespan just as each planet does. So it is through the lifespan of a Star or a grouping of Stars that the excess they all release forms what today is called the "Continuum." As the mass of Star matter comes together and forms a larger and larger collective of itself, it forms an unbreakable intricate weaving that is so tightly knit together that it **appears** to be completely seamless.

No, there are no visible openings in the Continuum, but the Star matter passes through the outer weave of the Continuum in order to gain access to the centralized area of the Continuum. The Star matter contains all recorded knowledge of each Star regardless of the period of existence it may have. As Stars eventually burnout what is left of them is matter that is returned to the Universal pool of Creation. The new Stars that are born as a result of the newly vacant area simply remain with the Star matter processing until the end of their lifespan. The Continuum itself then is both the recipient and the sender of all matter relating to the life of spatial events. It also functions as the transmitter of all knowledge that has been accrued by the Luminescents of each Universe and each of their Planetizens as well. Even the Creator and the Creation processing have all their own histories existing here. Life does not simply begin and end with the Akashic Library, you know. The Akashic is a library but the Continuum is far more than that. The Continuum is always in a state of flux, a motion that all realms of knowledge simply must exist in. She is always revolving and expanding, never diminishing in size, although the term "size" is really not adequate either. You see Children; there really is no beginning or end to the Continuum. She does blend all knowledge all histories, all possible and probable events thesis that have been either Created by all of Divinity, or by the Souls themselves who inhabit other worlds.

In some ways she is a massive memory bank in possession of all imagings that have ever been Created. In this way the Continuum is in a consistent state of **knowing** how and when the new Creation of worlds and Stars and new life forms who could inhabit each of those areas should enter into manifestation. No, Earth astronomers know nothing about this. How can they? They think they know more than they really do and they know far less than they should. I am often referred to as "All that Is;" I understand that, however that is a very limiting concept of "The All." In fact it is the Continuum who is "All that Is." Without the Continuum all life would cease to be. Yes, she does indeed provide a tremendous magnetic system that holds and maintains the core of each monitoring device that has ever been here. These devices constantly send her all information for her to store and review in her own memory banks. The very imaging of each Soul who has ever been is blended into her own cellular memory. Her memory capacity is infinite. It is in this manner that she assists all smaller versions of herself in assisting other life forms on other worlds. Her coloration is undeniably beautiful; but even the term "beautiful" does not really do her justice. She is every prism of color imaginable. And Children, you do not realize how many hundreds and hundreds of different prisms REALLY exist! Yet all her colorations vibrate, pulsate and BLEND together at all times. Many of these hues are extremely vivid while others are more subdued, but overall she is the personification of exquisite beauty. Beauty that is unparalleled. I did tell you that she blends all knowledge together so that each mote of data relative to a world and, or, its own inhabitants can be viewed by Us at any moment.

The Continuum is also known as "The Great Achiever." Universes must always be able to ADD their knowledge to her own accumulated data in order to see if there is anything that needs to be altered for the better during the

Creation processing for new Universes. All data needs to be added but nothing can be removed. The Continuum, as yet another multidimensional entity is here, there, and everywhere, ALL at the same moment. However because of her INFINITE ability to "know all and see all" even without the benefit of the accumulation of monitoring devices, she instantly knows if there is any change at all in her satellite Continuums. If this occurs because of an accumulated mass of duality being aimed at a satellite, such as the one here on Earth, she immediately takes that into account and can and does send massive beams of her OWN energy to the satellite in need. The reasons for the satellites is quite simple; as the Creator has set His plans to enlarging the areas needed for the Creation of new worlds into activated motion, it is a natural occurrence for the momentum of The Force to accelerate. As this occurs it has been seen that having satellites far improved the main Continuum's ability to access and assess all movements of energy.

As the new Earth here takes more form of herself the satellite here will of course activate more information relative to all that is occurring here. In time, the Earth satellite will move her own orbit and transfer her entire self into the main Continuum. As this occurs there is a simultaneous exchange of the former satellite to the newer version. This satellite "transformative process" continues for the duration of the life of a world. Terra, will now have a very, very, long lifespan. OK now, I do not expect anyone here to remember the swaying arcs and graceful movements of the Continuum that you once were completely familiar with. However, perhaps it will make more sense to you now that you are more aware of the Continuum and all she represents as a stabilizer of all Universes. So you see Children, there is much more to the Creative Processing that are ongoing events that are deployed for the good of all. The more your minds absorb the information I share with you about all pertinent situations, times and events, the more and better prepared you will all be to take part in the new world. Also, the more you remember or relearn NOW, the less you will need to remember on your next life journey. I ask you all to please bear in mind the fact that as you understand more about all the things you need to be aware of, you are either consciously or Super Consciously moving yourselves into a more prominent position of evolution. And it is not costing you a thing. What costs you everything however, is if you do not WANT to know. Understand please that it makes no difference if your intellect balks at any of the secret information or the spatial data I share with you. After all *the intellect is only human you know.*

I dedicate this writing to the Continuum and all those she holds dear. Which is everyone....*God*

Codex 11

Machinations

God... OK now, since a part of My mission in these books is to further instill truth in your minds while continuing to have truth displace illusions, I see no reason for Me to stop now. I have gone to great lengths to walk you through the convoluted and devious paths that the Illuminati have taken. They have done so in their desire to continue to deceive you, while still finding use for you until they had taken the last planned step in destroying the human races. So it is with sadness in My own heart that I must point out some things to you that they have managed to do right under your noses. Yes, yes, I am well aware that many of you are now realizing that much has gone on either unnoticed by you or simply seen by many of you as inconsequential. I assure you all, nothing they do is EXACTLY as it seems. They may be of a **much** lower based nature than you have realized, however that does not alter the fact that they are superior strategists. Although they do not exactly have a sense of humor, they do relish mocking all the beings they have been busy conquering. No, it is not any type of tongue-in-cheek humor on their part. It is their very disdain, their contempt for all those beings they have categorized as inadequate, substandard, ineffective and insignificant, these are the ones who they arrogantly and willfully seek to further demoralize. I suppose in an offhand way they are also always seeking ways to thumb their noses at the ones they despise. Which is everyone.

They really do enjoy edifices that are built which reflect their own origins, their own depraved indifference and they project these things to all life forms everywhere. They also possess an energy that you here would consider

185

"egotistical." However, this energy I speak of far surpasses anything that tame. It is a *need* they have to always leave markers, a way of lining a path that clearly denotes their invisible visibility in much the same manner that animals have been known to leave their scent or to mark their territory. For the Illuminati however, *this entire world has been their territory.* On this planet their NEED is to supplant any and all wondrous Creations that My Earthbound Children of all races have carefully and lovingly built and to replace them with their own creations. All worthwhile principles and more evolved standards of life to live by and ideas that reflect all civilizations' dreams, hopes and visions of the good they see in life and in one another, have been craftily and covertly changed by the shadow riders. When the earliest civilizations began here, even during the times when early people of all races used simple stones and used their fingers to attempt to draw the most basic although not always understood symbols, they did so to depict something they saw as important or prophetic. They were leaving their mark. It required almost no time at all for the shadow riders to know that mankind was trying to communicate with others of their own tribe. Humans were known to be extraordinarily curious. They were also known to be overly aggressive to one another. The shadow riders did not like the curiosity factor, but were overjoyed about the aggressive tendency. Although this aggressive tendency was in most cases a reflex of the simple survival instinct, it was the one principle area that the Illuminati KNEW could be used by them. It could be used to set into place the primary foundation they needed to strengthen their own positions within the human races.

Although the riders were well used to combating other life forms on other planets, it was a new experience for them to find such malleable beings that were representative of so many different worlds ALL on one planet. The early dark lords wasted not an iota of time in focusing on the gullibility of people here. They accomplished this through what would become a time-honored process of setting into place everything gory and everything preposterous, but as geographically well placed edifices TO themselves and OF themselves. The very simple mind thoughts of the early people here made this easy to accomplish. In no time at all those early civilizations' very curiosity contributed to the beginning of the beginning of humanity's downfall. Many deities were invented to help keep the people in line. One of the all-time favorite methods of the shadow riders was having parts of themselves that had been intentionally contaminated and then set in place in all areas of the known world. It was as mankind began to build structures of wood, stone and straw that they were "encouraged" to have grotesque statues of gorgons, viciously portrayed dragons and gargoyles posted atop various houses and ridiculously large castles.

The earliest evidence of this that We have seen were hideous replicas of the dark ones built of rather crude structures using sticks, straw and leaves to denote eyes, ears and teeth. Even when the homes were first either simple straw structures or homes inside of caves, the riders made very sure that certain outrageous symbols of themselves were prominently displayed by the people. This was easier to accomplish than you may think Children. The people of those times believed what they were told. They believed that these gruesome figures were not only to be their guardians, but that they represented the riders' gods, therefore whoever protected the riders would ultimately protect them as well. That is to say that they would be protected as long as they acquiesced to the demands of the riders.

Understand now Children, I have stated before that the shadow riders and their cohorts were and are supreme strategists. They have never done anything without scurrilous reasons. If energy was not matter that is living they would have been far less successful than they have been. However, be that as it may, they wasted no time at all in leaving their own indelible fingerprints on each and every "tribute to themselves" in all parts of the world. In a rather uncanny way, as the first overlords here began having children, they immediately began the process of indoctrinating their half-human progeny into the mindset of darkness. They then easily convinced the children that they were all royalty. The offspring also learned to believe that they were types of demigods who were invincible. As the children themselves grew into adulthood they were encouraged to always have the symbols of their secret heritage "hidden in plain sight." It was of vital importance to the Illuminati that they continued to breed for centuries with as many men and women as they could here. In this manner they succeeded in their plan of **planting their seed into fertile ground.**

Even if you bear in mind the lack of advanced ways of thinking in those earlier times, it would be difficult for many of you to imagine how people could be so gullible. That is if in fact you yourselves had not been equally gullible too. The times may have changed but the strategies have not. Even now stop to consider how many, many ancient buildings still stand today and still are adorned with gorgons and gargoyles. Unknown to but a few people...outside of the Illuminati children of today...the plan to maintain these buildings and to further spread the contagions embedded within those indelible fingerprints is still not at an end. YET. Even such things as trinkets, bowls, baskets and base metals were designed *by* the dark riders *with* the dark riders in mind. It is simplicity itself to pass these items on to succeeding generations. It is also very easy to sell them to people all over the world by placing an intrinsic monetary value on them. It has long been in this manner *that the beast goes on.* The beast does nothing that is of altruistic nature; in fact he absolutely

188

despises that belief and attempts to destroy the people or trounce that belief in all those here who do live their lives with altruism as their main precept in life. He does so every chance he can.

Once humanity began to explore new landmasses for the purpose of resettlement, it was immediately seen by the Illuminati that to continue to have tributes to themselves was the best way of leaving a trail for all those off-world beings on the dark planet to follow. It was also their supreme cockiness and their belligerence combined with their need to make haste and proceed to conquer all lands and subjugate and corrupt all races, which further propelled them to continue building their obscene tributes to themselves. OK now Children; here is where I ask you to lose all your preconceived ideas about what you would term "inanimate objects" being unable to impact, coerce or taint you in any manner. What began so long, long ago is still continuing today. It is pure irony itself from My vantage point. I have watched for so long and have seen so many millions of people become absolutely "ga-ga" over what they see as *"just incredible architecture," "so magnificent are these castles and OH, LOOK at the adorable "thingies" that adorn them. Aren't they just too much!"* These have been some of the times when I have thought, "Oh, if you only KNEW what you KNOW!"

So, one part of the creation of these diabolically placed icons was the further continuation of their saturation campaign to begin a race here of "half-breeds," until such time that the planet's people were no longer of any value to them. Then they would have proceeded to "Plan B." By the way, it was not until the late 16th. century that the Illuminati began to branch out more and more and mate with greater numbers of men and women who were the descendents of their own descendents. In this manner they foolishly believed that they could create a temporary PURER strain of beings here. The second part of their plan

189

here was to have these tributes of themselves function off-world as designated "points of interest." This meant that it would be these strategically placed statues and markers in other forms that would clearly show their brethren on the dark planet how, when and where, their ships could either try to land or to simply send more troops here. Although the Illuminati CAN simply walk into a human body or be born into one, they still rely to a great degree on those on their own home planet. In a way it is not much different than the functions of lighthouses or your satellites in the skies that are programmed to view and mark many different areas of the planet.

As civilizations progressed and became "Ages," it was when the landmasses changed and the earliest of the tributes collapsed or simply crumbled, that a new thought of the Illuminati emerged. They decided to remember to allow for the movement of the Earth by having stronger versions of some of their original tributes set into place. In this manner even if the hardier ones did eventually fall, they could be replaced with newer versions, ones that were more apt to withstand the test of time. To have monuments erected to themselves that still served their original purposes but to a more advanced degree, was seen to be a viable way to continually upgrade themselves and their mission. OK now, here is where it became very interesting. I do realize that all races are raised to believe in "something." Part of that "something" is **always** based on the concept that the presumed founding fathers of the country placed or built some type of monument dedicated to freedom, or to the earliest origins of the race, or to the presumed deity said to be the true god of the race, or simply dedicated to a religious organization. Well, those concepts are NOT true. None of them are. Even the founding fathers of a country had one or more "moles" in their group. It does not matter if the majority of these men really had the best of intentions for the people and the country, although many did not and still do not. The shadow riders are unparalleled in their ability to infiltrate any group they choose to and mentally seduce people into following the mind-suggestions of the dark riders, rather than their own original intentions. And they have chosen to do so in every country, with all groups of the countries' founders. It is what they do.

So Children, it has come to pass that certain monuments known as "Obelisks" for example, can be found in almost every country on this world. As part of the twisted minds of the Illuminati continued to revolve around the best ways to continue to hide things in plain sight, the obelisks themselves were originally created by them as perverted forms of daggers. They believed this to be something that no human being here would ever really see for what they truly are. Although many of the first builders of these edifices WERE the Illuminati, they still needed the human factor to take care of the manual labor. It was so easy to whisper to the minds of the truly dedicated men who wanted to erect something that would represent their ideals or the ideals of their country. A man or woman can be a very good person, but still be used by dark energy to accomplish nefarious goals, without the good person having any knowledge of what was really happening. THIS is how history has repeated itself. It recreates itself when under undue influences. Because all details needed to be taken into consideration by the shadow riders, it was originally decided, long before the very first LARGE obelisks were built, to have "**SPIRES**" placed atop churches. Should that surprise any of you, now that you may understand more clearly what has happened here and why?

Children, it was deemed to be physically impossible to have objects placed atop even the most simply built churches if the objects would be too heavy for the places of worship to adequately sustain. So their logic dictated that a symbol that would be relative to a church BUT still be a minor projection of the symbol of the Illuminati would best serve their purposes. All that the religious people see is that it is symbolic of a place of worship. As was intended. Obviously this also includes such structures as Minarets. Because not all countries follow Christianity, there still needed to be replicas of the Obelisks and spires on churches and other places of worship, in order for the Illuminati to maintain their tradition. Yes, even they have traditions, you know. Granted these are not ones I approve of, but they are the ones that best suit their purposes. Yes, as you are beginning to learn now the Illuminati have been the "grand architects and the supreme anarchists" of all time here. Please do not feel foolish because you are now finding out about things that you may believe you should have known all along. I have made it **very** clear that **I and only I,** am the one who has been permitted to give you all the information that you did not have before. Remember however, that even I had to wait until the dedicated gridline intersection arrived. This is the one that was the long time planned and long awaited event NOW taking place. Welcome to the timeline decreed to be the "**Time of the Great Revelations.**" These providentially important current nanoseconds in the lives and times of human affairs have finally arrived.

I am eternally grateful to the good Souls here who have been speaking out publically about the Illuminati though. I know far better than any of you do what terrible repercussions they each have endured as a result of their doing so. Although those such as Blue Star are off-world for extended periods of time, they still must speak out in their collective effort to assist in organizing peoples' beliefs by supplanting the illusions of truth WITH truth itself. I feel unlimited gratitude for all those Children here who serve as the vessels of My off-world Children. As is said here on Earth, "no one likes a whistle blower." Well I suppose I could add that label to My own repertoire as well! I do ask that you each understand what a terrible task it can be at times to stand firmly in the face of the unclean while steadfastly refusing to surrender or give in to the children of a lesser god. I also ask that you have merciful feelings towards all the men and women who are staunchly religious. Do any of you yet realize how shocking all this information will be to them? How about to yourself as well? What about all your OWN religious "training" in the past? How much did you believe then and how much of those teachings do you still believe today? Tell Me Children, what do you think their reactions will be when the very foundation of their lives is revealed to them all for what it really is? I will say this much about that-many people will not be able to live with that realization. That is all I will say.

Children, you have **each** walked in those footsteps yourselves, some to a greater degree than others. Let Us not forget that millions and millions of people still follow these religions because they simply do not know any better. Although there are others who do so simply because it is the easiest thing for them to do. At least that is how they justify it to themselves. And yes, many Children here still follow those beliefs out of sheer desperation and fear. *That does not make them bad people, they are just wrong, be VERY clear in your mind about this.*

I have been providing very detailed information about all that you need to know about the Illuminati, while still teaching you of more truths about your origins and the stages of your Souls. I am dedicated to speaking of both these worlds, the Spiritual world and the practical world. How else can you understand either the dependency that one world had on the other, or the interconnectedness of each world? The Spiritual worlds and realms will forever endure. The practical world however is changing **because it must.** As shall you, yourselves. I do not fault people who are now more so than ever before acting out in sickening displays of religious fervor, or their willingness to become

193

martyrs for their cause. I DO however hold them each responsible for the terrible anguish, the horrific acts of violence they are intentionally causing for others. I am well aware that there are millions of My Children on this planet that I can not reach out and touch. So, I must leave it up to you, all of "the yous" who read all of these writings to assist one another in balancing the scales of justice. To be informed IS the bastion as well as the foundation of the scales. To go on and teach others of what you are learning....as soon as your heads clear....will embellish the arms of the scales. In this manner right will defeat might. *It is so.*

I have been diligently informing you each in these writings, of many, many truths that have never been revealed before. I have done so as one means of shaking your "consciousness tree" with the intent of eradicating the last traces of your naivety. Remember, the more you understand about HOW all things have happened, the more prepared and less gullible you will be from now on. At least that is My hope. I am specifically requesting that you NOT become jaded because of the experiences that have been taking place here. Nor do I want ANY of you to run and hide! You can not hide from the truth for the truth will find you wherever you go. Under no circumstances do I want any of you who read My writings to become one of those people who live lives of contempt born of experience. *That simply will not do.*

OK, I ask that you take a moment and recall some of the markings, symbols, glyphs and so forth that you yourself may have encountered in your brief stay here. I would fathom a guess that even in your own home you have symbols and other cryptograms of the Illuminati displayed prominently. Masonic symbols, family crests, many forms of art, even some shrines dedicated to the past are just a few of the examples I speak of. The Illuminati want the people of Earth to hold on to the Illuminati's past, they

The Code

know that the past is what helps to make the people more controllable as well as even more predictable. It is your predictability that aids them the most and boy, you certainly have that in huge proportions! OK, those who continue to hold on to the past are the ones who have placed themselves in a form of stasis. No one can move forward unless they have released what has already been. This is what causes people to lose their dreams and their visions. For too long you have been caught up in a belief that life is some type of routine, where you work, marry, have Children and die. ROUTINES are but yet another pattern that has been foisted upon you by the shadow riders. They despise spontaneity because **it is not predictable.** Oddly enough people train their pets to respond to certain stimuli yet do not see that they themselves do the same thing. It has long been an Illuminati belief that if they tell people something and have it repeated over the centuries, then it will eventually be accepted as truth. They have taken that belief of theirs one step further through the simple but effective method of marking their trail. It is most unfortunate that those two ideas have worked as well as they have.

What you really long for is a life that you dreamed was possible, but not one that you necessarily thought you deserved. Over time, your dreams have dimmed and now many of you barely have the memories of them any longer. I have seen for so long now, that the very people who feel they do not deserve to have their dreams are the ones who cling to previous tarnished episodic moments in their families' histories and to some tainted memories of their own personal histories. They then retreat because their own cognition is no longer available to them and instead they kowtow to the propaganda that is replayed over and over and over again by their country's rulers. In time, they no longer can tell the difference between a good and just leader and one who is not. They give-up and give in to the established and long accepted standards and ways of life they are accustomed to. They do so because these are the known elements of their worlds, they then forget or give-up on their own ideals and visions. I find that appalling, Children. You all have the right to expect nothing less than the best. It is up to you to find the means to achieve it and you can begin by relinquishing the old and focusing on the new. Knowledge you are receiving now should assist you in this endeavor. Having abundance and happiness is a natural result of having lived a life you see is worth living.

Archeologists seek to retrace the past to better understand the present. Yet if they do not *really* have an understanding of the past beyond what is left behind in the remnants of previous cultures and civilizations, then how can they possibly understand the present for what it really is? It was never I who withheld your true history from you, you know. My Emissaries did speak with so many, many people of all races here for so very long. They spoke of the peoples' true lineage and issued warning after warning of the murderous intent of the shadow riders. All to no avail. Your true history has been intentionally withheld from you all this time by the Illuminati themselves. They convinced you that you have histories that you do not really have, while removing from your mind the history that you really do have. They convinced you that others died here in order that you could live. The truth of the matter is that the others would have died anyway. But their deaths, especially on the fields of battle, served an ignominious purpose. Your own warlike tendencies that had never served you well anyway, were forced to the surface of your minds by believing that you needed to seek retribution. Even though you never REALLY knew who the enemy was.

It further served to keep you in guilt and you forgot the fact that SOUL will never feel guilt, so it can not transmit that emotion to any human being.

196

By their actions and their application of reverse psychology, the shadow riders were able to keep you floundering in the dark.

Skyscrapers may be considered to be symbolic of a technologically advanced society; however they too are testaments to the superiority of the intellectual prowess of the shadow riders. All of you should know by now that the crust of this world is thin and prone to disturbances such as quakes. Most of you have forgotten or never knew however, that Terra MUST always release small amounts of energy in order to maintain the correct pressure within the deeper parts of Earth. You also should know that many of the skyscrapers on the various continents are strategically located near the oceans and waterways. Symbolically, they are just more tributes to the ego of the Illuminati. Of course the Illuminati know that when the tall structures tumble and fall, many lives will be lost, further promoting great sorrow and despair. Skyscrapers will definitely fall, especially when certain quakes have been engineered by mankind. The mazes of tunnels under the cities as well as all the millions of mine shafts all over this planet will eventually implode. Death, destruction and rampant **fear** are what the dark continues to feed on.

I explained in great detail that the Illuminati became aware that the current timeline you are all living in would be an unstoppable one. They accepted the fact that they would either be the masters of this world for the time they needed to be, or the forces of Light would come to reclaim this world and her races. Whichever occurred, they knew that they would still reap the benefits from the energies of fear that ensued. All of the Illuminati's tributes to themselves also function as direct energy signals and energy missives. The Illuminati do have their own form of *code* and I am hopeful that you are realizing that now. Inscribed within each of their monuments are subtle message markers that not only contain the lurid history of the building of these places, but also function as gateways to other dimensions. These are the dimensions that only the most adept of the dark riders can access. These are not dimensions that ANY of you should even consider venturing in to!

I would like to direct your attention to another aspect of their devious natures. Remember that everything the shadow riders do has purpose and their primary focus now more so than ever before, is pure intimidation. They intend to further intimidate those who might stand up to challenge their authority. This type of daunting maneuver has deterred a great many goodhearted Souls from recognizing the beast. This is how *the beast that hides its lairs in plain sight,* unbeknownst to the casual observer, has been able to thrive. This is part of what the beast has accomplished here. EVERYWHERE that the lore of the gods and other illusionary deities is present are the "placements of pleasure" that shadow riders had carefully planned in order to advance their own agenda of "obedience above all else." It is NOT that this planet has not been visited by ALL Luminescents at one time or another, because she has been. But not the way it is depicted. The placement and stories of war-intoxicated gods, is yet another of many sad attempts at discouraging the people from ever considering disputing the laws, that the Illuminati had written to enforce their own edicts. The shadow riders never did anything in an insignificant way, their obsessive attraction with and of themselves, always borders on the obscene, it is true lunacy. This has been well documented in the "Hall of the Sages" throughout the many ages of mankind.

Bridges all over this world may have made **your** lives easier, yet their original intended purpose was to make it easier for the dark overlords to move their precious commodities from one area to another and then to their compounds. Countries here have long been at loggerheads

198

with one another while each claims ownership of certain portions of this Earth. It is but more sad irony that no country here will admit to the fact that the country's leaders are but mere figureheads of a greater society. Bridges, heliports, drones, intrusive highways and automobiles that serve no real purpose other than to be ostentatious at best are NOT what should cause you contentment. If anything you should be dismayed at the fact that these civilizations of today are so UNCIVILIZED. Children, it is PEOPLE who are the civilizations; it is NOT machines, not the monetary system, certainly not many leaders in countries who have no moral CODE to live by.

No doubt there are those of you now wondering why I decided to have this codex included in this book. I have done so because I firmly believe that the more I am able to enlarge your abilities to see things in the right perspective, the less you are apt to remain as you are and the less likely you will be to believe in the things you have been accepting as fact. Tell Me, how do you think it would be possible to continue bringing technological advancements here now, while this world is winding down? There will be in the future, new and far more advanced methods of establishing bridges, moats, clean air systems and pure waterways, to name but a few. BUT that will not take place until there are TRUE civilizations here Children. That will not take place until you not only see what is going on here, but use your thought-processing ability to Create a better world for a better time. DO NOT discount the thought-processing! Universes themselves can be Creations of thought itself. Should you begin to falter in your desire to assist in enacting change here, then I remind you that "thought" was the nucleus of all that the Illuminati managed to do here.

I dedicate this writing to the new civilizations and the true civilized people...*God*

Codex 12

Decoding the Code

God... OK, as the Luminescent of this Universe, I reserve the right to change My mind when and if, I feel it is relevant to do so. I now feel it is. Therefore, I told Celest and David that I decided to have a question and answer session with them in this codex. As Celest just said to David, "God is doing so because He can." That sounds reasonable to Me, Children. Well then, lets proceed and see what questions Celest and David can come up with that will generate more provocative new thought patterns for you.

Celest... God, since you sprung this on us without any warning, my first impulse here is to ask you to explain more fully to readers why you speak in God Code and in what way do You think or feel, that this is affecting the thoughts of others.

God... Celest, in the earliest of the time periods here it was virtually impossible for Me to speak to the early Children with any type of word usage that was not too far above their heads. As the simplest of the races here, they only could fathom their basic needs, they were not able to nor did they want to, hear of anything more than that. So it began that I would speak only in brief monosyllables and only relating to their immediate needs. Of course a great deal of the time I used simple imaging to convey My words. They usually believed that it was some strange type of what you today would call "instinct," that gave them fresh ideas. Obviously this became the language of choice for not only Me for a very long time, but of necessity for all the Star keeper Children from other worlds who arrived here to assist the fledgling races across the world. As language progressed to develop an earlier form of literacy,

200

it was still difficult to have conversations with people because so few of them were permitted by their rulers to have even the most basic forms of skills in either knowledge or competency. Of course there were many spoken languages here that were still in developmental stages that were indigenous to each individual race, but for the most part symbolism and sign language was the norm.

However as linear time here progressed to different levels of simple literacy, I found that "speaking" symbolically was the easiest way to still communicate. Except for My animal Children of course, telepathy was simply out of the question. Descent into this lower gross dimension further eradicated any possibility of CONSCIOUS telepathy among the human races for a very, very, long time. Understand now please, because telepathy is the normal manner of communicating among all off-world beings, it has always been the use of telepathy and Sacred Universal geometry that function as accepted methods of "speaking." Yes, "at home" the God Code is always used however. It would not be in anyone's best interest if I and the other Luminescents did not do all We could to further fertilize the mind-thoughts of Planetizens in every Universe. And if you think that I speak in Code, *you should just hear how effectively and sometimes convolutedly some of the other Luminescents do!* I consider symbolism itself to be its **own** genus, its own unparalleled method of further connecting heart to heart, Soul to Soul and mind to mind. Celest, if I said to you, "the heart of a stone lies within its wake," how would you respond to that? Would you think of the "stone" as the principle part of the statement, would you think of "wake" as the dominant term, would you think of "principle" as the primary part of the statement, or would you fasten on "heart" as the core meaning and symbolic factor? No, I am not asking you for a reply Celest. I am merely giving everyone a tiny example of how symbolism can be effectively used as part of a descriptive process that defines a statement about

201

something, while challenging both your sentience and your mind. It really requires no time at all *when home* for all beings to immediately attune to the God Code Factor. And they always respond in kind. Since all beings possess sentience, it is the sentience factor itself that exists to greater or lesser degrees that encourages each being to always seek to enrich themselves. They are told to accomplish this through the Sacred Communions of telepathy, individual mind-thought and the advanced states of sentience. You see Planetizens of Earth; sentience is a never-ending story on other worlds, other realms.

Sentience itself can and does level off from time to time because it is simply a more proficient means of maintaining a healthy continuity between Souls and their natural abilities, than it is to assimilate too much at any given moment. In this fashion it is not possible for any Soul to integrate with more sentience than they are ready for, as far as their own evolutionary state is concerned. As far as My Earthbound Children are concerned however, symbolism seems to elude about 70 percent of them. I do know the reason. It is that they were never properly trained to understand symbolism in their hallowed schools of learning here. What a shame though. They have lost so much! Precognition is a given at home, here it too has been relegated to less than factual. Although this energy is highly important in order for Souls to flex their mental and Spiritual muscles, it is a much lamented loss that has taken place here.

As to the second part of your question Celest: I have seen minor miracles occur beginning eons ago, as people began to decipher God Code and then spontaneously progress to a better understanding of many other facets of life, both life here and life at home. Today however, I am gratefully and happily witnessing these events occurring on a massive scale at a massive rate. The parables of yesterday that have been attributed to Me, have given way to a more extroverted and more concise thoughtfulness that people here now have. They are better understanding all that I say while I am speaking in the God Code. No, I can not say this about the people who consider themselves to be the intelligentsia, that would not be true. Unfortunately. It is as it has always been My everyday, ordinary people who are the standard bearers of greatness that are the diligent and determined ones. Their minds <u>never</u> cease to consider the implications and additional meanings of what I say.

No, I am not suggesting that they all wake up one morning and announce, *I know God Code."* I AM saying that it is their minds that continually try to fathom the meanings within the meanings. Sometimes it requires a long period of introspective study on their parts; yet at other times they break through the cotton batting in their minds and simply KNOW. Each time this happens it is a monumental occasion. There is nothing ever trivial about it. This means that they are unconsciously stepping up; they are upgrading, and they are doing so both Spiritually and practically. It is the ones among them who are the most fearless who then go on and teach others and then Children, *step by step, one by one, My work is being done.* Next question please.

Celest... Thank you God, I am sure this will help many people to better understand themselves. All right God, would you explain, beyond what you already have, how your detailed writings about the Illuminati can help people to see more clearly who and what the enemy is, why You have been unable to simply remove all of them from everywhere, what can the people themselves do to aid in the massive undertaking of the annihilation of the Illuminati now and how your unveiling of these truths is so paramount to the survival of the human races?

God... Celest, I was hoping one of you would ask about these matters. OK, Children, when you see the enemy and understand who and what it really is, then you **can** defeat

203

it through sheer mind-thought. You can do this here because you are not under any constraints about "interfering in the lives of the humans." In **MY** situation, none of Us here can actively intervene or interfere here UNLESS We are specifically requested to do so by you, but even then only under special conditions. The Creator decreed that the timeline He set into motion, the one I have already spoken about with you all, is what He calls, "The permission zone." These are simple words that encompass a much larger, more complex picture than you are aware of. Certain criteria must be followed by Us to fully protect <u>all</u> Universes from total annihilation, but to do so by ALWAYS remaining within the laws of Universal protection, also known as "adhering to all Universal Laws without exception."

Certainly We have all known about the Illuminati for as long as they have been. But because Our own situations have been so tenuous in regard to actively interacting with them, the most We were able to do was to keep massive numbers of Star Keepers from other worlds, other Universes, always in battle formations. They all have Our own express orders to attack as need be in order to protect the Earth Star planet, which effectively protects all other Universes as well. The death toll among Our Star Keeper Children has been enormous. **You** however have the ways and means to further disable the shadow riders and their human counterparts through your own thoughts. This may not mean much to you now, but if you stop and consider the implications of what I am saying, then surely your mental "light bulbs" will begin flashing in recognition of the true power you each have. What makes this situation so unique for all of you here, is that it does NOT matter how evolved you are or how much you have retrained yourselves in the ancient art of "battle through thought." What matters is that you can do so without overextending your abilities to do this and by your understanding that THIS is what a Peaceful Warrior does. You Create peace by admonishing less hardy Souls thus curbing the progress of the dark. If you are willing to do this, your participation will be forever noted in the Continuum and in the Akashic Library as well. NO, I am not bribing you! I do not indulge in such petty behavior. Those of you who will participate in this thought-process however, need to be aware of certain rules here. YES, I am finally permitted to speak of this too.

<u>Never, ever, become what you detest!</u> You can focus either your individual mind-thought by yourself or engage with a cluster of other people such as yourselves, who are willing to do what they can to change the course of events, BUT for just cause. Do not begin to participate by having any thoughts of vengeance, no hatred, no ego based desire to show off, or for ANY self-serving reasons. Choose your own timing; be it a few seconds, a few minutes or a few hours a day and then focus your minds on your heart and Souls' desires and fill them with **pure** intent. Soul is indefatigable in these matters. Therefore, Soul will prompt you in selecting more and more thoughts for you to use. It does not matter if your sentience factor is as high as you would like it to be or not. What DOES matter however is that you maintain your focus on peace and the new and better world that will be here. If you can, picture in your mind's eye a world without the dark riders, a world where equality for all races is the new norm. A world where injustice and torpid states of mind no longer exist. Give serious thought to how wonderful it will be when you can all walk this world without any dark intrusive beings. Ask the Creator to assist you in your thoughts. He does that you know.

In other words you must *play the beast's game against the beast*, but play it better. IT can not tolerate good, loving thoughts. I ask you to proceed and send these thoughts upward while FORGIVING the beast for being what it is and FORGIVING it for all it has done here. You see Children, the beast simply can not tolerate these types of thoughts. The thoughts such as these actually cause it anguish on a level you can not yet even begin to understand. It is as the anguish accumulates more levels of pain that the beast's sensors actually transmit that pain to all shadow riders here AND to their human counterparts. No, it does not do so intentionally, but the very fact that each one of them is so incontrovertibly tied together, one to the other that forces them to share the commonalty of thought and TYPES of emotions. Ergo, as the beast feels and senses, so do they. This effectively helps to weaken them as a mass. This is a contributing factor to the mass confusion that begins among them. It is this confusion that affects them and causes them to act and react unambiguously. In these situations they tend to feed on one another and thus become even more parasitic to their own.

OK now, is it making more sense to you WHY we must try to enhance the goodness of each Soul here who is from the Light? Oh, oh, Celest is now singing, *"I got the power, I got the power."* I think she really needs to get out more! Yes, I do agree with her, however it is what you do with the information I am providing you with that is the real telling moment. What you do with it is yet another definition of yourself. There is so much irony in this entire situation; I have for so long told all of you about being in the Light and how to manage your mind-thought, but I rarely saw a glimmer from most of you that showed Me that you suspected or realized that there was MORE to what I was telling you than there seemed to be. *I told you before that you need to learn God Code!* Any more Celest?

Celest... Thank you God I will ask about just two more matters. By the way, I was also singing, *"I will survive."*

God... Celest, I know you were. I was just trying to ignore you. You did not walk-in with a.......spectacular singing voice you know. Now please, ask away.

Celest... All right God, would You please explain to everyone how the black beast came to be? Also, what future plans do you have for the people who are reading these books? Do You have plans that may assist them in becoming more aware of how much further they can go in life because these people are gaining a greater understanding now?

God... OK now, each world is composed of filaments of Light. Yet there have been worlds that have been born into dark matter. This is so because the gross amount of that type of matter is the all pervasive force in certain parts of Universes. These worlds give birth to themselves. They do so because all matter gravitates to the most dominant type of matter. They are not outside of the Continuum because nothing is, but they have very little Light particles, so there is not enough amassed Light to restructure itself and form together. People here tend to forget that "dark" IS Light, but that it is unilluminated. This may be a difficult concept for some of you to understand yet, but that does not negate the fact that it is true anyway. Normally these dark matter worlds do not have very long life spans, they simply wither away and burnout. On the particular planet that the beast came from however, that planet did not wither, it did not burnout. Instead an anomaly took place. One that would have long reaching consequences for all of Us.

This world I speak of was a fast moving world, one that hurled into great areas that infringed upon other worlds. At that point We set a perimeter into place to block that world from moving forward and becoming an intrusive, disruptive orb that could be injurious to any other orbs. However, the dark matter continually accumulated more dark matter in the core of itself which then gave birth to a type of gross, deformed entity. This entity had extremely long tentacles that would whip out and grasp other small particles of dark matter and inserted them into itself. In this manner the beast grew and grew and grew. The rest is

207

history. As this entity became more powerful on its world it then decided to detach itself from that world, while leaving many, many, remnants of itself there and began its journey to other Universes. Its appetite was insatiable. All other Universes had long known of the existence of the beast and were prepared to fight against it if necessary. However, as you now know, it was here to the Earth Star planet that the beast came to prepare itself for yet another period of the evolution of itself, thereby becoming and establishing the order of the one world.

As to the final part of your question Celest, yes, I do have plans for the Earthbound Children here that you are asking about. From the vey moment I released the first book in this series, I began to monitor very carefully all the attentive minds and other positive traits that the readers were displaying. I have continued to do so through each book. I want to tell you all that climbing mountains in the figurative sense in order to attain more knowledge, is always accompanied by certain periods of plateaus, or leveling off periods, presenting themselves. This is very necessary in order for the mind to absorb the information it is gathering and then process it in order to sort it all out. This process on an individual level will take as long as it takes. There should never be any fear of learning too much, but there should be qualms about learning too little.

Some people glide up these mountains while others take quantum leaps. Still others take small steps while looking around to see if anyone is watching. You should all feel better now to know that no one is watching you except **ME**. Others of My Children here are too much in fear to scale the mountains. They are afraid they will fall, but they do not realize that they can not fall. I have My arms and hands extended to help all those who make these treks. Those people who are the ones who after reading all My writings are still either too afraid or to callous to care anymore, are the ones who do not realize that without climbing the mountains they <u>will</u> fall. And I shall let them. So I have decided to issue a challenge to all those who read this series, or even a part of it. Children, *I am "raising the bar."* You can not go higher unless you go higher.

From this moment on I will be sending you each more and more information. I will use imagings, telepathy, sentience and everything else at My disposal. You will each undergo a transformative process as your cellular structures react to your "intake and output." I expect you each to do your best to understand and **act upon** all new thoughts, ideas, inspirations and dreams that you have for a better life. I shall **not** accept lip service from any of you. The moment I see those people who will not go ahead now and scale the mountains, will be the nanosecond I remove the mountains from them. And that is the way it is.

Celest... God, I thank you so very much for your ability to converse with everyone and to do so in such a way that You morally, intellectually and Spiritually are Your own "Cause and Effect." And You do so in such unmistakable ways that no one can deny Your willingness to be of service. I thank You, God. You are a credit to YourSelf.

David... thank you for sharing information about the origins of the beast, I believe it will be of great benefit to those who are still in the process of sorting through the God Code you have laid out in front of them. Many people believe that the beast started out as a Luminescent and that it simply tired of doing good and began the creation of fundamentally flawed types of lifeforms, many times crossbreeding just to see what would happen. Can you expand upon this? And were the remnants of the beast that the beast left behind when it left that world, were they the ones you now refer to as the shadow riders?

God... Many a goodhearted Earthly Soul has tried to decipher these questions. It has not always been easy, especially when considering the massive amounts of disinformation dispersed by the shadow riders themselves, as they tried to cover their tracks by layering illusions over truth. Hence another aspect of the Veil was placed over humanity's minds further steering them off course. Most of the ones I refer to as "shadow riders" are the ones left behind after the beast ventured beyond that world. These descendents or offshoots of the original mass of conscious matter eventually gained the ability to leave their home world as well. They, like My Children of the Light, also have the ability to walk-in to human form when the need arises. Others of the shadow riders are those who were once Souls birthed into the Light and for whatever reason were drawn to the allure of the unilluminated ones.

After all it is less challenging to skulk in the dark than it is to maintain integrity and honorable intent. I can not begin to express to you how this saddens all of Us who birthed them *OF* Ourselves, the Creator included. Those that believe that the beast, the one commonly know as the Devil or Legion had fallen from grace are in error. The beast is not a devil unless you are speaking metaphorically. The beast just as all other sentient beings was birthed with ample opportunities to be of grace and it chose not to. It chose to be OF the dark, to live IN the dark and to make a mockery of all that I am. Dark matter **can** be altered through the infusion with equal or greater proportions of Light matter, UNLESS the dark is so all-pervading that it intentionally leaves no room for the Light.

It is not that people here failed to understand the reality of the beast, nor is it necessarily because many people here at one time or another, did not studiously do their homework. These were not the reasons that they were so deterred from learning the truth. It was because the truth was buried beneath so many layers of deceit and illusion that the truth was often inaccessible. There has never been a time in Earth's recorded history that We did not make many attempts to set the record straight. The massive numbers of goodhearted, well-intentioned Souls that died as a result of the beast's marauding forces was staggering. To their credit these same Souls returned time and time again to change the tide of the beast's persuasion, one person at a time. This is very slow way of educating people, however it was deemed to be the only effective way to continue maintaining the balance between the dark and the Light. This had to last until this current Gridline intersection when truth could no longer be denied.

As I have previously noted, because of low literacy and the need of the many to focus all their attention on basic survival, it is not hard to understand how most people remained detached from a desire to know the truth. The pains of hunger and the basic survival mentality are strong deterrents for desiring a clearer understanding of the truth. For the record, at no time was the beast like Gabriel or Michael. I did already tell you all that during the Angel phases, some WERE weaker and less mature than others and DID become embroiled in the deceits of Legion. They then became what they were never initially intended to be. Yes, several of them then became types of commandants for the dark. In this manner their names or titles as Angels became vilified and the beast hid behind them while at the same time directing their actions. Not at any time was there an entire Soul cluster who did this though. These were random acts committed by individual Angels. Now shall we move on?

David... You have offered the readers more detailed information about the Illuminati and how the beast came into being. I am sure many people are curious or possibly wondering what happens to all the Souls that sidled up to the beast during this current lifetime. You spoke of a special place for them. What is the determining factor for placement on these lesser evolved worlds, these worlds that function on a level suited to their level of evolvement? What about all those who may have stepped off the path in

211

this lifetime, but for the most part have been good Souls during many previous human lifetimes?

God... Good question David, glad you asked. There are many determining factors to be considered when making these types of decisions. Obviously Souls that were fundamentally flawed by their life choices and had serious devious intent on being the worst they could be, are placed in strategic locations that are rightly suited to them alone. I will not go into all the locations at this time; however I will remind you that some of these places are worlds especially well suited to the needs of many of them. There is also much that you do not know about the place known as Nirvana, or Heaven. Nirvana has many levels; all levels are separated from one another so that there is no type of contamination from the lower levels to the higher more refined ones. OK now, the beings you refer to as being generally good Souls that may have strayed in this current lifetime are of course a different matter. Many times it is merely the choice of the Soul itself who ultimately has the final say. Soul always knows best. If it feels it is in need of some more intense rehabilitation rather then once again repeating the same degrading previous life experience at a different time, then it knows the correct placement. In decisions of this magnitude there are many beings involved.

Of course there is MySelf or another Luminescent that may have originally given birth to a particular Soul. There are those of the High Council and along with those who were the Soul's Spirit Guides whose input is vitally important as well. I do want to caution all of you from making snap judgments about someone else, for never is it in your place to judge another. That is simply not done and is in direct violation of Universal Laws. Many Earthbound Souls' arrive here for the specific purpose of being extremely bad examples in order that others may learn from their being so. Generally, these are people who are in

212

very public positions. But of course this is not the "rule of thumb." I could write an entire book explaining all the intricacies and nuances describing the hows and whys any Soul does what it does, but doing so would not benefit you at this time. I have already offered you the information you needed in My previous books, so this is as much as I am prepared to speak on this subject. If you have doubts about yourself, then by all means ask Me directly about them, but please do not ask Me about another person. That is their affair, not yours. If you are worried about yourself than perhaps you should ask yourself why? Have you done something that you have not forgiven yourself for? If you have wronged another and have not made peace with the fact that it happened, then do so now. If you no longer believe the illusions that you once did and if you have acknowledged this to your Soul Voice, then trust that you have done what you needed to and move on, you are wasting time. Now, next question.

David... Will Atlantis rise again?

God... No. Not in the manner you are thinking. She has arisen in many parts of this world already. Let's move on shall We?

David... Will the Moon be a part of Terra's new Universe?

God... Wait and see. I would like to remind all of you who have ventured this far into this current book of Mine, that the Moon serves many purposes, not the least of which is to impact upon your dreams. Reach out to her as you would Terra or MySelf and give thanks for all that she does on your behalf. Time is short. You each should use the remainder of your time to put together all the pieces of the puzzle, thus ensuring the future for humanity that you all desire.

David... What do we do with all our watches and clocks when the NOW is accepted by the masses?

God... Glue them all together. They will make a nice conversation piece.

David... Will verbal language become a thing of the past as humans relearn to use telepathy? If so, then what would be the purpose of having vocal cords?

God... Only you would think about the vocal cords. The future generations of humans will utilize both. You know as well as anyone that many different Universal races of beings speak audibly *when they choose to,* as well as using telepathy. Animals and others of the animal kingdom communicate through telepathy, but still use their vocal cords to reach out to one another with their songs do they not? David, trust Me, the human race will find a use for them.

David... I know, I just thought I would ask.

David... I am curious, what will become of all the automobiles, homes and buildings that are left abandoned and vacant by the masses of people who will not be continuing on with Terra?

God... Leave that one to Terra for the moment. As I have previously said, "nothing is ever lost or destroyed." It is an easy enough task for those who are much more knowledgeable than the human race currently is, to show all of you how to transform them. Remember that all matter is energy fluctuating at variant frequencies and vibrations. What Terra does not reabsorb naturally as she continues the process of altering the continents, will be dealt with by the upcoming generations. In the interim home prices will continue to fall as supply exceeds demand.

David... Is having a Light body anything like being on the moon where there is less gravity? In other words, will we have the ability to travel great distances with little or no effort?

God... Light in this sense refers to cellular structure. In answer to your specific question I will give you two responses. As you raise your vibration and enter into the NOW, you will find that with practice you will be able to be in two places at once, much the same as I do, only I refer to it as "multitasking." Consider it like having your own teleportation pad only without the pad. The laws of physics are not fully understood by humanity as of yet, that will come with time. Also, many people will learn to glide rather than to walk. Not that I am trying to imply that you could use some finesse and charm. It is much more natural to glide and requires a great deal less effort. I may address this subject more at a later date.

I believe this is enough information for you to mull over until the next book presents itself. In adhering to My own personal directive, "never give too much information at one time," I will call an end to this question and answer section. My desire is that those who take the time to understand what I have shared will find many ways to implement these Codices into their own lives. The better prepared you are, the easier the mountains will be to climb. I will be waiting at the top.

I dedicate this writing to all those who take the time to question, understand and *"keep on truckin."* ... *God*

From the Eye

God... (received by Celest) Well Children, here We are yet again, We have arrived at the completion of another one of My books. I do not expect most of you to understand what I am about to say to you; however you need to hear this anyway. I want you to know that it actually requires great courage to read these books, this one in particular. I define *courage* as, the willingness to hold on to **the eye of the storm** while all around you many people are still seeking to follow the path of least resistance. Courage is *valor* that has no equal. Valor is the purity of heart and Soul linked together and working in tandem to assist you in assisting others, even in the face of their disbelief. *Honor* is part of courage and a Child of valor. Honor is remaining true to yourselves regardless of what mockery, insults or threats of violence may be hurled against you because you speak the truth. *Grace* is a highly sought virtue that allows you to walk on water Spiritually while trudging up yet another mountain in life, but doing so as a free flowing Child of Spirit. This is an attribute that can only be achieved by confidence **in** yourself and **of** yourself. *Courage, valor, honor and grace;* these are the necessary components that your Soul must be able to flow with exponentially in order to continuously affect your cellular level and thus enhance and elongate your cellular memories.

Children, although you were all born-into or walked-into this life and previous lives with all these aspects of your Soul intact, literally billions and billions of people over time have allowed those natural parts of themselves to remain in a dormant state throughout each life experience, for the most part. On an unconscious level for <u>many</u> of you now, you have each agreed to participate as part of the collective consciousness. Those people however who are

216

participating on a conscious level are seeing more and more clearly every day how important it is that you each maintain your placement in this massive grouping. Remember now, I have explained to you all how Light impacts and then saturates each cell in your body as you continue to strive forward, as you continue to walk away from those whose minds and hearts are diseased. These uncomely ones are representative of all that was, all that still is existing in all countries of this planet and all that will change, with or without their consent. The time for "semi-consent" is well over. *The Time of the Courageous Ones is here.*

Children, I commend each of you for all that you do, especially the people of all races who simply do not understand their own greatness. *Greatness is defined by Courage;* Courage *is the definition of a true human being.* I ask that none of you ever forget this! Do not expect that you will always feel that you have courage; you have been living in a wilderness, one that does NOT support courage, rather it admonishes the courageous and does so in support of NOTHING. I define this "nothing," as "people who do not actually have life, rather they simply exist."

I know that many of you began reading these books out of sheer curiosity, while many others had a true desire to find out what it is that I could say that they needed to hear. *How do I know these things?* I know because I am God. OK, I also know because I listen to your thoughts. You do not understand how well pleased I am with the nonverbal declarations of your individual decisions to remain more alert, more attentive to reading and understanding truth. You are each facilitating in further Creating for yourself an unbelievable amount of brilliant energies that are far more evolved than the ones you have had in many a year now. Truth does this you know. She always responds to those such as yourselves by rewarding you for your efforts. Truth is aware of your quiet strength and of the times when you have such fierce determination to change yourselves for your own betterment. Children, I feel so much empathy for you each and all! I can not dry your tears for you, but I can encourage you not to cry. I can not change the attitudes or refusals to believe truth that so many of your cherished loved ones still have. I can not force them to become true human beings, but I can offer them ample opportunities to do so.

I can not change the Illuminati in any fashion, but I can remove them from this planet. I can not change the beliefs of the religiously indoctrinated Children here, but I can offer them My loving arms when they arrive in Nirvana. You yourselves have most reluctantly in many cases, finally accepted the truth that I have told you each before, this truth is *"You can only change what you can and accept the fact that there are things that you can not."* This is even truer now than ever before My Children. In time, over the next 100 years, this time period of course has already begun, as the new civilizations here become completely attuned to the new heartbeat of My Golden Terra Child, they too will discover the reasons why they will not be able to change the things that are not their responsibility to change. The storms of change here are increasing on a minute by minute basis. As recently as 2010, they were infrequent bursts of change instigated by My NESARA CHILD, in accordance with the wishes and the decrees of the Creator and the Creation Processing and with Terra herself.

Now however, the necessary acceleration of the Winds of Change is taking place. These storms are the heralds of a larger, more encompassing storm. This is the storm of total cleansing that has already arrived here, but is not yet in full force. So many, many, times I have implored you all, as have My more evolved teachers here, to **"hold on to the eye of the storm."** *Have you forgotten?* You each are Souls who entered into a human body. You descended into matter

218

and prepared to walk your walk into the unknown. As multidimensional beings living in a world that has been grossly dimensional at best, you lost your way for a while. Your only afterthought was your mortality. You did not remember to always hold on to the eye of the storm and you forgot to "touch the face of God."

Remember, I always speak in *God Code*, so tell Me please how many of you truly understood the storm I have for many months now referenced to? If you reply that it is the storm of change, then I will reply to you that "yes that is PART of it." If you say that it is climatic and environmental, then I will say to you, "That it is only a long overdue conciliatory arrangement between Terra and Divinity." Terra has long reconciled herself to the fact that as part of Divinity herself, she can no longer tolerate those who are not. Total cleansing is the term to best describe the complexity of the nature of the storm of which I speak. Imagine for a moment the most massive tornado you can think of. One that actually covers the entire face of this world. The scope of this tornado is gargantuan and nothing and no-thing can withstand its self-controlled fury. It is a dedicated paragon of Spiritual righteousness possessing spatial monitors that have exquisite sensors that seem to be in constant motion. In actual fact they always are. The sensors and the monitors contain unlimited amounts of empathetic ability that function as the truest of attribution qualities, capable of knowing who the friends of the Earth are and who are the violators. No, Children, you will not see this formation in the way I am describing it to you. You will however see magnetic storm after storm of great magnitude here. They will be proportionately impacting on this planet and carrying with them strong electrical charges. Magnetic energies will unleash and assist in the cause and **assess effect** to alter land and waterways. **This** is but part of what will be visible to you. What you will **not** see is the tornadic form that is the actual OverSoul of the storms and the further elongation of the Winds of Change.

No, these are not to be feared, but welcomed. The OverSoul is one of great magnanimous nature; this OverSoul is both noble-Spirited and fair in her dealings with this planet and with all of the races here. We do not need to inform the OverSoul or her companion energies of who the just are here and who the unjust are. *It is already known in the Continuum.* Although I have striven to do My best in sharing so many long held secrets with you, it has not been easy for Me to speak of these things. It is not because I am too well aware that this information will elicit many emotional responses from some people. These are the people who will falsely believe that they have been denied the truth of these matters for far too long. They will believe that you all should have been told of this information sooner. OK Children, truth can be a double-edged sword; too much revealed at an improper time does nothing except contribute to mass confusion and detrimental behavior. Truth must always have its own timeline. But once that timing element comes into view, NOTHING can stop or impede its momentous unyielding surges. There is sad irony present here in this matter; if these long withheld secrets had been revealed to you by Me as recently as 10 years ago for instance, what do you think that would have accomplished? *In truth, none of you then were ready to KNOW, except for "the few!"* The human races never seem to function better than they do during times of great upheavals, great unrest and the threatened loss of their safety nets. I told you there is sad irony in this matter!

The races here tend to pooh-pooh any and all concerns of "future possibilities and probabilities" until **the future** stares them in the face. It is then that they feel their personal sanctuaries have been violated. And **the future** is now staring because she has arrived! I can speak these secret truths on behalf of all Luminescents and all other forms of Divinity, including OUR collective of Star Keeper Children from all Universes now. And now is when I say,

"We have waited since time immemorial for the collective consciousness to form itself and start asking QUESTIONS. Do NOT give Me reasons of plausible deniability as to why the human race as a whole has not until now arrived at an apex of **fear** and **uncertainty**. It is these two elements which are causing them to rebel against their "keepers." Do NOT indulge in self-denial here. You all knew that much was wrong on this planet, but you all felt that there was nothing you could do to change it, you all accepted the *same old, same old,* routine of living <u>because you knew no other way to live.</u> But again I ask you, how do you know another way if you never tried?

We were all so saddened by humanity's refusal to not want to know more truth, but by their refusal to accept what We wanted them to know as true reality. We know this because We sent many of Our own most evolved teachers here to assist you. *You see how well that went!* Just as it has always been since the TRUE beginning of Our recording the history of the people of this planet, *only the few listened; only the few believed and only the few HAD COURAGE.*

Another interesting and ironic footnote in the history of this planet is that it has always been the people who have had the least who have <u>given</u> the most.

It is only as people began to feel helpless and hopeless about the conditions of this world that were "SUDDENLY" impacting on their own personal worlds, that the timeline SET IN STONE by the Creator, has availed Me of the opportunity to now speak openly. No Children, needing to make you all aware of not only the true nature of the Illuminati but of what was planned for ALL of you and Terra as well, was not easy for Me. There have been so many, many, times, far too many, that We have all had to listen to the silent screams of anguish from the human race overall. I wish that everything could have been so different here. I wish that humanity had not groped the dark hem of illusions, trying to hide beneath those tattered and dank veils. I wish this had not provided contentment for humanity. But it did. *Except for the few.* I can not, even if I was permitted to do so, change the turning of the tides here.

For those of you whose minds are still asking why I am going ahead with My instructions and JUST BEGINNING to tell you of so many things now, I must question your reasons for asking. You see, I KNOW some of you have these thoughts because you can not see what you can still change. Others here wonder what good this information will do for you at this time. I will now give you My further responses to those questions: Speaking on behalf of We who are of Our own collective, *We want to see you survive.* We want to see you live, even though many others shall not. I can not change "those who have been the many." But I CAN and AM initiating certain measures to ensure that the "few" now become "the many." This I CAN do.

Too many of you still do not truly understand the "productivity changeability" that energy has. I will make one last attempt here to explain this. Those who have long been "the many" have energies that became dull and began to flat-line. These energies became non-productive entities that slowly transmuted themselves into stagnant pools of lesser Light, thus fracturing and functioning erratically, at best. When this occurs the very cellular structures of human beings then changes. These people are caught up in a total loss of inspiration and of aspiration. Physical and mental apathy then ensues. As this happens free flowing energies WITHIN the human body slowly become more static. You see, bodies and minds must work together in a devoted relationship. Because of the loss of the required elasticity and the further loss of the cohesiveness of the struggling energies, the body begins to create illness. This then is a direct causation due to the lack of nourishment that body so dearly craves. The mind then finds itself in direct opposition to the body and begins to slowly lose its ability to function as it should. The energies rot. Energies when not properly used, when not properly distributed within the human body, then leach the body's systems, as the energies then begin to struggle for their own survival. It is really no different than watching a plant die from dehydration.

All of the body's natural energies lie within the physical vehicle and expand and grow as a body matures. So it is that a young Child will have the juvenile energy streams that will go on to become adult forms of themselves as the Child matures. This is SUPPOSED to be a continuous exchange between body and mind throughout the mortality of a human being. However, too many people here have forgotten that these energies have a tangibility that far surpasses in physical power anything that is a mass of **physical** strength. There is <u>nothing</u> intangible about this. However body and mind must rely on these free-flowing energies because they are inherent to the well-being of each. This is but one primary reason why life expectancy here is not nearly as long as it had been intended that it be.

As to "the few," that is a different matter entirely. The few possess absolutely awesome energies. These selective forms of energetic matter are electrical in nature. They continuously pulse throughout the physical vehicle and the mind, prompting each to carry on and Create even more of these pulsations. The nature of electricity here should be obvious, even to My more obtuse Children. It is the electrical matter of these highly conductive energy conduits that combines with one's own electromagnetic system to provide a healthier physical vehicle. This then spontaneously ignites quiet and steadily paced stages of vibrational furor within the entirety of the mind. This is "the enabling principle" causing body and mind to continuously step-up and Create higher vibrations, higher frequencies for mind and body to occupy in serenity. The "few" may have been small in number but their greatness is **without equal**.

The enabling principle exists within the Soul matrix of every life form. Yes, this includes all of Divinity. For Us however it simply operates at a far different vibration and frequency than it does for other life forms. For Us it is the great enhancer as well which continuously propels Us to extend and add to the quality of Our own Creative abilities; Our own Creative gestures. We may not inhabit a physical vehicle, unless there is a reason for Us to do so for a brief moment in time, but the overall principle remains the same. You see Children; I too have an OverSoul, as do We all who are part of the higher dimensions. We also have an OverSoul that connects each of Us, one to the other, who are the collective of the Luminescents. Our own OverSouls, as well as the collective OverSoul, also has a main OverSoul Cluster who oversees each of our own. In some ways We are not that different than you are. *I said, "In some ways!"*

I believe I have now fully expressed My feelings in the writing of the reasons why so much has been hidden from you. Now that you are learning what you need to, tell Me Children, what shall you do? Will you alter your lifestyles, will you be more selective of those you associate with, will you be able to stand firm in the faces of the now known enemy, or will you do nothing at all? Will you wisely teach others, those people who still have an opportunity to survive and thrive, or will you hoard what you now know while thinking that I will not be aware of what you are doing? Will you be willing to take a major leap into the void and assist in getting My words out to this world, or will you think that "it is not your job, not your responsibility?" Will you live out the rest of your mortality as true human beings or not? *Ah, decisions, decisions.* What WILL you do Children? I will not override any decisions you make.

THAT is NOT MY responsibility. Those who make the wrong decisions will be the ones who will suffer more grievously than will any others. Soul is always in a state of awareness, especially when the most important decisions of a lifetime are being made or being ignored. In this sense, you arrange your own court date with yourself.

I have given each of you great and wonderful gifts. It is what I do. I ask you all now **for the final time;** hold on to the eye of the storm and touch the face of God. The greatest gift for you if you do this, is one I have been longing to give you for so very, very long. The greatest gift I can give you now, is to give you back to yourself.

I dedicate this writing and this entire book to those who will hold on to the eye of the storm. For those of you who do not know this, I **AM** the Eye of the storm...*God*

*Due to the nature of this Blue Star transmission it has been suggested that this writing be included in this current God book.

Dream Voices

Greetings chelas, welcome to my realm. Now, it is due to the extraordinary preponderance of fear running amuck even more so than usual on Earth that I have selected this topic to discuss. The goals here are as always to provide you ones with all truths relative to the level of conscious understanding of each of you, on an individual basis. So it is that some of you may grasp the upcoming situations quite easily, while it may require a *few days* for others to do so. What you term "evolution" is a wondrous event, yet it can at times be perceived as a painful instance, fraught with "unknown" or "unaccepted" and "unacceptable" realities. As you each evolve to the best or worse of your ability, you will indeed encounter many things that go bump in the night for many individual reasons. As part of your Soul Progression, "evolution" is a heightened process of acting and reacting in accord to the "no-fear, no-consequences to be paid" agendas. On the other side of the coin, this simply means that those others amongst you ones who still live in the dark ages of the mind, those "misinterpreted and misunderstood" times that have lingered and enlarged themselves out of all proportion in the far recesses of your minds, regaling many people with illusions of truth and non-acceptance of Greater Belief Systems, are in fact experiencing some rather rude awakening experiences. And well they should!

You see, there exists a plethora of true knowledge of "The Great Inspiration" that is unknown here by humanity as a whole. It is true Soul Desire to observe and bear witness to all that Soul knows is not palpable as vehicles of truth. It is the experience of Soul to first discern the situation without capitulating to the dark abyss, then to

Create the formation of the mind-to-heart energy streamer necessary to adjudicate then dissipate the direness of the situation, in order for the person and that one's personality to undergo the transfiguration process necessary to break free of the bonds of ig-norance and dis-ease. At times this can be accomplished most easily if the individual, or groups of people of like-mind and desires for great change, are receptive to the knowledge that they have been duped by the agents of the Dark Agenda. These have been rare instances at best until most recently. Soul possesses the unique ability to render useless the tiny fragments of unease experienced by these above mentioned individual types, when these people have a polarity which is in direct opposition to the masses. In this case the masses would be those who follow the old idem that the world should be based on material principle. This is the antithesis of what we know should be the correct form of living life on this planet. This world was meant to be based on Spiritual Principle. This is the one that some people have for many a life experience desired and attempted to wholeheartedly embrace, that which is of the good and pure, rather than the evil agents and those Spiritual polemic dissidents who are hell-bent on usurping the good.

Now, there are times that are meant to cause the ascension of Spirit within the individual. It is during these "Soul Rhapsodies" that men and women are afforded the opportunities to slowly regain a Spiritual balance; one that is dependent upon their ability to "just say no" to those who deplore the "new" actions and thought patterns of these "In-Change Souls." This term in this sense denotes those who are indeed becoming something that others are not consciously aware of, the metamorphosis can be rapid for a few but for most it is a step by step progression. As Soul has correctly gauged the tiny, or in many cases, gigantic amounts of mis-information substituted for truth, Soul can and does eliminate the Dark thought forms projected by the "pattern makers," one thought at a time. Soul is

227

cognizant of the impact that intellect can and does have on the ordinary person. Soul is also well aware of the limitations of so many minds which have been successfully compromised by the Dark Overlords. Now, The Creator, the God of this universe and the Creation were All in accord that intellect and Soul Voice were to share a Sacred Merger, One that would facilitate the God I AM manifestation as the human being walking, talking, BEING the ultimate consummation of mind (matter) and Soul.

It was known that intellect would be a tremendous tool for humans to use to convey the intelligent aspect of themselves. This would facilitate the Creation of an easier life experience, not one fraught with indignities. Soul was to be of course the Guiding Light, the font of wisdom that intellect would always cherish as a NECESSARY aspect of the integration of the two. It was to be the marriage of these two, one tangible and learned, one intangible and just as vital, that would ultimately enable the human race to live as God on the Earth Star Planet. Now, during the more primitive eras of humanity, intellect was quickly discovered by the Illuminati to be "quirky" and able to absorb false information by accepting that it was true. Intellect knew no better. Still does not by my reckoning. As early man slowly moved into different epochs of linear time, the intellect became even more of a focus, one to continue to be used as a weapon by the Dark Energies and their human counterparts, against naïve people, insipid people and particularly those not mentally stable. There were indeed people who truly did want to initiate changes, to teach others that cruelty, bias and prejudice were not aspects of freedom of thought or speech. However so many of these ones were unable to cast off the Dark existing in their surroundings. Because of that conundrum those plans which they wanted to implement languished and existed as *loose energies,* movements of thought forms that eventually became static. Although they still remained in existence, the destination was lost; they were energies with nowhere to go.

Now, as the Illuminati progenitors and later their spawn became more and more aware of the easy access to the human being that the intellect could provide, their early strategy of conducting invasive forays into the minds of humans through manipulating the intellect, seemed to them the greatest of ironies. You see they were of course aware of the great considerations bethought by the Creative Forces in determining that a "governor" energy which could function under First Cause for the alignment of mind with Spirit would be a great asset to all human races. This conjunction although deemed a necessity in the beginning times could "carry over," thereby aiding all the generations of the human species. The Illuminati saw that it could also be utilized by the Dark Overlords and literally trained to function not in unison with Soul Voice, but independently and turned into a "loose cannon." These Dark ones found it both intriguing and laughable that the same Forces of Divinity would gift humans with "free expression." The Illuminati Forces of course do not believe in any free expression; their philosophy was and is, all must succumb to the Dark way or die. So it was that intellect which simply meant originally, "intelligence at work in tandem with Voice," became its own behemoth. The easiest way of explaining to you ones the deviousness of their programming of the intellect which has taken place over the centuries, is to ask you to consider the work required to program your computers.

When the program is finally in place, the computer will only respond in a certain manner, to certain commands. You can if you have the knowledge, go into the brain of the computer and realign the commands and set many options that can be used, rather than affixing the menus and guides to one set program. Now, please to remember the computer and its programming are only as good as the programmer. Now, what the dark forces have done and have achieved is this....they simply implanted a type of "computer virus," into the mainframe of the intellect. It began centuries ago by the instilling of fear and the birthing of ego. "The intellect is the home of the ego;" as intellect "goes" so "goes" ego. Fear is a correlated response to outside stimuli existing as situations/ events/ people/ philosophies, which intellect cannot understand, cannot accept through ego as truisms. Fear, which is actually tendrils of nonattached energy streamers, receives subliminal and subconscious commands from intellect when intellect fears itself to be in mortal jeopardy. Fear then "attaches" itself to the gestalt of the idea/ person/ event/ situation/ philosophy, which the individual(s) is being exposed to. The intellect only accepts that which it has been trained to. In a very real sense, ITS belief system is what you are mirroring to it.

Fear then is the recipient of the intellects' belief system. Fear immediately enters into defensive action by radioing a high frequency throughout the central nervous system, alerting the body to what fear perceives as a hostile, dangerous action. The human mind which is an incorporation of brain hemispheres, reacts to the stimulus fear is providing instantaneously. So it is that in these instances body and mind are working together, but not in any harmonious way, rather they are accepting what is occurring as "alien and hostile." They then file that information into a "saved information" file. This can be readily pulled out again and again throughout a person's life for easy reference and the ultimate reinforcement. This is indeed the sorry state of affairs you ones are in today. The Dark Overlords KNOW your Achilles Heel; it is all in your MINDS! Fear is shaped and molded by you. The Dark Forces merely impact upon your fears by adding new "old" fears and further instilling more "controlled viruses" designed to bring fear and its companion, intellect, as the dominating force in your individual lives. Do any of you chelas ever wonder how it was possible for this situation to become so far out of your control? Have you ones not yet gleaned the insurgence of fears among religious and political figures and everyday people as more and more small clusters of humans are refusing to promote fear; are recanting in many cases that which they used to espouse? Why are all these ones SO afraid of those who would Create, stabilize and maintain "right action and correct change?"

Is anyone paying attention to how quickly friends, families and other loved ones turn against those who are recognizing the diabolical hands at work inside the human mind? How often, if you ever have, have you sat down and listed all those many things that cause you fear; how often have you looked at your own words written by your own hand and felt amazement at the duplicity that has held you in captivity AND your own role in this? Your irresponsible non-use of a God given Gift, your lack of using your free expression to clean your own house is lamentable, to say the least! *Free Expression is the Infinite ability of the Soul in VOICE and ITS perception of great NEED to exercise discernment in all matters; to rightfully exert the movements necessary whether of mind, body or Spirit, to enhance an individual's need for Creativity and experience predicated by the individual's desires.* Free Expression is Creation in motion; it is the God Bestowed Rite to BE Freedom in activated form! Free expression can only be restricted by the intellect/ego. The intellect/ego which has for so long been governed by the Dark Overlords can only be reprogrammed by you, yourself. YOU broke it and now YOU fix it!

Now, so many of you fret about the days long past when you as students and parishioners only did and learned as you were taught. Must I be the one to remind you ones that that was then, this is another "now?" The Illuminati then and NOW have played upon the human responses to teachings rendered to the masses by allegedly learned persons, by the words and judgments of the clergy and those exercising undue force parentally. It was in the long ago "discovery" times of the Illuminati's understanding of the vulnerability of the intellect and its affect on free expression, which first gave rise to the ability of manipulating the intellect, which caused the Dark Overlords to gain their first great triumph. It was at first a trial and error situation, however it required no time at all to see with great clarity not only the conditioned responses that could be elicited by humans, but also to learn that humans are "creatures of habit." Who do you ones think were the founders of all religions? Who do you ones think orchestrated all witch hunts; who do you ones think relished the telling of great lies designed to keep your minds enslaved? Who do you ones think convinced people that "the earth was flat?" It was deemed *essential* to the Illuminati control here on Terra, that humans be carefully regulated by restricting their free expressions and enforcing the need for humans to remain dumbly unaware of the constancy of the Illuminati in the human races' everyday thoughts and belief systems. They have succeeded far, far too well. Up until the recent 70's and 80's in particular, the Illuminati made humanity a congealed Spiritual pariah.

The intermittent movements throughout the centuries of isolated, very small groups of *Courageous Souls,* who quietly defied the ancient voices of darkness by refusing to believe in the dark rhetoric issued forth by those in charge of their lives, bore fruit centuries later. This happened because as all gardeners should know, seeds must first be planted before they can germinate. Even though no one here on Terra remembers the names of those early ones, those ones who despised the dark despots and their LEGIONS, they were the ones who re-birthed countless times here, still looking for intelligent-Spiritual life on this planet. Today, particularly in this current year of massive revelations on all levels, they have returned yet again and are now the main fulcrum of gathered voices demanding change and the freedom of expression as promised by the God of this universe and the Creator. To this end they are indeed fulfilling their personally designed Soul Contracts through the unmasking of the corrupt and those Spiritually senile who have been corrupted. These "change forges" are also hard at work re-educating those who they can of the importance and benevolence of intellect when it is in harmony with Soul Voice. Long, long ago they had their finger in the dike, so to speak. In the "now" today of present linear timing, they are discovering that many people are finding the information these ones have to share as captivating and "feeling right." That is not to say that "mainstream" people and those of corporate worlds are yet willing to believe in something that has not been part of their "training." Nor does this mean that this has been "easy acceptance" by those who now believe. So many people have had to experience rather severe wake up calls," before they "got the point." Oh well.

Now, this is in fact one of the most crucial battles the Illuminati has had to face in a very long time. They are used to dealing with combat situations where they are confronted by those who are the warrior teachers and "warrior warriors" on this planet. The Illuminati know during these daily conflicts, that one or the other in this combat will cease to exist. This reawakening of those "lost in mesmerized slumber" however is a different kind of war. The same ones who battle in immortal combat with the Dark Overlords are also battling by using truth as a noninvasive tool and asking for Spiritual Inspirations to be given to those people who truly do want to awaken. The Illuminati can and do inspire fear and feed off the fear at the same time. However they cannot inspire great Spiritual Truths, yet they are "in awareness" that in times of despair, Soul Voice can and does urge the receiver of Its Voice to "listen for truth, to rise above the intellectual

233

chaos and seek true guidance." So the Illuminati and their human counterparts are currently masquerading as ancient prophets and Ascended Masters in order to garner more naïve people into their dark fold, thus preventing many people from using free expression and relearning truth. There is a tremendous learning curve here; it is apparent by the ways and means that Earthizens are either succumbing to the dark or reestablishing themselves as Children of The Light of All Lights. Either way, they are casting their own die.

Now, as more and more of you ones release yourselves from all prior con-ditioning and dis-tress, you will find most easily that your thoughts and thought formations are rapidly changing. All Earthizens who are altering their thought formations, experience feelings that are almost indescribable by them, feelings of exhilaration at times bordering on a "floating sensation." This is "freedom of thought" in activated form; the most desirous and priceless gift you ones can give to and OF yourselves. It is as the tempo of this sense of freedom, slowly in most cases, continues to rise in spiral fashion until it arrives at a crescendo pitch, which causes the individual or those of a Spirit Roots Movement, to discern that Soul Voice is speaking to and with them in tandem with the freedom-of-thought motion. The motion of this collaboration of Mind and Spirit Force is of such magnanimous proportions that all empathic and/or telepathic connectivity literally bursts wide open. All it ever awaits is the correct catalyst. Now, with the progression of this energetic form in activated flow exists also an aspect of what is known by many as *"Dream Reality."* The reality of dreams is... that they are! If you're initial response to my brief statement just now was "they are only dreams then, they hold no validity," then I say to you, you have just signed yourself up for yet another remedial education in a future life on this planet. Mea Culpa, Mea Culpa.

If in fact you understand the words..."that they are," then you are aware of the true meaning of this statement. Dreams are a VOICE; they are an aspect of the SuperConscious mind on a level that is separated from the conscious and the subconscious mind. Dreams exist in a realm of thought *imaging,* as such they have the power to not merely influence your thoughts, desires, hopes and aspirations, they have the ability to bring the imaging process into activated manifestation as a birthed thought form. They are NOT, contrary to popular belief, relegated to occurring only in your sleep states. Many people are part of the "Dreaming Awake Ones." You see, this means that they have the gift of forming, molding and modulating their "dreams" while consciously wide awake. These ones have relearned the ancient art of Creating through conscious imaging all they desire, BUT performing this alchemy for the right reason, without any hidden agendas. I speak here of those who carry themselves with the inner pride of KNOWING the truths, KNOWING their ability to Create without limit, without prejudice, without intentionally attracting dross entities or indulging in chatter with mindless people.

Other Earthizens and those who are our volunteers here, can either be a part of the Dreaming Awake Ones, or choose to experience both the realities of a dream realm while sleeping AND while Awake. It is but a matter of choice. Now, many of you should remember that I have repeatedly stressed to you ones the importance of understanding "thought" as Creative matter. No "thought" is unimportant, no "thought" goes unnoticed by the subconscious or SuperConscious mind. The genesis of thought is what balances the Creativity of the human race. It is also both how and why the Dark Overlords have been so readily able to "mind-link" with those among you who harbor fears, possess damaged psyches and those who think they have no beliefs. "Dreams are realities existing on different levels, different frequencies and of different times and different worlds." Please to remember this! <u>Your own personal world may depend on it.</u> All dream realities are REAL! <u>YET</u> many are implanted in the minds of those of weak mind and Spirit. I speak here of dreams that are illusions; they are used to suppress your struggles to rise above the decadent energies that have been intruding here and which continue holding you captive. All dreams are relevant to your "present now moment" as well as to each "future now moment." The term "dream" is a misnomer. The implication is that "it is a matter without substance, events without purpose," all of which is untrue. The place of dreams is actually called the "thought formation processing realm."

Dreams are an important fragment of Soul Voice as well. Soul expresses ItSelf through the dream state; in this manner <u>many</u> of you receive pertinent information of upcoming times and events that you call "prophecies." At times Dream Voices can relay to you a particle of what your own Soul Contract has stipulated as "right action" for you to commence. Other times Dream Voices impart the necessary information relative to incoming people or incoming Star Keeper Forces awaiting your meetings with them. Soul as Dream Voice cannot be interfered with intellectually when one is sleeping. The conscious mind, that place where the intellect and ego merge as one entity, are at rest during your sleep periods. So it is that the intellect is prevented from any further interference with Soul Voice during those times. Many of you attempt to retain CONSCIOUSLY, dreams that you feel suddenly "without reason" dissipating upon awakening. Of course all attempts to retain what you are <u>not</u> meant to, is wasted effort. Dreams can and do guide your paths, even without your recognition of this fact. All dreams are contained within a minute level of your SuperConscious mind. Here they remain while subtly and at times intangibly, rising to the conscious mind as "inspirations, ideas, NEW thought forms." You do not retain this knowledge consciously for they are guides, landmarks... not land mines.

Dream Voices speak in loving, comforting and inspirational fashion while portraying the imaging necessary in symbolic terms. Dreams are the language of the Soul. These terms are relevant to you only, each one of you has a different relevancy in the dream state; "imaging" is an aspect of your mind that relates to you individually, to your mind alone. Many times Soul Voice remembers past lives and prior events during those times which can and will impact on the dreamer in this present life experience. Soul Voice will never torment, taunt or threaten you at any time. Ergo, Dream Voices resplendent in Divine Attunement assist in honing your natural ability to discern Dream Voice from De-Vile Voice. All Eartizens who have ever been, have always had the ability to tell good from evil, BUT a funny thing happened on the road to evolvement...they FORGOT! Now, just as each of you ones have been imbued for as long as you have been, with a "fail-safe mechanism" designed specifically to retain in minute increments all dream knowledge, you have also been gifted with the ability to choose to allow the Dream Voices to work with you or against you. It is when Soul Voice appraises the situation and concludes that you are not working with Dream Voice that dreams become even more vague, more elusive to remember. So many of you ones fervently believe that you do not dream at all. This is but an ignoramus conclusion.

Dreams are what your "psychologists and psychiatrists" have field days with! Most unfortunately these men and women, these "sacred cows" know naught what they speak of! Now, just as Dream Voices were the original concept of Soul Voice masking Itself as Dream Realities to further your life experience completions in a good and honorable manner, this "portal" of beyond Earth realities is also a conduit by which the Dark Overlords have gained entry. Even though the main Overlords have abandoned their sinking ships here, they have left behind a full contingent of their LEGION to carry out their orders and their Dream VIOLATIONS. As you should know by now, tis the depraved energetic forms, those who despise your goodness and Light-ness that seek to undermine you through further instilling fears into the Dream Voices. They viciously and cunningly seduce you as you sleep. They are far more aware of those of you who protect yourselves before the dream realities begin than you think. They know who does and who does not. They know where you live. They know of your secret foibles, your quirks and your perversions. They know the hearts and minds as well as the degree of formidability that you each possess. Although they are adepts at locating the unclean minds which they have always sought, over the last millennium they began to turn their attention to the clean, clear minds of the then-upcoming teachers and prophets, just as they are now. This did not preclude their attacking the minds of ordinary Earthizens however, just as they are now.

People who are already tarnished are easy prey at all times, but most especially while they dream. The Dark Agenda Agents are privy to all the mental and physical debauchery that humans indulge in. Why should they not be? THEY created it! However the days of merely sucking on the life force of lower evolved humans is now passé. A great part of the "Changeling" times that is being experienced on Terra in the present time, is the determined need decreed by the present day Illuminati members, to infiltrate the minds through the Dream Voices of those who are the most astonishingly pure among you. You see the battle plans have altered. As more and more of you ones are becoming aware of the true nature of evil and the means used by dark forms to permeate your societal groups, your family ties and most especially your youth movements, the dark sources' perceptions of inveigling humans to willingly become a part of the unholy alliance had to change. They knew many of you would suspect the true realities taking place here, but they did not expect the disgust with political arenas and the religious formats to be the instruments to usher in the now overwhelming conscious voices demanding truth, even at great personal cost. It was because the Illuminati created the corrupt political systems and created the unnatural organized religions that made it so difficult for them to understand this "sudden" turnaround. They know that they can still invade your minds through the intellect, but it recently has come to pass that SOME people are now questioning the roles of the intellect in their lives and the reliability of that governing energy to render truth as it REALLY is.

So, as the dark forces had need to rebound and reformat their long planned final coup of the human race, they have once again followed an old plan that has not failed them before. You need to understand this very clearly; love, joy, inspiration, evolvement, clarity and all else that is of any Light permeated energetic mass, has its equal opposite. What these dark forces do is to use against you all that you know is true, all that you resonate to or with, especially your capacity to love. Those of you who are already deeply entangled in the intellectual morass of the deceit of true realities, pose no threat to these ones. You already are where they want you to be. They merely feed off you slowly until such time you lack the sustenance they require. Then you die. It is all the others, the millions and millions of others, who have not only answered the Creator's "Wake-Up Call," but are in their own way bringing this Light and the need for the relevancy of truth to all peoples, who are now the real threat to the Illuminati. So a cosmic game plan has been initiated by the dark agenda hierarchy. One that is geared to casting intense mistaken sensory deception and hindering truth; one that is causing deep seated fears to take hold among people who are struggling "to understand."

By using your God Given Realities and Truths against you, they are keeping you in Spiritual bondage. **There can be no freedom from wars, no freedom from poverty, no FREEDOM without first establishing Spiritual Freedom!** They know this! You do not! Now, the oldest form of attack that has proven to be the most fruitful to the dark Overlords is to slur and distort the Soul Voice. Obviously those listening to the intellect rather than Soul Voice would not understand this, nor can they. The dark forms are aware that the blatant arrogance of the intellectual people is working in favor of the dark agenda without the conscious knowledge of those people...for the most part. Over the last century in particular, much more emphasis was placed on the ego part of the human in relation to knowledge and wisdom. By convincing people that this is the way to success in life, the reinforcement of ego based issues and realities has come full circle. It was known that in this manner the conditioning of the human race would arrive at a completion carefully orchestrated by the dark ones. What the Illuminati failed to take into consideration during those years, was that the gift of "free expression" could deftly intervene in the minds and Spirits of many people, causing great epochs of consternation and disbelief to the Illuminati. It had been hoped by the dark overlords that by taking the physical lives of these Right-minded people, it would end the "perceived insurrection." It did not. The hallowed process of reincarnation has merely brought forth the same people; those deemed "instigators and troublemakers," who are determined to make a difference.

As the last century became the present century, a battle of "wills" began in earnest. Those who for generation after generation returned here again and again, still following the proscribed Illuminati plan of following the ego dictums, have become aghast with those who follow Soul Voice. Those who follow Voice have become disillusioned with the people whose intellects indulge in "scientifically,

240

medically, politically and religiously correct agendas." Although it has taken a long time linearly speaking, those who live and follow Voice are beginning to realize more and more, that they cannot compromise with intellect. They cannot change what they cannot change. They can only do what they can only do. It has not been an easy realization for these ones. They so much desire to convince others of true realities and the deceptions of the dark ones. Yet *in time* they will understand that their non-understanding of these other people shall become personally, their greatest triumph. Now, this present century did indeed again herald the arrival of the Time Walkers who have been for so long now guarding their Soul Voices with great care, and well they should. They are currently teaching others to "be aware and beware" of those who can and will attack them when least expected, WHERE least expected. We have many, many times impressed upon all those Souls who experience the lassitude and moral ineptitude of many of the human race, that all which they, those ones now living here and teaching of the appendages attached to so many by the dark forces, are making a difference here in spite of what they may think.

Now, as the Truth Talkers clashed with those who are the Deceit Talkers, an anomaly occurred. The Dark Overlords who had long before devised a plan to bring down Soul Voice were angered to see Light, one that was but a feeble spark existing within many Deceit Talkers that would always begin to burn but a bit higher during the confrontations with the Truth Talkers. It gave rise to the speculation that in future incarnations those minute Lights could possibly gain a momentum that would ultimately cause the cessation of the engulfing dark within the matrix of these ones. This meant that "in time" nonlinearly speaking, these tarnished and worn down Souls could eventually regain all that they had "lost." This is not true of the worst of the caste among them however. So it was then as it is today, that the only viable conduit available as the most pertinent, most valuable means to savage all Soul Voices, is to await "the midnight hour" and render useless the Soul Voice imaging as Dream Voice. The egregious discarnate entities have set many traps for Dream Voice now in this present linear time, as the final showdown between the Voices of the Light and those voices of the Dark, the Voices of De-ceit reaches new heights.

Dream voice is a superb rendition of Soul Voice ascending to different aspects, different octaves of ItSelf. What Soul Voice cannot achieve during the times of consciousness of the individual, Dream Voice Can. They are inseparable for they are the same, yet different. Now, as part of your self-designed blueprint for this present life experience for example, you gave permission for Soul to express ItSelf in all means available to It at any given time. This means that "premonitions," visions, brief glimpses into the past and the probable futures, are relegated to the realm of Soul to disperse to you as needed, all in your own best interest. Soul as Dream Voice has the capability to mimic others' words and facial expressions during the dream state in particular. This is the exponential method of indelibly imprinting upon your memory banks events, people, possibilities and probabilities for you to expect in your "near future" or at times, in your "future future." All are relevant to your Soul expansion and personal evolvement, most times there are hidden message within the messages. In time, you shall discover the secret ones. They are usually hidden in plain sight. In this manner the intellect does not recoil in fear from information which is earmarked to be discovered by you later. It cannot fear what it does not see or hear.

Dream Voice can and does also mirror to you events transpiring to others within your Soul Cluster. The irony here is that most of those people are ones you shall not meet in this lifetime, yet it was because you expressed a "need to know" about their life experience situations when

242

you Created your blueprint, that this information is solemnly given to you. Soul Voice understands that your desire to know this is part of a Sacred Trust to be honored. On one level you shall understand this information about these people very well, but it is not the conscious level. There are occasions when you and hundreds of other people most you have not heard of, shall share the same dream experience at the same time. Inevitably this type of dream information is about a portentous event about to occur that shall touch many lives. It is not sent to you for the purpose of your attempting to change the event! These are *preparatory dreams.* They are also a test. Far too many of you ones run in circles when receiving news that some may construe as bad; the desire to hurry and change it becomes a prevailing issue for you ones who do this. What many fail to realize is that often these types of dreams are merely to impart the event-to-be to you, so that you may make ready for it with NO FEAR!

The test then is the result of how you react. That is the determining factor of Soul/Dream Voice as to whether or not you are yet ready for Higher Forms of information. What is misunderstood also of the Dream Voice is that nearly all dreams bear more than one meaning. Also it is recommended that you learn how to tell past events that you may have participated in long, long ago and the relationship of those dreams to life situations you are either currently involved in, or shall soon be. There is indeed great relevance there. Dream Voice during slumber can also bring to you many of your "off world" mentors and true family members. These visitations are important; they are to give to you encouragement and infinite love for all that you are, for all that you do. It is here where your off-world mentors can visit, encourage you and share with you ones quiet moments without expectations. Those of you who have asked for visions and information pertinent to you as individual Soul receive these. You may not remember them at the time but "in time" you shall.

Without Dream Voice in activated form, Soul Voice would be constricted in ways that are not healthy conditions for Soul Voice. Those who have the finely honed ability to hear and see Dream Voice while fully awake and conscious, have undergone a subtly varied metamorphosis that causes Dream Voice to be integrated with the conscious mind, while being perceived by the intellect as "non-threatening." This is the juncture where a sentience of "clarity" known here as "clairvoyance" is actually Dream Voice in the conscious state of <u>BE-ing.</u>

Dream Voice is a wondrous instrument of conveyance for the heart, mind and Spirit of each life form. Just as Soul does not indulge in placebos, yet the intellect can, neither can or will Dream Voice ever resort to such demeaning behavior. Now, I spoke earlier in this transmission of the viability of Dream Voice being used by the dark agenda in its newest helter-skelter dash for survival and dominion. Although the dark entities have always sought to enter human consciousness by any of the most expedient routes, it is only in the Earth Star's most recent history that Dream Voice has become so targeted by the un-illuminated. Those dark beings are running in helter-skelter fashion. The advance on the parts of the sordid dark energies to the Dream Voice Realm was instigated by the very voluminous numbers of incarnated Ancient Souls who either walked-in or were born-in. Just as the Creator Forces know well that the Light shall indeed win in this final battle, the Dark Overlords also know they must do all they can to prohibit that from happening, or die. Those dark energies can no longer depend on merely sending dark energy streamers to encase the human beings here. Those who are here to continue this last great battle can easily decimate those streamers when they are the ones being targeted. Those who are of the fighting forces fear not what the Illuminati hurls at them. The growing numbers of Soul Clusters aligning for sanctuary and becoming the voices of peace and reason, rely on those who know how to defend themselves to teach others how to defend themselves as well. This Creates a win-win situation for our teams.

The best way perceived by the Illuminati to counterattack the Light Weavers here and all the ordinary people as well, is to encapsulate them during the dream state. It is to this end that such massive "terroristic" attacks have been launched against you ones. The perpetrators of this invasion have suffered severe damage as a result of attempting to enslave Soul Voice as Dream Voice when the personality possessing this non-physical Aspect of themselves, refuses to allow the entrance of the dark into the Light of the Soul. Also, when the personality adheres to Universal Law and is not timid nor afraid to cast the Sword of Truth at the incoming invader. Now, unfortunately there are those millions upon millions living on Terra who do not believe in the reality and validity of dreams and those who pay no attention to their dreams. Instead they revert to the psychological meanings thereby negating the true information. They usually end up "hating mom or dad because the dreams were translated as "feelings of worthlessness and betrayal beginning with the parents," these ones are easy prey for the dark "Dream Caster."

One year ago, a specific mass consciousness began that had been "seeded" on this planet. Men, women and children of all ages, all cultures, all countries took issue with the dictatorial policies of world governments spearheaded by the Illuminati based American Administration. As the peoples' dissatisfaction rose with each lie and unfair policy directing them to continue to engage in a war built on a foundation of lies and greed, the body count of thousands upon thousand of men, women and children, gave credence to the worlds' peoples that they had been badly deceived. Their subconscious minds became a volatile area of seething disquiet and not always silent rage. For a short period of time, their focus strayed from their own everyday practical concerns to "the greater good." In a bizarre twist, this interfered with the dark dream caster's plans. The plan was to effect an implanting of thoughts, of subjugating these people through the implanting of off-world terrors within their minds. The people were then too concerned with on-world terrors. It goes to show that the dark Overlords can and do underestimate Earthizens and the peoples' impressively large capacity to rebound during times of great catastrophes. Now, it was during that time of turmoil that Dream Voices began in earnest on a global scale, to infuse all peoples with imaging and words containing "new" visions and "true" freedoms and denouncing the monsters posing as political and religious Overseers. This situation has undergone many levels of peaks and valleys since then, but the Dream Voices are still remaining as the unknown catalyst they truly are.

Now, as the previous Earth year progressed into this year of 2006, the dark forms became more blatant in connecting with their contactees and more arrogant in what they were publicly stating. Their collective non-understanding of the minds of the human race caused them incalculable losses in this battle for Soul dominion.. Although they were still able to subdue the weak-minded humans and cajole many to act as their human counterparts it was the others, those who had "had enough" who became the most difficult to subjugate during slumber times. So, desperate measures were enacted. You see when dark battle lines are drawn all strategies are already prepared; all those whose positions require an accounting and answerability to the hierarchy "off world," are kept in place as long as the dark commanders here on Terra are producing the results needed. Because time is of the essence here and the Illuminati know this, they cannot allow anything less than a massive wave of brutality and mayhem to be enacted as a means to counterattack those who are changing their minds about life, religion and politics in particular. So a plan hastily formulated came into being on February 28th. of this year, 2006.

A humongous mass containing the nucleus, the matrix of the energetic form of the god of the dark universe began its slow travel to the Earth Star planet. It is the father of all monstrosities. It was decided that my Celestial daughter bear witness to this event; without any forewarning to her. We were not concerned about her for she will never fail herself. So it was that she not only witnessed the final landing of this dross creature but maintained strict eye contact with it...and well she should have. Although we have seen this "landing" occur on other worlds during a time of massive transitions, I for one have not seen it happen here before. This is a congealed mass that is a compendium of all the lowest based energies that have coupled with the higher-level dark mass, which is much older than this planet. It contains all the density and blackness that so long ago formed this matter; there is no Light present, there is decay, blackness and a layered thickness such as is unknown to this planet. This energetic formation when in motion, is a massive slowly whirling physical quantity that can cause more density to occur on gravitational levels. It effuses a type of "suppression" of oscillation as it travels through different dimensions. It moves in relation to the amount of gross matter it contains. Therefore it does indeed move very slowly, yet it does have intelligence. It is cannibalistic by nature, that is to say it must survive at all costs, even devouring its own in its attempts to remain the central base of the damned. It is of course androgynous and its parasitic needs are the Light beams that it can corrupt and turn into a bastion of darkness. In order to compensate for any inability to capture Light, it must multiply itself whenever possible. This is the main cell of the damned, the main cell of the Illuminati. It is a thing without mercy, without compassion, without love. It will capture as many Souls as each person allows. It is from the world that had no end, no true beginning.

Now, do not consider this to be frightening or "bad news." It is neither. It is a complement in its own way. Humanity in many cases is "giving the devil its due," therefore "the big guns" must appear and attempt to thwart you in your successful endeavors at teaching others of true realities and defeating this force. We do know its plan and are prepared, as you shall also be. The only way left for this maelstrom of madness to continue to attack you is...in the dream realm. What is known here as "psychic attacks" are actually psyche attacks. The dark forces use this mainstream opening to attempt to invade a person's mind and Spirit. They are blatant and ruthless in this endeavor. They stop at nothing when they enter this orifice to convince you that they are entities other than what they truly are. Please to understand, it is not that you are unprotected while in this realm, it is not that your Master Teacher, your Spirit Guides, those of the Angelic Realm and we also who are Star Keeper family forces, are not there to defend you when necessary. A vital part of your own Soul Contract calls for you as the "personality" of the Soul, to be ready and able to fend off those dark ones by using your God Created abilities to act in accordance with Universal Law.

It is in many ways a test of your abilities, your knowingness and your determination that rises to the occasion when these silent audacious attacks occur. You see these dark ones will attempt to cajole many by stroking the persons' egos at this time. This is the Great Pretender in action, seeking your downfall by tricking you with words of praise, words geared to cause you to wish vengeance upon others who have taken wrong action against you; imaging of people who are actually very dark but dressing them in the guise of Light Beings. Oftentimes they will attempt to convince people to reunite with others that are no longer good for the individual under attack. They will seek to alter the current life style or life-way of a person by suggesting that he or she return to former addictions. They infuse dreams with sexual overtones ranging from incest to orgies. When all else fails to convert a person, this ogre force attempts to instill condemnation in a person and serious guilt feelings for things that the person did in the recent past.

They will use your innocence and any uncertainties against you. Certain people will be led to believe that he or she is responsible for all that goes wrong in this world. Those who are descendants of the Illuminati who have long ago detached themselves from that ill-begotten race, are primary targets. These dream entities will exhibit threatening behavior if you in your dream state confront them and order them to depart from your life experience. They will know that you know. Whatever "secret" fetishes" you have will also be used against you in dreams. Now, anytime you dream and experience horrifying events occurring to you personally, dream of vampires and other things that go bump in the night, be assured <u>you are being attacked.</u> When you dream of being chased, being "out of control," of fighting evil demons, take note here: you are being attacked. In the fighting sequences you experience in the dream state, be aware you are LITERALLY engaged in battle in this realm. As you consciously acknowledge this when you awaken, a series of events will take place. First, the fear factor will begin to fade and justifiable anger will take its place. Those who are *"in awareness* will have no problem calling upon their guides and other family members consciously for assistance.

This then permits the cluster of benevolent forces to offer assistance to you in your "combat endeavors." Your anger, when used PROPERLY can be a great tool in this. Allowing the dark forces to know that YOU KNOW what the ongoing scenario is in the dream realm, puts them on serious notice. They seek easy prey, not those who are able and willing to battle back and order the beasts to return from whence they came. If they cannot succeed in duping you while awake, then they shall attempt to do so while you sleep. It is the nature of the beast. Now, a Soul will only find ItSelf set against a dark entity that is of the same evolutionary level as that Soul Itself. Those Souls who are of 10th. grade level will be confronted by entities on that same level, and so forth. Now, if you bear in mind that there are indeed certain guidelines to assist you in your determining the True Voices from the false, then you shall have no problem distinguishing the voices. The Dream Voice of Soul Voice does not ever capitulate to De-Vile Voice by instilling fear and/or attempting to perpetrate untruth. Dream Voices bring warmth, Light and understanding. They render pertinent information to you ones that is predicated on your ability to understand and your READINESS to accept.

They reveal truth of times, places and events without any underlying distress, no compromising situations on your parts. Airiness and innate understanding permeates their Voices. They often shower the dreams with such a force of love that it would be difficult for you to explain the sense of it to another. Never, never, under any circumstances do they judge you for anything you have done or failed to do. Often they will show you glimpses of your near future, sometimes you may see yourself in the dream observing yourself throughout an event that will take place. Never do they encourage you to kill another human being, nor do they claim that they are killing on your behalf. They advocate peace without violence and speak of loving without condition. When it is perceived that specific warnings should be sent to you of upcoming events, they will issue these warnings without instilling fear. In this manner the warnings are given with passionate detachment, as they should be. You see it is important that you understand this because of the huge influx of psyche attacks beginning now, as never before.

It is in this manner that you can "serve and protect" yourself. All manner of assistance is given to you and will continue to be especially when you are in this realm, by those who love you best. It is not necessary that you remember their fighting on your behalf, just remember that YOU must also fight on your behalf. The Black Beast that has had to leave its lair in order to be an active participant in its war on humanity, can only attempt to subjugate you while you slumber. This is not true for those on this planet who are "the sleeping awake." However I can only address these issues to you ones who are "in awareness." That is all I can do at this point. In time, many of you will go on in this life to awaken those who have had enough. Until then you must guard your Dream Realm well and saturate it with golden Light and infinite love prior to going to sleep. The beast is here and now present as was foretold long, long ago in ancient prophecies. You see it had to await a certain timeline, the one that is here and now quickly gaining momentum on the Earth Star planet. It awaited the time of "the Second Coming."

Now that this Sacred Event is taking place within the consciousness of those "in awareness," the last vestiges of the mass of dark powers held over Earth are aware that a "new game is afoot." They are now more so than ever, deeply dedicated to obtaining as many Souls as they can capture. Here begins a battle of "numbers." **The children of a lesser god in combat with the children who are God**. How many among you ones realize that there could not have been this "Second Coming" that is now permeating this globe, without the "time of the emergence of the beast" as well? The Second Coming, this which is the ultimate sanctified sweeping Consciousness of Jesus The Christ would never have been necessary if the Illuminati had not controlled this planet. The forced emergence of the matrix of the beast NOW, is because of the Infinite Christ Consciousness which threatens the beast's very existence. The time of capricious living is over; the time of the middle roaders is over, the time of the reinforcement of Soul Voice as Dream Voice has begun. You are what you dream, you are SOUL. Just do not confuse those Voices, not for any reason.

Dreams are not an imitation of life, yet dreams are life existing in Its own unique way. So...let the dreaming begin.....again and again and again...Be not afraid, for so many of you who make our hearts smile shall continue to walk forth AS Truth and justice, none who follow Universal Laws shall live a non-life. NOT ON MY WATCH!

Salude...Blue Star the Pleiadian

Reflections of Thought

By Celest and David

As we look back over all that God has shared with us these many days, we are reminded that His words are in some ways mirrored reflections of our own thoughts and remembrances. We are reminded that during the time that we are safely tucked away in the protective cocoons of our Souls that we **do** know much, but certainly not **all** of the information that He has been sharing with us. It is remembering all that we DO know and remembering that there is much that we DO NOT know while incarnate, that can be a puzzle; it is not always easy to put the pieces together. The other day God said...*"Trying to get everything right the first time is like shooting darts at a comet. It can not be done."* This does not in any way imply that we should give up and not try, it just means that we should arm ourselves with more darts (knowledge) so that we can do the best we can with the time that we have available to us. The more we know, the more thoughts we can understand, define and expand upon. This will help us to better understand our existence, our purpose for being. God has repeatedly told us all not to underestimate the power of thought. There is undeniable truth in this statement. The more we think about this power the more sense it makes.

For example: it is like taking the time to first think, then sense and feel the words, "by doing nothing you are doing everything." What is it that most people are doing when they are doing nothing....they are thinking, rationalizing, assessing and building new thoughts based on the old. As they do so, somewhere down the line they will replace the former with the newer versions. The power of thought has moved mountains and swayed entire governments without people brandishing a weapon. When expressed correctly it has turned hate and violence into love and peace. That should be worthy of further thought. With clarity and purity of intent a focus can be quickly shifted, so why not use the one gift that is freely at hand? One that has no strings attached and should be used to bring into manifestation the world we all dream of and Spiritually hunger for. Thought IS free expression. If you use it badly you will not lose it, you will just not be where you ultimately would desire to be. If you do not use it at all it becomes harder to recall the thoughts, the free expression, when the times arise that you need to recall them the most. Everyone who ever walked upon the Earth Star has special gifts, some of these gifts are just more difficult to access and require patience and determination to bring them to the surface.

We know we are not guessing when we say, "the end result makes the effort worthwhile," and that any attempt to better yourself is worthy of at least trying. If a racehorse were to give up before it left the starting gate because it was intimidated by the horse standing next to it, then its thoughts would be forever..."what if?" "What if," works both ways, it can either be viewed as a dealmaker or a deal breaker. It is all about how this act is applied. Evil or good, whichever one prevails or is the dominant factor, is dependent on which one is supported the most. When not infected by the brutality of the dagger of the beast, every being that has ever been, has glided thoughtfully up the mountain path. It is while in human form that many people forget about their origins and they forget about the mountains and why the mountains are present in life. They forget that all life is considered precious, no matter what its current level of evolvement is. This is not an afterthought. Guy Red Owl of the Lakota Sioux was once heard by us to say, "How can you have an afterthought? Is it not a thought in itself?" Whether this was something that he instinctively knew or some truth that he had arrived at by trial and error is not up to us to say. He, like

254

so many great teachers, offers his sage advice sparingly and conditionally, he first gently prompts people *to think for themselves*. If **all** the answers were given to people by the great teachers, then what would anyone learn about the test of life? Honor the thought; honor the prayer, for they alone hold power supreme that is aligned with destiny and direction.

If Soul wanted the person who is the expression of ItSelf, to be nothing more than a lifeless cumquat on a deserted island, then it would not have bothered taking the time or putting forth the effort to wait for *the person* to come into being. It could just be a cumquat on a deserted island without a physical body. Soul is forever in search of more and more knowledge and of finding new ways to express and expand upon ItSelf as a means to evolve. Utilizing the power of thought to examine all options, to Create new opportunities, to figure out what others may not have thought of yet, is in great part each person's responsibility as Co-Creators of the Creation Processing. It just does not get any better than that. The physical world as part of the practical world and everyday ways of thinking is limited. Thoughts, ideas and inspirations are ethereal; they have buoyancy without boundaries or limitations. Imagine gazing upon the mirrored reflections of a still pool of water. Above the water and below the water are two scenes that are distinct representations of one another. Yet when combined together they display a perspective that traditional thought processing does not register. Bounce thoughts off the mirrored water and magically they possess depth and dimension, neither of which is limited by time or the perception of space.

Examining your thoughts - thoughts like life is much like playing a game of Chess. You have to look over *the whole board* before making your move. The more you practice this technique the better off you will become at knowing what your next move is to be. You can always stay

255

three moves ahead by Being, by strategizing in the NOW. You CAN do that, you know. As we reflect back over the time we have participated with God in these books, we can clearly see and understand where He is leading everyone and why. No longer are you bound by the limitations of a practical world. You can exist in the timelessness of the NOW and view past, present and future as one, enhancing your abilities to Create a better future for yourselves, far beyond your short stay here on Earth. This planet is our sister, our home away from home. She, like God is as much a part of us as we are of her. The more people become aware of what *IS* reality and the truths that God is awakening in everyone, then the more people will discover that no one should ever have to feel so utterly, desperately alone, ever again. To be alone is one thing, but to be in fear of BEING alone is just not acceptable.

Here is our own question and answer section for you:

Q...What if God was not throwing "stones" into the waters here to cause ripples to build a momentum that would effectively displace smaller bodies of water, thereby causing larger bodies of water to come into existence?

A...The "stones" would be all the seeds of truth that have now gestated into a massive size. The stones will no longer allow people here of ANY race to keep their minds idle and infertile. If necessary the people CAN be replaced, but the planet can not be.

Q... What if He decided to throw people in instead?

A... For one thing it would be an act of reprehensible irresponsibility if He did that. For another thing, God loves all people here so much that He is STILL willing to help them to help themselves. However, that having been said, we can think of many people who could use a good "baptism by truth."

Q... What if there were not any good people still on this planet? Would this planet still be worth saving or would Divinity have to find an alternate action to take?

A... If there were not still many good people here, then we have all come to the wrong place at the wrong time. Terra would be saved because she has an important destiny to fulfill. She would just have to assist in the Creation of new, **improved** life forms, for she will <u>never</u> forget what mankind has done to her. She will forgive because that is what she does. But she will never forget.

Q...What if we (Celest and David) and all others like us here in human form, simply gave up and said, "All right, I have had enough. Beam us all up Scotty." Who would be the biggest losers here and what staggering losses would there be worldwide in any of these scenarios?

A... We would all lose. Everything would be lost. Besides, Scotty does not really exist.

Q... What if many of the young Children of today, those whose goals are still muddied at best and the many young adults who still live lives of eroticism and "noncompliance," all changed over the next few years?

A... Ah, if only wishes were horses! No one would need a car. Considering the fact that it is the young Children and the young adults who will be so much needed to reeducate and train the new generations to be, we say it is **critical** that they change, while they still can. There has been far too much collateral damage here as it is.

Q... What if the Mayans decide to haunt humanity because of the chagrin they no doubt feel over the controversy and totally misunderstood interpretations of their calendar?

A... Oh boy, you would all be in trouble! We say "you" collectively, because we know what the calendar really means. So, we're safe! Of course they know how terribly maligned their work has been. As some of the greatest teachers to ever walk this planet, they are also some of the most forgiving. Saddened, but forgiving.

*Q...*What if the doom and gloom people, especially those who belong to different religious organizations, wake up on their self-styled, well prophesized, apocalyptic day in 2012, to discover that not only are they still here..*so is everyone else?*

A... We truly pity them. They have wasted their lives believing in a non-happening event. In so doing they have managed to bring down a great number of normally good people who are far too naïve for anyone's good. The doom and gloomers deserve what they will get.

These are some of our own thoughts, what are yours?

Salude...Celest and David

Our three websites are

www.bluestarspeaks.com

www.awakenedhearts.com

and

www.godumentary.com

Who's Who

Celestial Blue Star - For 22 years now I have been on an extended journey on this planet, seeking other likeminded people. At times I have felt like a lone individual walking and holding a bright lantern to attract others such as myself. In the last 10 years I have seen many people making much needed changes in their lives and this has heartened me to a great degree. Over the years during my private conversations with God, I have expressed to Him that I felt great sadness as I watched so many people who were not changing but were continuing to fall deeper and deeper into the chasm of ignorance. Even though I remain passionately detached as I watch this happen, these are always trying times for me. God of course always manages to pick up my Spirits by reminding me of all the beautiful people, places, animal life forms and new plant life to be. Of course walking in a human form can at times cause me to feel that I want it and I want it now.

Even though God, my father Blue Star and all my other Sources understand how devastated I sometimes feel as I watch the madness overtaking good people here, I always bear in mind that there really are many other "me's" here too. But boy, are we spread out all over this planet! David and I are fortunate to have one another to hold on to now, yet it is during the periods of the great aloneness that we wish so fervently that everything was already different here. Readers, I want to impress upon you all that YES, I do understand the desperation so many people feel here. I do understand that more people now than ever before are banding together and are part of the new collective consciousness, even though many people have no idea that they are. That is all right with me though; I do have the understanding that in time **they** will better understand what they ARE doing, as opposed to what they HAD been doing.

Someone who obviously did not know me at all, once asked me who I am and what do I do. I believe to this day there was a communication failure going on there. How do I explain myself to people who have no understanding? How do I explain what I do, to people who do not inhabit "my world?" How do I explain myself to people who are not even trying to understand either themselves or life? I know that many of you have had similar experiences with other people. I can not tell you how to answer them, but for myself, yes, I have Created an answer. Of course they still do not understand what I am telling them, but at least I have forged an answer. At times I have been known to speak in God Code too. *Who am I?* "I am all that I am." *What do I do?* "I am dancing as fast as I can."

Salude... and I send my gratitude to each of you who is trying, whether you know who you are or not... Celest

David of Arcturus... I, like most of the human inhabitants of Earth, did not come in with any conscious recall of who I was or why I was here. I was living an ordinary life. Well, ordinary to me, although I suppose others would consider it to be extraordinary. I rarely gave any thought to why others were attracted to me. I figured it must have been my "award winning smile." Since I have awakened and jumped headfirst into the process of remembering all that I had forgotten, I have not stopped remembering and rarely take the time to look back. Ten years ago I would have told you that Celest and I lived a lifetime in every year that went by. Now if I were asked if it is the same today, I would now have to say that we live an entire lifetime every month. So I guess I could say that I have lived ten to thirty lifetimes since Celest and I reunited in this lifetime, with no possible end in sight to how many more we will be blessed to share together.

Somewhere. I can honestly say that I live in the NOW. I wouldn't, I couldn't return to the way things were before, even if I wanted to and I can sincerely say, I have no desire to do so. I am mentioning this so that those who have not arrived at this state of being in "Grace," will have something to look forward to. I have an honest respect for not wasting time, yet I learned I can still be consistently *living in the moment* while being busy.

In other words, time has no meaning. What a wonderful gift, one that I wish for everyone. I am not in competition with anyone, not even with myself. I have all the time my immortal Soul gives me and although I will never stop "leaping when I am ready to" and I will not stop resting when I need to. I guess what I am trying to say is that we have all the time in the world but not a minute to lose. I have no idea where or what God will have me doing next and I am at peace with that. If He wanted me to know He would tell me. I am here to serve, ready to serve, just point me in a direction. In between times I will playfully work on embracing other interests that have drawn my attention. Life is never dull or boring; anyone who says so should open their eyes. In every second life is waiting for us to join in. The other day as we were busy doing practical things, Celest suddenly burst out in the insurance office, "I JUST LOVE THIS PLANET." I echo her sentiments.

My world would be boring without ME! Au revoir... David

God... I suggested to Celest that We not use "biographies" this time; I suggested that We use *Who's Who*. I felt that it is a more definitive way for each of Us to speak. Obviously if you do not know Our biographies by heart by now, then it is more than likely that you never will. Celest just called Me, "the Speaker for the House of the Gods." Well, I rather like that idea; perhaps I should enlarge upon that in the future! I do want it to be clearly understood that I am the same God, the same Luminescent that I have ever been. There is no "new God in town." I mention this because after reading one of My previous books, a reader wrote and announced that I was "the new God," that the "old" one was replaced by the new one. Sorry everyone, but you are all stuck with Me. *This is as good as it gets!* I evolve, I do not devolve, nor have I been replaced. As a continuously evolving Luminescent, My own Creative abilities always "upgrade." I then Create more EVOLVED thought-forms to share with others. I AM I Share and I care. Perhaps this best summarizes an aspect of MySelf that you each should understand. I hope so anyway. I was very amused by Celestial Blue Star's description, "I am dancing as fast as I can." I was amused because it reminded Me of a conversation I had recently with David.

David said, "ever since Celest and I reconnected I hit the ground running every day." I replied to David, "David, I do know what you mean; every time she enters this world I hit the ground running too, just to keep up with her!" I mention this because there are others here such as Celest who set such a pace for themselves that I sometimes wonder how they are able to do so and still retain their sanity. From My observation points the Lights that you each are flash, stream, slide, fall, glide and become so much brighter when faced with dilemmas, than do those other Lights who fade into obscurity. From My observation points you, who are the determined ones, become the new WHO you are and replace the former WHO you once were. You all make Me very proud of you AS INDIVIDUALS. Please excuse this analogy, but you are the salmon who swim upstream. No, I am not implying that you then die! But boy, can you fertilize others' thought-patterns and that is half of the battle here. *I am taking care of the other half.* You are rebels with a cause while other Children here manage to do as little as possible in as much time as possible.

I also agree with Celest that you must each Create your own answers when asked the most troublesome of questions. Since she already presented the questions to you, I will not do so. Children, do not despair because WHO you are, was not always WHO you were, rather be overjoyed in knowing that you have been searching for the victor and the victor is yourself. By the way Children I am encouraging you one and all to ALWAYS remind yourselves to hold on to the eye of the storm. I have good reason to tell you this. Only here, is there safety, only here, is there peace, only here, can great change occur. Only here, will the times of the great aloneness cease to be while you are in mortal form. You must remember this. Also remember that I Created you in love and I now leave you in love...

I AM the *eye of the storm... God*

Books currently available from Celest and David

And Then God Said... Then I Said... Then He Said...
Volume One - first book of the God Book series.

Beyond the Veil ~ Epiphanies from God
Gods Truths and Revelations for Today and Tomorrow
Book number 2 of the God Book Series

And Then God Said... Then I Said... Then He Said...
Volume Two - third book of the God Book series.

The Code
Book number 4 of the God Book Series

Blue Star the Pleiadian
My Teachings through Transmissions
A Three Volume Series

Star Tek - **Perspectives through Technology**
Volume One
Star Tek Volume 2 will be available in the near future
Celest and David's Websites
www.bluestarspeaks.com
www.awakenedhearts.com
www.godumentary.com

New Book News

On July-11-2010 Celest was told that God wanted us to write a complete series of His books. David later talked to God about this matter and was told that this was predestined long, long, ago. God has said that there will be a total of eight books in the God Book series. In accordance with this new responsibility we will post the titles of these upcoming books. Stay tuned for these and more from Celest and David...

The entire God Book series consists of:

#1 And Then God Said... Then I Said... Then He Said... Volume One

#2 Beyond the Veil~Epiphanies from God

#3 And Then God Said... Then I Said... Then He Said... Volume Two

#4 The Code

#5 Beyond the Journey

#6 Advocates for Justice

#7 Winter People who Ride the Wind

#8 Avatars in the Valley of the Ancients

If you wish to be added to our "private" *new book notification list* send us an email to creation@godumentary.com

For information on how to order our books please go to:

http://rainbowproducts.awakenedhearts.com/

Note:

The God Books are currently in the process of being translated into Spanish and Dutch. Check "Rainbow Products" or Update Notices on our websites for updated information about when these will become available.

Made in the USA
Lexington, KY
13 March 2013